Youtube — Mandarin corner, Chinese podcast, kevin in shanghai, Jared

Apps - Tandem, tiny cards, duo lingo

web — character pop

教材规划小组
Teaching Material Project Planning Group

许琳　夏建辉　张健　郝运

海外咨询小组
Overseas Consulting Group

洪　玮	美国普渡大学
周明朗	美国马里兰大学
王命全	美国塔夫茨大学
陈山木	加拿大不列颠哥伦比亚大学
吴小燕	加拿大多伦多大学
王仁忠	加拿大麦吉尔大学
白乐桑	法国巴黎东方语言文化学院
顾安达	德国柏林自由大学
袁博平	英国剑桥大学
吴坚立	澳大利亚墨尔本翩丽艾森顿文法学院
罗　拉	俄罗斯莫斯科国立语言大学
三宅登之	日本东京外国语大学
李充阳	韩国首尔孔子学院
朴兴洙	韩国外国语大学
希夏姆	埃及艾因夏姆斯大学

孔子学院总部/国家汉办
Confucius Institute Headquarters (Hanban)

荣获"优秀国际汉语教材奖"
Won the Award for Outstanding International
Chinese Language Teaching Materials

刘珣◎主编

1

英文注释
Annotated in English

NEW PRACTICAL CHINESE READER

新实用汉语课本

3rd Edition

TEXTBOOK
课本

编　者：施家炜　刘　珣　郑家平　裴珊珊
英文翻译：Helen Xiaoyan Wu(吴小燕)
　　　　　John Edward Stowe(司徒祥文)
英文审订：余心乐

（第3版）

北京语言大学出版社
BEIJING LANGUAGE AND CULTURE
UNIVERSITY PRESS

© 2015 北京语言大学出版社，社图号 15191

图书在版编目（CIP）数据

　　新实用汉语课本：英文注释 . 1，课本 ／ 刘珣主编
. ——3 版 . —— 北京：北京语言大学出版社，2015.10（2018.11重印）
　　ISBN 978-7-5619-4277-2

　　Ⅰ. ①新… 　Ⅱ. ①刘… 　Ⅲ. ①汉语－对外汉语教学－
教材 　Ⅳ. ① H195.4

　　中国版本图书馆 CIP 数据核字（2015）第 223456 号

新实用汉语课本（第 3 版 英文注释）课本 1

XIN SHIYONG HANYU KEBEN (DI 3 BAN　YINGWEN ZHUSHI) KEBEN 1

项目负责：付彦白
责任编辑：付彦白　　　　英文编辑：孙玉婷
封面设计：张　静　　　　版式设计：李　佳　　　　插图绘制：李慧麟　刘　谱
排版制作：北京创艺涵文化发展有限公司
责任印制：周　燚

出版发行：北京语言大学出版社
社　　址：北京市海淀区学院路 15 号，100083
网　　址：www.blcup.com
电子信箱：service@blcup.com
电　　话：编辑部　　8610-82303647/3592/3395
　　　　　国内发行　8610-82303650/3591/3648
　　　　　海外发行　8610-82303365/3080/3668
　　　　　北语书店　8610-82303653
　　　　　网购咨询　8610-82303908
印　　刷：保定市中画美凯印刷有限公司

版　　次：2015 年 10 月第 3 版　　　印　　次：2018 年 11 月第 3 次印刷
开　　本：889 毫米 × 1194 毫米　1/16　　印　　张：21.25　插表 1
字　　数：438 千字
　　　　　12800

PRINTED IN CHINA

第 3 版前言

　　《新实用汉语课本》是新世纪之初，主要为以英语为母语或媒介语的海外成人汉语学习者编写的一套零起点的综合教材，是《实用汉语课本》系列的第二代产品。本版为修订后的第 3 版，主要供海外大学、孔子学院及高中用作汉语课教材，也可自学使用。

一部世界广泛使用的汉语教材

　　《新实用汉语课本》自 2002 年作为中国国家汉办重点规划教材陆续问世以来，得到世界各地汉语学习者和汉语教师们的欢迎与关爱。最初推出了英文、俄文、泰文、西班牙文 4 个文种注释本。2009 年在孔子学院总部/国家汉办的大力支持下，又陆续推出了英文、法文、德文、俄文、西班牙文、阿拉伯文、日文、韩文、泰文等 9 个文种注释本的入门级分册；同时我们对原版（英文注释本）进行了局部修订，出版了第一册到第四册的第 2 版。现在，从南北美洲、东西欧洲到大洋洲，从亚洲到非洲，都有第 1 版和第 2 版的大量的使用者。以西班牙文注释本为例，2014 年的发行量是 2009 年的 6 倍。13 年来，各种版本的第一册，总共已印刷 31 次。一些国家还购买了该教材的版权。这些都表明《新实用汉语课本》正如它的上一代产品（上世纪八九十年代的《实用汉语课本》）一样，已成为世界上最广泛使用、最具有影响力的基础汉语教材之一。2010 年，《新实用汉语课本》荣获"优秀国际汉语教材奖"。

教学目标

　　《新实用汉语课本》的教学目标是通过汉语语言结构、语言功能与相关文化知识的学习和听说读写技能训练，逐步培养学习者综合运用汉语的能力。首先是培养学习者跨文化交际能力，并提高多元文化意识；同时在这一过程中让学习者掌握一些汉语的学习策略，增强学习汉语的兴趣。

　　全书共六册，第一册到第四册为初级（基础）阶段，围绕几个年轻的外国留学生在中国的生活及他们与中国朋友和教师的友情与交往，展开一系列贴近学习者真实生活、有趣的故事。其中，第一、二册结合校园及日常生活，介绍与汉语表达和理解有关的习俗文化；第三、四册围绕青年学生感兴趣的话题进行文化对比和讨论。完成这四册的学习，学习者可掌握汉语的基本结构和表达功能，达到新 HSK 四至五级水平。第五、六册为中级阶段，内容反映了中国社会的众多方面，体现中国当代国情、文化和传统文化。语言结构除扩大和深化词语和语法教学外，把重点放在复句和语段层面，培养学习者理解和表达中高级的功能和话题的能力，特别是成段表达的交际能力。完成这一阶段的学习，学习者可达到新 HSK 五至六级水平。

编写和修订理念

　　近年来国际汉语教学已出现前所未有的大发展的新形势，世界第二语言教学理论和教学方法的研究也有很多新的进展。这些变化促成了《新实用汉语课本》第 3 版的问世。

　　本教材的编写和修订，以学习者"更容易学"、教师"更方便用"为宗旨，继承中国对外汉语教学半个多世纪以来的优秀传统，汲取国内外语言教学理论和教学实践的新成果，特别注重研究汉语教学本身的规律，坚持贯彻能体现汉语教学特点的"结构—功能—文化相结合"的教学理念。我们认为，牢固地掌握语言结构，是培养语言运用能力的基础。这就需要既要让学习者通过大量操练和练习获得四种基本技能，又要让成人学习者懂得必要的语法知识和组词造句的规则。对像汉语这样与绝大多数学习者母语的谱系关系相去甚远的"真正外语"，尤其要强调语音、词汇、句型、语法和话语等语言结构的学习和掌握，而且要特别注意体现由简单到复杂、由易到难、循序渐进、不断重现的原则，才能使学习过程更为容易，更为顺利。语言教材还应该有助于学习者了解目的语国家的文化和社会，从而更好地运用目的语进行交际。这就是我们编写和修订《新实用汉语课本》所主张的主要理念。

新版（第3版）的新特点

修订后的第3版教材，更重视学习者主动的、创造性的学习，使学习者不断增强学习动力并获得成就感，每课增设了课前"热身"以及最后的"自我评估"环节。

新版强调用中学，加强课堂互动和合作学习，在坚持以语言结构教学为基础的同时，加强交际性、任务型的活动。

新版课文内容更体现时代感，更有趣味性，更适合学习者的需要；话题更加集中、明确；功能更加突出、实用；语言更加真实、自然；生词选取更注重常用词，加强补充词；语言点的安排更为科学合理，更突出难点、重点；练习更加注意处理好机械性、交际性、任务型练习的关系。内容采取板块式的安排，方便学习者根据需要进行选择。

修订后的《新实用汉语课本》，海外专修或选修中文的学习者可用作听说读写综合教学的汉语教材。全书每册有10课（第一册另设两课语音预备课，供学习者选用），每课约需4～5学时。一学期可学完一册。

新版《课本》体例

语音预备课

学习者从一开始就重视汉语的语音和声调的学习，这一点非常重要。新版编写了两课语音预备课，除系统地教语音外，还配合声韵母和声调的练习，学一些常用会话和课堂用语。（注意：预备课中不进行任何语法、句型教学，语言结构的教学将从第一课开始。）同时，开始学习汉字的基本知识。教师可根据学生的具体情况决定这两课的使用。

正课

1. 热身　每课的开始，提出三个启发性的问题。然后结合当课内容，设置一个富有趣味性、挑战性的活动。作为课前预习的一部分，有助于引起学习者的兴趣，将学习者引进本课。

2. 课文　为学习者提供他们所需要的话题和典型的情境，进行汉语基本结构和功能的学习和运用。课文中凸显功能，并多次重现本课要学的语言结构。第一、二册课文基本上采用对话体（每课两段），以利于基础阶段在听说读写全面要求的基础上加强听说的训练。课文中拼音与汉字的呈现方式，由利用、突出拼音到逐步摆脱对拼音的依赖。

生词　一方面对组成生词的语素（汉字）进行分析，便于学习者理解和记忆生词，进而掌握汉语构词的规律；同时强调通过词语搭配，掌握生词的用法。

注释 主要内容为：解释词语的用法；介绍必要的文化背景知识；补充已学过的语法点；对课文中已出现但暂不讲解语法点的句子，通过译文让学习者弄懂意思。

3. 语言点

核心句 体现了本课所介绍的主要语言结构及主要功能，是本课必须要熟练掌握的句子。

语法 针对汉语的特点和难点，对本课出现的主要语言结构进行必要的说明。着重介绍句子组装的规律，不求语法知识的全面系统。每个语法点讲解后，即有理解性（机械性）的练习加以巩固。比较复杂的语法点或词汇用法，常分几课介绍，注意在当课不要一次超前讲完所有用法。课文中尽量重现前一课的主要语言点。每册有 1～2 次语法小结，帮助学习者对已学过的语法点进行梳理。

4. 练习与运用

补充词语 紧密配合课文内容，扩大相关词语，有利于学习者进行交际性、任务型课堂活动，并由学习者量力吸取。

语音练习 在学习语音预备课的基础上，针对汉语语音的特点和难点，坚持有重点地加以练习，巩固并提高语音学习的成果。

会话练习 根据本课的话题和主要功能，运用所学的语言结构，进行有意义的会话练习。

听后复述 根据本课的话题和主要功能，运用所学的语言结构，在变换情境的情况下，做听和说的练习。

阅读理解 用叙述体短文重现已学过的句型与词汇，着重培养语段理解与连贯表达的能力。

任务与活动 在操练和有意义练习的基础上，进一步进行交际性、任务型的活动，培养学习者综合运用汉语的能力。

写作练习 由于汉语自身的特点，学习者读写能力的提高一般说来难于听说能力，读和写中又以写的能力难度为最高。在学汉语的开始阶段就要重视写的技能的培养，从写汉字、生词、语段开始，读写结合，逐步由控制性写作提高到开放性写作。

5. 汉字 加强部件的教学，介绍汉字的结构规律和书写规律，帮助学习者认写汉字，逐步化解汉字难的问题。

6. 文化知识 开始多用学习者母语或媒介语介绍，便于学习者了解、学习与汉语有关的、必要的文化知识。随着学习者汉语水平的提高，文化知识将逐渐融合到课文中去。

7. 自我评估 自我小结本课的学习情况。

此外，为增加汉语学习的趣味性，启发学习者对汉语特点的思考，每课还在最后增设"趣味汉语"小板块。

配套资源

《综合练习册》 主要供学习者课下练习用。除了汉字练习外，还有语音、句型、词汇的练习，以及听说读写全面的技能训练。此外还设有一些交际性、任务型的练习。

《教师用书》 就每课的教学目的、教学步骤和方法等提出建议，并对教材内容进行说明。对语音、语法、词汇的有关知识做较详细的介绍，并尽可能提供教案和教辅资料，供教师参考。

《同步阅读》 加强语言输入，培养阅读技巧，使课内学到的语言结构得到重现和运用。

《测试题》 每课有一个小测试卷，期中和期末各有一个单元测试卷，最后还有一个大测试卷，方便教师准备课堂或学期测试及学习者自测。

《汉字练习册》 主要围绕《课本》每课课文中出现的汉字，进行汉字的认读、书写与识记练习。

网络资源专区 提供教案、课件及教材的练习参考答案等，实现资源共享。

网络课程平台 辅助教师授课，同时提供智能化的班级和学生管理系统，实现学习者在线智能学习与互动。其网络沟通功能可实现全球的《新实用汉语课本》用户联络和在线交流。

鸣谢

《新实用汉语课本》第3版的修订工作，得到孔子学院总部/国家汉办一如既往的关心、指导与帮助。北京语言大学副校长、前北语社董事长戚德祥博士，北语出版社董事长兼总编辑张健博士和北语出版社社长兼北美分社社长郝运博士，自始至终给予支持与帮助，为修订工作提供了可靠的保证。特向他们表示衷心的感谢。

考虑到《新实用汉语课本》国际通用的现状，在此次修订过程中我们向分布在各大洲、长期使用本教材并从事汉语教学研究的多国学者们提出了咨询，得到他们宝贵的意见和建议。他们还同意担任本教材新版的咨询小组成员，继续关注教材在各地的使用情况，并继续提出建议。特向他们表示我们的谢意。

加拿大多伦多大学吴小燕博士和怀雅逊大学司徒祥文博士担任本教材第3版的英文翻译工作，北语社责任编辑付彦白和孙玉婷、美术编辑张静和李佳、画师李慧麟和刘谱为本教材的编辑出版工作付出了辛勤的劳动。没有他们的通力协作，也不会有我们面前的这套亮丽的新版本。

本教材是在第1版的基础上修订而成的。第1版的作者为张凯、刘社会、陈曦、左珊丹、施家炜和刘珣，主编为刘珣。是他们的辛勤工作为《新实用汉语课本》打下了坚实的基础。由于种种原因，部分原作者未能继续参与第3版编写的工作，特向他们为第1版所做的努力致以衷心的感谢。

我们要特别感谢本教材第1版的加拿大主要协作方——不列颠哥伦比亚大学亚洲学系中国语文部的老师们，特别是陈山木主任和郑志宁先生，为本书第1版的完成做出了出色贡献。

《新实用汉语课本》第3版从内容到形式都是全新打造，我们希望它能以更专业、更国际化的新面貌呈现给世界汉语学习者，让学习者感受到选择它来学习汉语，更实用、更有效、更容易；也让我国对外汉语教学界的这套已有30余年历史的品牌教材，继续为汉语加快走向世界服务，为帮助各国朋友们学习汉语做贡献。

期待使用本教材的教师和学习者提出宝贵意见，以便我们今后继续对本教材做新的改进，使之不断与时俱进。

编者
2015 年 5 月
于北京语言大学

As a product of the second generation of the *Practical Chinese Reader* series, *New Practical Chinese Reader* (NPCR) is a series of comprehensive Chinese textbooks compiled at the beginning of the 21st century for adult beginners who are native English speakers or who use English as their language of instruction. This is the third edition of NPCR, mainly targeting students at overseas universities, Confucius Institutes, and high schools. It may also be used for study on one's own.

A Popular Chinese Language Textbook Series Used Worldwide

Ever since its publication in 2002 as a key textbook series planned by the Office of the Chinese Language Council International (a.k.a., Hanban), it has been well received by students and teachers of Chinese all over the world. It was first published with annotations and translations in four languages: English, Russian, Thai, and Spanish. In 2009, with the strong support of Hanban/Confucius Institute Headquarters, a beginner-level Chinese language textbook, was added to NPCR, annotated and translated into nine languages: English, French, German, Russian, Spanish, Arabic, Japanese, Korean, and Thai, which were published one after another. At the same time, we partially revised the English edition and published the 2nd edition from volumes 1 to 4. At the present time, from North and South America, East and West Europe to Australia, from Asia to Africa, there are a large number of users of the 1st and 2nd editions. For example, the number of copies of the Spanish edition sold in 2014 was six times the number in 2009. Over the past 12 years, all the first volumes of various editions have altogether been reprinted 31 times. Some countries also bought the copyrights of NPCR. All these indicate that *New Practical Chinese Reader*, like its previous generation *Practical Chinese Reader* in 1980s to 1990s, is one of the most widely used and influential basic Chinese language teaching materials. In 2010, NPCR won the Award for Outstanding International Chinese Language Teaching Materials.

Teaching Goals

The teaching goals of this series of textbooks are to gradually develop students' ability to use Chinese through the study of its structure, functions, and related cultural knowledge, as well as the training in listening, speaking, reading, and writing skills. The textbooks will cultivate students' cross-cultural communicative skills and raise their multicultural awareness, and at the same time help students master some strategies for learning the Chinese language, and increase their interest in learning the language.

The whole set consists of six volumes. Volumes 1 to 4 are at the basic level, focusing on the interesting stories of the lives of a few young foreign students in China and their friendships and interactions with their Chinese friends and teachers. Volumes 1 and 2 introduce Chinese customs and culture relevant to some Chinese expressions and ideas within the setting of campus and daily life. Volumes 3 and 4 encourage cultural comparisons and discussions on the topics that young students are interested in. Upon completing the four volumes, students will have a good command of the fundamental structures and functions to express themselves, and may reach Level 4 or 5 of the new HSK (Hànyǔ Shuǐpíng Kǎoshì – Chinese Proficiency Test). Volumes 5 and 6 are at the intermediate level, with the contents reflecting various aspects of Chinese society, embodying the current situation and traditional culture in China. In addition to expanding and deepening the teaching of vocabulary and grammar, the teaching of linguistic structures emphasizes complex sentences and paragraphs, which will help to develop students' ability to understand and use high-intermediate functions and topics, especially their communicative competence to express themselves using sentences extensively. After that, students' Chinese proficiency may reach Level 5 or 6 of the new HSK.

The Concept for Compiling and Revising NPCR

Recently, a new situation, an unprecedented advancement in the teaching and learning of Chinese as an international language, has emerged. Theories and methods of second language teaching have also undergone new developments. Many of these changes have led to the creation of the 3rd edition of NPCR.

The compilation and revision of this series of textbooks aim at producing a series of textbooks that are "easier to learn" for students and "easier to use" for teachers. The 3rd edition carries on the fine tradition in China of teaching Chinese as a foreign language for over half a century. It absorbs the new findings in theories and methods in language teaching in China and abroad, particularly emphasizing the research in the patterns of Chinese language teaching itself. It maintains the pedagogy of "the integration of structure, function and culture" that embodies the characteristics of Chinese language teaching. We believe that firmly mastering the structure of a language is the foundation of developing the use of a language. This requires numerous drills and exercises to obtain the four basic skills of listening, speaking, reading, and writing. It should also help adult learners to understand the necessary grammar and rules to form phrases and make sentences. As for a "genuine foreign language" like Chinese, which is entirely different from most students' mother tongues according to the language families, it is particularly important to emphasize the study and mastery of pronunciation, vocabulary, sentence patterns, grammar, and discourse, etc. It is essential to pay close attention to the principle of going from simple to complex, from easy to difficult, with constant repetition. Only then can learning become simpler and smoother. A language textbook should also help students understand the culture and society of the target language, thereby better communicating in that language. These are the main principles for compiling and revising NPCR.

New Features of the 3rd Edition

Having been revised, the 3rd edition emphasizes learners' initiative and creativity in learning, continuously motivating them and giving them a sense of achievement. Each lesson has a Warm-up section added at the beginning, and a Self-evaluation section at the end.

The 3rd edition emphasizes learning by doing, strengthening classroom interactions and collaborative learning; while insisting on the teaching of linguistic structures, it gives priority to communicative and task-oriented activities.

The part of the Text of the 3rd edition offers present-day contents, and is more interesting and more suitable for the needs of the learners. The topics are more focused and explicit; the linguistic functions are more clear-cut and practical; the language is authentic and natural. The most commonly used vocabulary has been chosen, and more supplementary words are added. The arrangement of the Language Points is more logical, with stress on the difficulties and key points in the language. More emphasis is given to the coordination of mechanical drills, communicative activities, and task-oriented exercises. The contents are arranged by categories, making it convenient for students to select a section based on their needs.

The revised NPCR can be used as comprehensive Chinese textbooks for foreign students who major in Chinese or take Chinese as an elective. Each volume has 10 lessons (the first volume also has two optional preparatory lessons on phonetics). Each lesson requires approximately 4-5 class sessions. One volume can be completed in one semester.

The Layout of the 3rd Edition Textbook

Introduction to Phonetics

It is extremely important that students, from the very beginning, pay attention to the pronunciation and tones of the Chinese language. The 3rd edition contains two preparatory lessons on phonetics. In addition to teaching phonetics systematically, these two lessons provide many exercises on initials, finals and tones, as well as some daily conversations and classroom expressions (N.B.: These two lessons don't teach any grammar or sentence patterns. The teaching of the linguistic structures starts from Lesson 1). The basic knowledge of Chinese characters is introduced concurrently. Teachers may decide how to teach these two preparatory lessons based on the specific needs of their students.

Main Lessons

1. Warm-up

At the beginning of each lesson, there are three probing questions as well as a fun and challenging activity based on the lesson to stimulate the interest of students, leading them into the lesson.

2. Text

This section provides necessary topics and typical scenes for students to learn and use basic structures and functions of the Chinese language. The Text highlights the functions and repeats the linguistic structures in this lesson. The Text in Volumes 1 and 2 primarily uses the format of dialogues (two in each text) to strengthen listening and speaking, two of the overall requirements of the four language skills at the basic level. In the Text, *Hanyu Pinyin* and Chinese characters appear together, going from heavy use of *pinyin* to gradually reducing the reliance on it.

New Words

Each lesson analyzes the morphemes (characters) which make up each word, making it easy for students to understand and memorize, and thereby helps them to grasp the rules of word formation. At the same time, through various word combinations, they are reinforced to master the usage of the new words.

Notes

The main contents explain the usage of the words, introduce the necessary cultural background and knowledge, and supplement the previously learned grammatical points. Some sentences whose grammar has not yet been covered are accompanied by translation to help students understand.

3. Language Points

Key Sentences

They embody the main language structures and functions of the lesson, which must be thoroughly mastered.

Grammar

Focusing on the characteristics and difficulties of the Chinese language, this section gives necessary explanations for the main language structures that appear in the lesson. It stresses the regular patterns of the sentences instead of systematical presentation of the grammar. After each point is explained, exercises, although may be mechanical, are immediately provided to reinforce students' understanding of the point in question. The relatively complex grammatical points and vocabulary usages are often introduced using several lessons and are not meant to be taught all in one lesson ahead of time. Each text repeats, as much as possible, the main language points of the previous lesson. Each volume has one or two summaries of the grammar covered so far, helping students to progressively review all the grammatical points already studied.

4. Practice and Application

Supplementary Words

This section closely coordinates with the content of the Text and expands related vocabulary, facilitating communicative and task-oriented classroom activities, and allows students to absorb the supplementary words according to their ability.

Pronunciation Drills

In view of the characteristics and difficulties of pronunciation in Mandarin for foreign students, this section places special emphasis on practicing challenging sounds, reinforcing students' achievements in the pronunciation skills they have acquired.

Conversation Practice

Building upon the topic and main linguistic functions of the lesson, this section allows students to use the grammatical structures learned to conduct meaningful conversations.

Listening and Repeating

This section, based on the topic and main linguistic functions of the lesson, facilitates the application of the grammatical structures learned through listening and speaking exercises in different scenarios.

Reading Comprehension

Using short narrative passages to repeat the already learned sentence patterns and vocabulary, this section focuses on training in paragraph comprehension and smooth expression.

Task and Activity

Based on the drills and the meaningful exercises, this section provides more communicative and task-oriented activities, developing students' ability to use Chinese in a variety of ways.

Writing Exercise

Due to the characteristics of the Chinese language, the progress in reading and writing is generally more difficult than listening and speaking, of which writing is the most difficult. Writing should be learned from the very beginning, starting with writing Chinese characters, new words, expressions, and through the integration of reading and writing, gradually progress from guided writing to free writing.

5. Chinese Characters

This section emphasizes the importance of teaching Chinese character components by introducing the composition of a character and writing rules, thus assisting students to recognize and write characters, gradually reducing the difficulty of learning Chinese characters.

6. Cultural Knowledge

This section is first introduced in the students' mother tongue or intermediary language so that they can gain insight into the cultural information related to and necessary for their language studies. As their proficiency in Chinese improves, cultural knowledge will be incorporated more and more in the Text in Chinese.

7. Self-evaluation

This section checks students' progress in the lesson.

Besides, a section Fun with Chinese is added at the end of each lesson to increase the interest in learning Chinese and to stimulate students to think about the special features of the Chinese language.

Supplementary Resources

The *Workbook* is primarily for students to do exercises while out of class. In addition to Chinese character exercises, there are exercises on pronunciation, sentence patterns, and vocabulary, as well as comprehensive skill training in listening, speaking, reading, and writing. There are also some communicative and task-oriented activities.

The *Instructor's Manual* gives suggestions for the goals, steps, methods, and so on for teaching each lesson, and also explains the teaching materials. It introduces the relevant knowledge about phonetics, grammar, and vocabulary in detail, and provides teaching plans and supplementary materials as references for teachers.

The *Companion Reader* strengthens the input of the Chinese language and develops reading skills, repeating and applying the language structures learned in class.

The *Tests and Quizzes* provides a quiz for each lesson, as well as a mid-term test and a final exam. All these facilitate teachers' preparations for classroom teaching, testing and students' self-testing.

The *Chinese Characters Workbook* provides exercises for students to recognize, read, write and memorize the Chinese characters taught in the textbook.

Online Resources provide teaching plans, courseware files, and answer keys to the exercises and so on to be shared by all users.

The platform for online courses helps teachers to teach; at the same time it provides computerized classroom and student management, facilitating students' online learning and interaction. This online platform allows the global NPCR users' exchanges and interactions to happen.

Acknowledgements

The revision work of the NPCR 3rd edition has been under the ongoing guidance of and with the assistance of Hanban/Confucius Institute Headquarters in China. Dr. Qi Dexiang, Vice-President of Beijing Language and Culture University (BLCU) and the former President of BLCU Press, Dr. Zhang Jian, Chair and Editor-in-Chief of BLCU Press, and Dr. Hao Yun, President of BLCU Press and President of Phoenix Tree Publishing Inc. in North America, have given constant and strong supports to the revision of NPCR. We express our heartfelt thanks to them.

In view of the worldwide use of NPCR, we sought consultations from the international scholars who have been using the first two editions of this series in teaching for a long time and have been engaging in the research of teaching Chinese as a foreign language, whose valuable opinions and suggestions have been incorporated into the revisions. They agreed to serve as the consultants to continue to care about the use of this series in their localities, and keep on giving feedback. We express our sincere gratitude to them.

Dr. Helen Xiaoyan Wu at the University of Toronto and Dr. John Edward Stowe at Ryerson University, the two Canadian translators of the 3rd edition in English, Mr. Fu Yanbai, Managing Editor, Ms. Zhang Jing and Mr. Li Jia, Artistic Editors, and Mr. Li Huilin and Mr. Liu Pu, artists, all made significant contributions to the compilation of this edition. Without their concerted efforts, there would have been no new edition.

The 3rd edition is based on the revision of the 1st edition. The authors of the 1st edition are Zhang Kai, Liu Shehui, Chen Xi, Zuo Shandan, Shi Jiawei, and Liu Xun, with Liu Xun as the Chief Compiler. Their hard work laid a solid foundation for NPCR. For various reasons, some original authors were unable to continue to participate in the compilation of the 3rd edition. We truly appreciate all the efforts they made for the 1st edition.

We would like to give special thanks to our main Canadian collaborators of the 1st edition, the Chinese language teachers in the Department of Asian Studies, University of British Columbia, particularly to the Coordinator Dr. Robert S. Chen and Mr. Zhining Zheng, who contributed greatly to the completion of the 1st edition.

From the contents to the format, the 3rd edition has been completely revised. We hope that this new edition will encourage international students to choose NPCR for its greater practicality, effectiveness, and easy use, and will continue to allow the world to access this series of textbooks of Chinese as a foreign language that has been popular for over 30 years, thereby supporting our international friends in learning Chinese.

We sincerely hope that teachers and students who use our teaching materials will offer their valuable suggestions so that we can keep these textbooks up along with the times.

The compilers
May 2015
Beijing Language and Culture University

目 录 CONTENTS

课号	标题	话题	功能
1	你最近怎么样	问候	1. 日常打招呼 2. 问名字 3. 问候 4. 问候他人
2	你是哪国人	介绍	1. 问好 2. 介绍他人 3. 问姓氏 4. 问国籍 5. 告别 6. 指认物品 7. 问喜好
3	你们家有几口人	家庭	1. 问家庭 2. 问职业 3. 招待客人 4. 问年龄（1）
4	你明天几点有课	学习	1. 谈学习（1） 2. 约会 3. 问时间（1） 4. 问专业
5	祝你生日快乐	生日	1. 说日期 2. 表歉意 3. 表遗憾 4. 问年龄（2） 5. 祝贺生日
6	图书馆在食堂北边	方位	1. 问路 2. 描述位置 3. 劝慰 4. 表达未听清 5. 问不懂的词

课号	标题	话题	功能	
			1. 称赞与回应	
			2. 问价	
7	**苹果多少钱一斤**	购物	3. 遇到语言困难求助	
			4. 砍价	
			5. 付钱	
			6. 请求与允许	
			7. 挑选衣服	
			8. 结账	
			1. 催促	
			2. 道歉	
			3. 询问身体状况	
8	**我全身都不舒服**	看病	4. 表示必要	
			5. 表示可能	
			6. 挂号	
			7. 陈述病情	
			8. 看病	
			1. 谈论季节和天气	
			2. 谈打算	
9	**天气凉快了**	季节与交通	3. 提活动建议	
			4. 问时间（2）	
			5. 讨论出行交通	
			1. 谈已经发生的事情	
			2. 谈某人的变化	
			3. 谈论节日	
10	**祝你圣诞快乐**	节日	4. 问年龄（3）	
			5. 节日祝愿	
			6. 打电话	
			7. 转达问候	
			8. 谈学习（2）	

Lesson	Title	Topic	Functions
			1. Praise and response
7	How much is half a kilo of apples	Shopping	2. Asking about the price 3. Encountering a language problem and asking for help 4. Bargaining 5. Paying for something 6. Making a request and giving permission 7. Choosing clothes 8. Settling a bill
8	I am not feeling well at all	Seeing a doctor	1. Urging someone to do something 2. Apologizing 3. Asking about someone's health 4. Expressing a need 5. Expressing a possibility 6. Registering in a hospital 7. Talking about one's health 8. Treating an illness
9	It's getting cool	Seasons and transportation	1. Talking about the seasons and the weather 2. Talking about one's plans 3. Suggesting an activity 4. Asking about time (2) 5. Talking about transportation
10	Merry Christmas	Festivals	1. Talking about something that has happened 2. Talking about someone who has changed 3. Talking about a holiday 4. Asking about one's age (3) 5. Holiday greetings 6. Making a phone call 7. Passing on someone's regards 8. Talking about studying (2)

《Xīn Shíyòng Hànyǔ Kèběn》 huānyíng nǐ!

《新实用汉语课本》欢迎你!

New Practical Chinese Reader welcomes you!

In the two lessons of Introduction to Phonetics, you'll come across the complete Chinese phonetic system: 21 initials, 38 finals, 4 tones, and tone sandhi in the flow of speech. When you have learned "Hànyǔ pīnyīn 汉语拼音", you can read out any syllable in Chinese (There are only some 1,200 syllables in Chinese). Of course, these two preparatory lessons only give you a phonetic foundation. In each of the future lessons, we will continue to practice the sounds and tones until you can pronounce them as correctly as the Chinese do.

The purpose of learning phonetics is to communicate. In these two lessons, you'll learn 16 sets of common dialogues and more than 30 classroom expressions and will also come across many useful Chinese words and phrases.

What is extremely important is that you'll learn 14 most basic Chinese characters and come to understand the strokes of Chinese characters and the writing rules. These most basic characters can help you learn the relatively complex characters and learn by heart more words and phrases.

Are you ready? Here we go!

1

Nǐ hǎo
你 好
Hello

Chinese is a tonal and musical language. You will want to use accurate Mandarin to communicate with Chinese. These two preliminary lessons will help you from the very beginning to establish a sound foundation in phonetics. The picturesque Chinese characters, one of the world's oldest written languages still in use today, with more than three thousand years of history, might have seemed quite mysterious to you. These lessons will also tell you how to recognize and write Chinese characters, in a relatively easy manner. In the current lesson, you will learn six basic characters. In addition, you will learn how to say some essential daily expressions. Are you ready? Let's begin.

热身 WARM-UP

Listen to the following syllables. On the lines below, write the numbers of the three syllables that you think are Mandarin. Listen a second time and imitate the Mandarin syllables you hear.

(1) _____ (2) _____ (3) _____ 1-01-01

第一部分 PART ONE

一、课文 TEXT

1-01-02

Nǐ hǎo!
A: 你 好!

Nǐ hǎo!
B: 你 好!

- -

A: Hello!
B: Hello!

Communication activity

Greet your classmates and teacher in Mandarin.

二、语音 *PHONETICS*

1 语音知识 Knowledge about Phonetics

1. The basic sounds in Mandarin

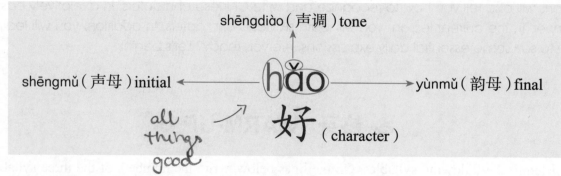

In Modern Standard Chinese, a syllable usually has three parts: the initial, the final, and the tone. The initial is the consonant at the beginning; the rest of the syllable is the final. A final is made of one to three vowels or a combination of a vowel plus the consonant "n" or "ng". A tone mark is placed above a vowel. For instance, in the example "hǎo 好", "h" is the initial, "ao" is the final, and the tone is the third tone. A syllable may not have an initial, such as "ai", but it must have a final. Altogether Mandarin has 21 initials, 38 finals, and four tones.

The structure of a Hànyǔ pīnyīn syllable is as follows:

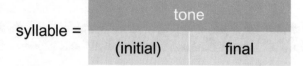

	tone	
syllable =	(initial)	final

2. Phonological items

(1) Initials: b, p, m, and f

The initials b, p, and m are bilabial, but f is labiodental. They are pronounced similar to English.

(2) Initials: d, t, n, and l

When pronouncing d, t, n, and l, the tip of the tongue is in the alveolar position. They are pronounced similar to English.

Note:

The initials b and d are unaspirated; p and t are pronounced in the same position as b and d, but they are aspirated.

(3) Single finals: α, o, e, i, u, and ü

When the final o alone is combined with b, p, m, or f, there is usually a short u in between the initial and the final. So, the actual pronunciation of bo, po, mo, and fo is buo, puo, muo, and fuo.

The *pinyin* final e and the English letter e are pronounced differently. When pronouncing the *pinyin* e, approximate the sound er as in the British English word "her".

The final ü is a rounded high front vowel. When pronouncing it, place your tongue as if you were pronouncing i in pīnyīn and then round your lips.

(4) Tones

Chinese is a tonal language. Each tone has the function of differentiating meaning. Mandarin has four basic tones.

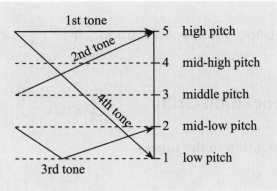

Example

| bā (八) | bá (拔) | bǎ (靶) | bà (爸) |
| eight | to pull out | target | dad |

Tone marks: the first tone is marked " − ", the second tone is marked " ∕ ", the third tone is marked " ∨ ", and the fourth tone is marked " ＼ ".

When a syllable has only one vowel, the tone mark is marked above the vowel such as "lù 陆" and "hěn 很". If the tone mark is above the *pinyin* vowel i, the dot above i should be removed such as "nǐ 你", "nín 您", and " píng 平". When a syllable has a compound final, the tone mark should usually be put above the vowel which requires your mouth to be open the widest. When the degree to which you open your mouth is the same, put the tone mark above the second vowel, such as "liú 留" and "duì 对".

The order of vowel sounds based on how wide the mouth is opened:

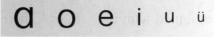

(5) The neutral tone

Mandarin has a neutral tone. The neutral tone must be read lightly and quickly. When spelling the syllable, there is no tone mark.

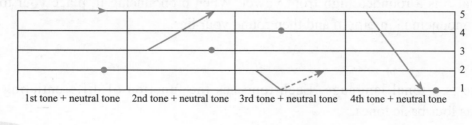

| 1st tone + neutral tone | 2nd tone + neutral tone | 3rd tone + neutral tone | 4th tone + neutral tone |

Example

| māma（妈妈） | bóbo（伯伯） | nǐmen（你们） | bàba（爸爸） |
| mom | uncle | you | dad |

2 语音练习 Pronunciation Drills 1-01-03

1. Read aloud and pay attention to the tones

ā	á	ǎ	à
bō	bó	bǒ	bò
lū	lú	lǔ	lù
yī	yí	yǐ	yì
wū	wú	wǔ	wù
yū	yú	yǔ	yù

2. Sound discrimination

bà (father) —— pà (afraid)　　bó (uncle) —— pó (mother-in-law)

dà (big) —— tà (to stamp)　　dǔ (to bet) —— tǔ (soil)

fǎ (law) —— mǎ (horse)　　mò (ink) —— mù (wood)

lì (strength) —— lǜ (green)　　nǚ (female) —— nǔ (to exert)

3. Tone discrimination

mǎ (horse) —— mā (mom) mù (wood) —— mǔ (mother)

yī (one) —— yí (aunt) lì (strength) —— lǐ (in)

dǔ (to bet) —— dú (to read) yǔ (rain) —— yú (fish)

4. The neutral tone

bàba   māma   dìdi

bóbo   pópo   Nǐ ne?

三、课堂用语 *CLASSROOM EXPRESSIONS*

● Nǐ dú.   Read aloud.   1-01-04

❧ 第二部分 PART TWO ❧

一、课文 *TEXT*

（一） 1-01-05

　　　Nǐmen hǎo!
A：你们 好！

　　　Nǐ hǎo!
B：你 好！

- - - - - - - - - - - - - - - - - - - -

A：　Hello, everyone!
B：　Hello!

（二）  1-01-06

Nǐ máng ma?
A： 你 忙 吗？

Hěn máng.
B： 很 忙。

- -

A： Are you busy?
B： Very busy.

Communication activity

Based on the pictures and scenes below, complete the dialogues, using the designated words.

(1) A： _____！ (2) A： _____！ (3) A： Bàba, _____? (máng)

　　B： _____！　　　　B： _____！　　　　B： _____. (máng)

二、语音 *PHONETICS*

1 语音知识 Knowledge about Phonetics

1. Phonological items

(1) Initials: g, k, and h

When pronouncing g and k, raise the back of the tongue against the soft palate. The initial g is pronounced like "kir" in the English word "skirt".

When pronouncing h, raise the back of the tongue and place it close to the soft palate.

Note:

Though g and k are pronounced in the same position, g is unaspirated and k is aspirated. The initial h in Mandarin is pronounced in a similar position as "h" in English.

(2) Front-sonorant compound finals: ai, ei, ao, and ou

Front-sonorant compound finals are composed of a primary vowel and a secondary vowel. The first vowel is the primary vowel (the tone mark is put above it), the pronunciation is relatively clear and loud, and the length of the sound is longer than the secondary vowel; the length of the secondary vowel is relatively short and the pronunciation is less stressed.

A primary vowel + a secondary vowel: ai, ei, ao, and ou

The final ei is similar to "ay" as in the English word "play" and the final ou is similar to "o" in the English word "so".

(3) Finals with nasal endings: an, en, ang, eng, and ong

A final that ends with n is called a front nasal final; a final that ends with ng is called a back nasal final.

When pronouncing a front nasal final, first pronounce the vowel in the final. Then immediately pronounce n along with the flow of the air. The nasal n is pronounced similar to "n" as in the English word "in".

When pronouncing a back nasal final, first pronounce the vowel in the final. Then immediately pronounce ng along with the flow of the air. The pronunciation of ng is similar to "ng" as in the English word "belong".

2. Third tone sandhi

(1) When appearing on its own, a third tone is fully pronounced.

Example   nǐ   hǎo   mǎ   nǚ

(2) When two third tones are read aloud together, the first third tone is read as a second tone, but the tone mark remains the third tone.

ˇ + ˇ ⟶ ˊ + ˇ

Example   nǐ hǎo (hello) ⟶ ní hǎo

hěn hǎo (very good)   hén hǎo

yǔfǎ (grammar)   yúfǎ

kěyǐ (all right)   kéyǐ

(3) When a third tone is followed by a first tone, second tone, or fourth tone syllable, or most neutral tones, the third tone is read aloud as a half third tone.

Example   hěn gāo (very tall)

hěn bái (very white)

hěn dà (very big)

nǎinai (grandma)

2 语音练习 Pronunciation Drills 1-01-07

1. Read aloud and pay attention to the tones

nī	ní	nǐ	nì	
hāo	háo	hǎo	hào	nǐ hǎo
mēn	mén		mèn	nǐmen
tā		tǎ	tà	tāmen
	hén	hěn	hèn	
māng	máng	mǎng		hěn máng

2. Sound discrimination

kàn (to look) —— gàn (to do)   kǒu (mouth) —— gǒu (dog)

fēi (to fly) —— hēi (black)   bǎi (hundred) —— běi (north)

dāo (knife) —— dōu (all)   tán (to talk) —— táng (sugar)

fēn (minute) —— fēng (wind)   dōng (east) —— dēng (lamp)

3. Tone discrimination

dāo —— dào   kàn (to look) —— kǎn (to cut)

pái —— pài   hěn (very) —— hèn (to hate)

páng —— pàng (fat)   děng (to wait) —— dēng (lamp)

4. Third-tone sandhi

děng tā	hěn gāo
nǐ máng	hěn máng
nǐ hǎo	hěn hǎo
kělè	hǎokàn
nǎinai	hǎo ma

三、课堂用语 CLASSROOM EXPRESSIONS

❶ Hěn hǎo!   Very good!   1-01-08

❷ Nǐmen dú.   Please read aloud.

❸ Kàn hēibǎn.   Look at the blackboard.

❧ 第三部分　PART THREE ❧

一、课文 TEXT

（一）🔊 1-01-09

A：Lǎoshī hǎo!
　　老师　好！

B：Nǐmen hǎo!
　　你们　好！

- -

A：Hello, teacher!
B：Hello, everyone!

（二）🔊 1-01-10

A：Zhè shì shéi?
　　这 是 谁？

B：Zhè shì Chén lǎoshī.
　　这 是 陈 老师。

- -

A：Who is this person?
B：This is Teacher Chen.

（三）🔊 1-01-11

A：Nà shì shéi?
　　那 是 谁？

B：Nà shì Zhèng lǎoshī.
　　那 是 郑 老师。

- -

A：Who is that person?
B：That is Teacher Zheng.

Communication activity

Based on the pictures and scenes below, complete the dialogues, using the designated words.

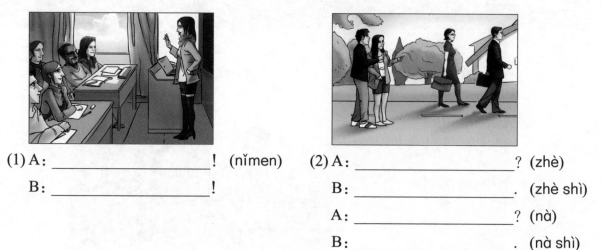

(1) A: _____! (nǐmen)

   B: _____!

(2) A: _____? (zhè)

   B: _____. (zhè shì)

   A: _____? (nà)

   B: _____. (nà shì)

二、语音 *PHONETICS*

1 语音知识 Knowledge about Phonetics

(1) Initials: zh, ch, sh, and r

The initial zh is similar to "j" in the English word "jet", but the tip of the tongue curls toward the back a bit, and it is unaspirated.

The initial ch is similar to "ch" in the English word "church", but the tip of the tongue curls toward the back a bit, and it is aspirated.

The initial sh is similar to "sh" in the English word "ship", but the tip of the tongue curls toward the back a bit.

The initial r is similar to "r" in the English word "right", but when pronouncing r, the lips are flat, and the tip of the tongue curls toward the back a bit. First try to make the sh sound, next vibrate your vocal chords, and then the r sound will be produced.

(2) The final: -i [ʅ]

The -i [ʅ] in zhi, chi, shi, and ri is not pronounced in the same way as the single final i [i]. After pronouncing the aforementioned zh, ch, sh, and r, the tongue remains unmoved.

(3) Finals that begin with u: ua, uo, uai, uei, uan, uen, uang, and ueng

The structure of this group of finals is as follows:

Medial u + the primary vowel	ua, uo, uai, or uei (ui)
Medial u + the nasal final	uan, uen (un), uang, or ueng

When pronouncing a final that begins with u, first pronounce the sound of "u" as in the English word "youth", then naturally glide to the vowel or the nasal final.

2 语音练习 Pronunciation Drills 1-01-12

1. Read aloud and pay attention to the tones

lāo	láo	lǎo	lào	
shī	shí	shǐ	shì	lǎoshī
chēn	chén	chěn	chèn	Chén lǎoshī
zhēng		zhěng	zhèng	Zhèng lǎoshī
	shéi			shì shéi
	rén	rěn	rèn	lǎorén

2. Sound discrimination

guī —— kuī   shǔn —— zhǔn

chūn —— tūn   lù (road) —— rù (to enter)

zhǐ —— chǐ   kuài —— kuà

wán (to finish) —— wáng (king)   huài (bad) —— huì (can)

3. Tone discrimination

shì (to be) —— shí (ten)   shuǐ (water) —— shuí (who)

chá (tea) —— chà (poor)   zhū (pig) —— zhú (bamboo)

rén (people) —— rèn (to recognize)   wǒ (I) —— wò (to lie down)

4. Practice reading the disyllabic words

shuōhuà (to speak)   zhīdào (to know)   chídào (late)

shàngwǔ (morning)   wǎnshang (evening)   rènshi (to know)

Zhōngguó (China)   Měiguó (USA)   Rìběn (Japan)   Hánguó (South Korea)

三、课堂用语 CLASSROOM EXPRESSIONS

 1-01-13

❶ Shàngkè le.   Let's begin the class.

❷ Gēn wǒ dú.   Please repeat after me.

❸ Duì bu duì?   Is that right?

❹ Duì le.   That's right.

❺ Bú duì.   That's not right.

❧ 第四部分 PART FOUR ❧

一、课文 TEXT

（一） 🔊 1-01-14

Nǐ hē kāfēi ma?
A：你 喝 咖啡 吗？

Wǒ bù hē kāfēi.
B：我 不 喝 咖啡。

- -

A：Do you drink coffee?
B：I don't drink coffee.

（二） 🔊 1-01-15

Nǐ hē shénme?
A：你 喝 什么？

Lái yì bēi chá.
B：来 一 杯 茶。

- -

A：What would you like to drink?
B：A cup of tea.

Communication activity

Small group activity: In groups of four, look at the picture on the right, and take turns asking and answering questions regarding what each person wants to drink. Find out the most popular drink in the group, then report your finding to the whole class.

二、语音 *PHONETICS*

1 语音知识 Knowledge about Phonetics

1. The tone sandhi of "yī 一" (one)

The original tone of "yī 一" (one) is the first tone. When it appears alone or appears at the end of a word or a sentence, it is read in its original tone. When it is used as an ordinal number (i.e., dì-yī 第一 first), it is also read in its original tone. However, when "yī 一" appears before the first, second, or third tone, the tone is changed to the fourth tone. When it appears before the fourth tone, the tone is changed to the second tone.

$$
\text{yī} + \begin{cases} - \\ \diagup \\ \lor \end{cases} \longrightarrow \text{yì} + \begin{cases} - \\ \diagup \\ \lor \end{cases} \qquad
\begin{aligned} &\text{Example:} &&\text{yì bēi (a cup of)} \\ & &&\text{yì píng (a bottle of)} \\ & &&\text{yì běn (a volume, a copy)} \end{aligned}
$$

$$
\text{yī} + \diagdown \longrightarrow \text{yí} + \diagdown \qquad \text{Example:} \quad \text{yí biàn (once)}
$$

2. Summary of the spelling rules (1): Rules for separation of syllables

(1) Spelling rules for i, u, or ü as a syllable itself

When the final i itself is a syllable, or when i that is combined with a nasal consonant n or ng is a syllable, add y before i.

i ⟹ yi   Example: i → yi   in → yin   ing → ying

When a compound final starts with i and this final itself is a syllable, i should be changed to y.

i ⟹ y   Example: ia → ya   ie → ye   ian → yan

When the final u itself is a syllable, add w before u.

u ⟹ wu   Example: u → wu

When a compound final starts with u and this final itself is a syllable, u should be changed to w.

u ⟹ w   Example: ua → wa   uan → wan

When the final ü itself is a syllable, or when a compound final that starts with ü is a syllable, add y before ü, and remove the two dots above ü.

ü ⟹ yu   Example: ü → yu   üe → yue   üan → yuan

(2) The apostrophe

When a syllable starts with the vowel a, o, or e with no initial, an apostrophe is placed before the vowel to separate it from the previous syllable. For example, Tiān'ān Mén 天安门 (Tian'anmen), Xī'ōu 西欧 (Western Europe), and 天鹅 tiān'é (swan).

3. Brief review of phonetics (1)

(1) Summary of the initials

	Unaspirated Stops	Aspirated Stops	Nasals	Fricatives
Labials	b[p]	p[pʻ]	m[m]	f[f]
Blade-Aveolars	d[t]	t[tʻ]	n[n]	l[l]
Velars	g[k]	k[kʻ]		h[x]
Blade-Palatals	zh[tʂ]	ch[tʂʻ]		sh[ʂ]、r[ʐ]

(2) Summary of the finals

Single finals: a, o, e, i, u, ü, -i[ʅ]

Compound finals: ai, ei, ao, ou, an, en, ang, eng, uai, uei, uan, uen, uang, ueng, ong

(3) The combinations of initials and finals in this lesson

Initials / Finals	b	p	m	f	d	t	n	l	g	k	h	zh	ch	sh	r
a	ba	pa	ma	fa	da	ta	na	la	ga	ka	ha	zha	cha	sha	
o	bo	po	mo	fo											
e			me		de	te	ne	le	ge	ke	he	zhe	che	she	re
i	bi	pi	mi		di	ti	ni	li							
u	bu	pu	mu	fu	du	tu	nu	lu	gu	ku	hu	zhu	chu	shu	ru
ü							nü	lü							
-i[ʅ]												zhi	chi	shi	ri
ai	bai	pai	mai		dai	tai	nai	lai	gai	kai	hai	zhai	chai	shai	
ei	bei	pei	mei	fei	dei	tei	nei	lei	gei	kei	hei	zhei		shei	
ao	bao	pao	mao		dao	tao	nao	lao	gao	kao	hao	zhao	chao	shao	rao
ou		pou	mou	fou	dou	tou	nou	lou	gou	kou	hou	zhou	chou	shou	rou
an	ban	pan	man	fan	dan	tan	nan	lan	gan	kan	han	zhan	chan	shan	ran
en	ben	pen	men	fen	den		nen		gen	ken	hen	zhen	chen	shen	ren
ang	bang	pang	mang	fang	dang	tang	nang	lang	gang	kang	hang	zhang	chang	shang	rang
eng	beng	peng	meng	feng	deng	teng	neng	leng	geng	keng	heng	zheng	cheng	sheng	reng
uai									guai	kuai	huai	zhuai	chuai	shuai	
uei (ui)					dui	tui			gui	kui	hui	zhui	chui	shui	rui
uan					duan	tuan	nuan	luan	guan	kuan	huan	zhuan	chuan	shuan	ruan
uen (un)					dun	tun		lun	gun	kun	hun	zhun	chun	shun	run
uang									guang	kuang	huang	zhuang	chuang	shuang	
ueng															
ong					dong	tong	nong	long	gong	kong	hong	zhong	chong		rong

(4) Brief summary of the rules for tone sandhi

① The third tone sandhi

When two third tone syllables are read aloud together, the first third tone changes to the second tone.

$$\vee + \vee \longrightarrow \diagup + \vee$$

When a syllable with a third tone appears before the first, second, fourth, and most of the neutral tones, it is read aloud only as a half third tone.

$$\vee + \left\{ \begin{array}{l} - \\ \diagup \\ \diagdown \end{array} \right. \longrightarrow \vee\!\cdot + \left\{ \begin{array}{l} - \\ \diagup \\ \diagdown \end{array} \right.$$

② The tone sandhi of "yī 一" (one)

$$yī + \left\{ \begin{array}{l} - \\ \diagup \\ \vee \end{array} \right. \longrightarrow yì + \left\{ \begin{array}{l} - \\ \diagup \\ \vee \end{array} \right.$$

$$yī + \quad \diagdown \longrightarrow yí + \quad \diagdown$$

2　语音练习 Pronunciation Drills   1-01-16

1. Read aloud and pay attention to the tones

kā   kǎ

fēi   féi   fěi   fèi   kāfēi

shēn   shén   shěn   shèn

                                              me   shénme

yī   yí   yǐ   yì

bēi   běi   bèi

chā   chá   chǎ   chà   yì bēi chá

2. Sound discrimination

bǐ —— pǐ   duì —— tuì

kě —— gě   shì (to be) —— rì (sun)

zhǐ —— chǐ   zhōng —— chōng

kuài —— kuà   rì —— rè

huān —— huāng   gēn —— gēng

ròu —— ruò   dōu (all) —— duō (many)

3. Tone discrimination

ní —— nǐ   shí (ten) —— shī (lion)

zhě —— zhè (this)   chéng —— chèng

guāi —— guài   ràng (to let) —— rǎng (to shout)

4. The neutral tone

nǎinai	bóbo	pópo	
mèimei	gēge	gūgu	shěnshen
nǐmen	wǒmen	tāmen	

5. Third tone followed by other tones

Half third tone:

lǎoshī	hǎochī	nǐ shuō	
Fǎguó	nǐ dú	hěn máng	
kělè	nǐ yào	wǒ mài	
nǎinai	wǒmen	hǎo ma	
wǒ gēge	nǎ guó rén	nǐ bàba	nǐ wàipó

Two third tones:

nǐ hǎo   hěn hǎo   wǒ mǎi

6. The variations of the tone of " 一 (yī)"

shíyī	dì-yī	yī lóu
yì zhāng	yì bēi	yì zhī
yì tái	yì rén	
yì běn	yì bǎ	
yí gè	yí kuài	

7. Practice reading the disyllabic words

kāfēi (coffee)	hē chá (to drink tea)	lǜchá (green tea)	hóngchá (black tea)
shénme (what)	yǔfǎ (grammar)	dǎkāi (to open)	kǎoshì (exam)
Hànyǔ (Chinese)	chī fàn (to eat a meal)	yígòng (altogether)	yìshēng (whole life)

三、课堂用语 CLASSROOM EXPRESSIONS

❶ Bǎ shū dǎkāi.   Open your book.

❷ Kàn kèwén.   Read the text.

❸ Dǒng le ma?   Do you understand? / Have you got it?

❹ Dǒng le.   Yes, I do. / Yes, I have.

❺ Bù dǒng.   No, I don't. / No, I haven't.

1-01-17

四、汉字 CHINESE CHARACTERS

1 汉字知识 Knowledge about Chinese Characters

1. The origin of Chinese characters

Chinese characters originated from pictographs. From ancient times to the present, the shapes of Chinese characters have undergone great changes. Modern Chinese characters are square in shape. They evolved from ancient Chinese characters. For example:

Pictograph	Oracle Bone Script	Bronze Script	Small Seal Script	Official Script	Traditional Character in Regular Script	Simplified Character in Regular Script
				馬	馬	马

2. The basic strokes of Chinese characters

Chinese characters are composed of strokes with different shapes. The strokes of Chinese characters are divided into basic strokes and compound strokes.

Basic strokes of Chinese characters

Stroke Form	Name	Example	Way of Writing
一 [→]	héng	一 yī (one)	From left to right, like 一
丨 [↓]	shù	十 shí (ten)	From top to bottom, like the 2nd stroke of 十
丿 [⟋]	piě	八 bā (eight)	From top right to bottom left, like the 1st stroke of 八
乀 [⟍]	nà	八 bā (eight)	From top left to bottom right, like the 2nd stroke of 八
丶 [⟍]	diǎn	六 liù (six)	From top left downward right, like the 1st stroke of 六
乛 [⟋]	tí	我 wǒ (I; me)	From bottom left upward to top right, like the 4th stroke of 我

3. Basic rules for the stroke order and the way of writing Chinese characters

Example	Stroke Order			Rule
十 shí (ten)	一	十		Horizontal before vertical
八 bā (eight)	丿	八		Downward left before downward right
好 hǎo (good)	女	子		From left to right
个 gè (*measure word*)	丿	人	个	From top to bottom
月 yuè (moon)	几	月		Outside before inside
国 guó (country)	冂	国	国	First outside, next inside, then close
小 xiǎo (small)	亅	小	小	Middle before left and right

2　认写基本汉字 Learn and Write the Basic Chinese Characters

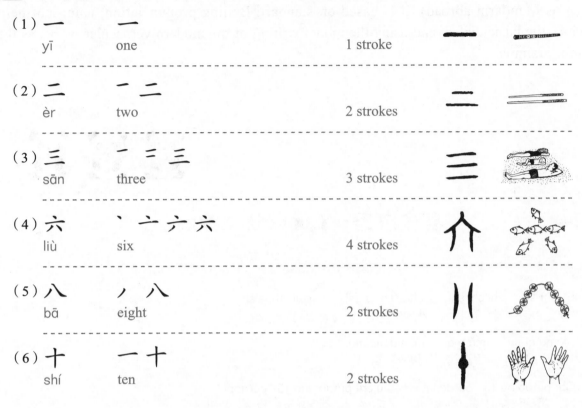

（1）一	一	one	1 stroke	
	yī			
（2）二	一 二	two	2 strokes	
	èr			
（3）三	一 二 三	three	3 strokes	
	sān			
（4）六	丶 一 六 六	six	4 strokes	
	liù			
（5）八	丿 八	eight	2 strokes	
	bā			
（6）十	一 十	ten	2 strokes	
	shí			

五、文化知识　*CULTURAL KNOWLEDGE*

Chinese and Pǔtōnghuà (Mandarin)

Chinese is the primary language of the Chinese nation with a long history. It belongs to the Sino-Tibetan family of languages. It is one of the languages with the longest history. According to UNESCO statistics, currently about 1.6 billion people in the world can speak Chinese. The extensive use of Chinese is second only to English in the world. Chinese is one of the six official languages of the United Nations.

There are 56 ethnic groups in China, of which the Han, Hui, Man (Manchu), and some other ethnic groups use Chinese, accounting for 94% of the Chinese population. Overseas, many people in Chinese communities in Singapore, Malaysia, and some other countries also use Chinese. Over one billion people worldwide use Chinese as their mother tongue.

The Chinese language is divided into seven main dialect regions, of which the northern dialect region (also called the Mandarin dialect region) accounts for approximately three fourths of the total area of China. The northern dialect speakers of Chinese account for two thirds of the total population of China.

Modern Standard Chinese is "pǔtōnghuà 普通话" (literally the Common Speech, known as Mandarin abroad). It is based on standard Beijing pronunciation, using northern speech as the basic dialect and using the model writing of the modern vernacular works as the norm for grammar.

趣味汉语 Fun with Chinese

Tongue Twisters

Sì shì sì,　shí shì shí,　shísì shì shísì,　sìshí shì sìshí.
1. 四是四，十是十，十四是十四，四十是四十。

Māma qí mǎ,　mǎ màn,　māma mà mǎ.
2. 妈妈骑马，马 慢，妈妈骂马。

Chī pútao bù tǔ　pútaopír,　bù chī pútao dào tǔ　pútaopír.
3. 吃 葡萄不吐葡萄皮儿，不吃葡萄 倒吐葡萄皮儿。

(1) Four is four; ten is ten; fourteen is fourteen; forty is forty.
(2) Mom rode a horse; the horse was slow, (so) Mom cursed the horse.
(3) When eating grapes, don't spit out the grape skins.
　　When not eating grapes, spit out the grape skins.

2 Xièxie
谢 谢
Thank you

After studying this lesson, you will have learned almost all the initials, finals, and tones in Chinese. You should also be able to pronounce all of the syllables, recognize and write the eight new Chinese characters, and say many useful words and phrases. Perhaps you have already realized that it is quite interesting to learn to speak Chinese and write Chinese characters. Although it could be a little strange at the beginning, studying Chinese is not difficult at all as long as you use the correct method as suggested in this book. You still have lots of time and many opportunities to continue to improve your pronunciation in Mandarin and write Chinese characters.

๛ 热身 WARM-UP ๛

The Chinese words below are transliterations based on English pronunciations. Try to read aloud these words and guess what they mean.

kāfēi　　　　qiǎokèlì　　　　hànbǎobāo　　kělè
（1）咖啡　　（2）巧克力　　（3）汉堡包　　（4）可乐

๛ 第一部分 PART ONE ๛

一、课文 TEXT

（一）　🔊 1-02-01

please

Kěyǐ jìnlai ma?
A: 可以 进来 吗?

Qǐng jìn.
B: 请 进。
请 进

A: May I come in?
B: Please come in.

· 21

宀 冖 shelter/roof radical

（二）　 1-02-02

Qǐng hē chá.
A: 请 喝 茶。

Xièxie.
B: 谢谢。

Bú kèqi.
A: 不 客气。

A: Have some tea, please.
B: Thank you.
A: You are welcome.

Communication activity

Following what you see in the pictures, split into groups of two, with one acting as the guest and the other acting as the host.

（1）　　　　　　　　　　　　　　　　（2）

二、语音 *PHONETICS*

1 语音知识 Knowledge about Phonetics

(1) Initials: j, q, and x

The initials j, q, and x are voiceless palatal affricates.

When pronouncing j and q, first raise the tongue to the hard palate and press the tip of the tongue against the back of the lower teeth, and then loosen the tongue to let the air squeeze out.

The initial j is unaspirated while q is aspirated. When pronouncing q, the airflow is very strong.

When pronouncing x, first raise the front of the tongue toward (but not touching) the hard palate and then let the air squeeze out. The vocal cords do not vibrate.

Note:

The only finals that can be combined with j, q, and x are the single finals i and ü, as well as the compound finals that start with i or ü.

(2) Finals: ia, ie, iao, iou, ian, in, iang, ing, üe, üan, ün and iong

In the finals that start with i or ü, the primary vowel is the sound after i or ü (e.g., ia and üe). The final i or ü glides over to the primary vowel. If there is another vowel (e.g., iao and iou) or a nasal sound (e.g., ian, iang, and iong) after the primary vowel, the secondary vowel or the nasal sound is pronounced lightly.

2 语音练习 Pronunciation Drills 1-02-03

1. Read aloud and pay attention to the tones

jīn		jǐn	jìn	
	lái		lài	jìnlai
qīng	qíng	qǐng	qìng	qǐng jìn
xiē	xié	xiě	xiè	xièxie
kē	ké	kě	kè	
qī	qí	qǐ	qì	kèqi

2. Sound discrimination

jī (chicken) —— qī (seven)　　　　jiāo (to teach) —— qiāo (to knock)

jué (to feel) —— xué (to study)　　　qǐng (please) —— xǐng (to wake up)

yuè (moon) —— yè (night)　　　　jiǎo (foot) —— jiǔ (nine)

jìn (to come in) —— jìng (quiet)　　　qián (money) —— quán (all)

3. Tone discrimination

xià (down) —— xiā (shrimp)   shuǐ (water) —— shuí (who)

xīn (heart) —— xìn (letter)   líng (zero) —— lǐng (to lead)

xiǎo (small) —— xiào (to laugh)   juān (to donate) —— juǎn (to roll)

4. Combination of tones

– + –	– + ╱	– + ∨	– + ╲	– + ∘ [1]
kāfēi	Zhōngguó	hēibǎn	shēngdiào	tāmen
yīshēng	hē chá	shēntǐ	chī fàn	gēge

╱ + –	╱ + ╱	╱ + ∨	╱ + ╲	╱ + ∘
túshū	chángcháng	niúnǎi	liúlì	péngyou
(books)	(often)	(milk)	(fluent)	(friend)
chénggōng	yínháng	píngguǒ	chídào	yéye
(success)	(bank)	(apple)	(late)	(grandpa)

5. Practice reading the disyllabic words

yǔyán	xuéyuàn	xuéxí	xuésheng
(language)	(institute)	(to study)	(student)
xǐhuan	jiāoshū	péngyou	yuèliang
(to like)	(to teach)	(friend)	(moon)
qìshuǐ	Yīngguó	gāoxìng	xiūxi
(soda water)	(United Kingdom)	(happy)	(to have a break)

三、课堂用语 CLASSROOM EXPRESSIONS

1-02-04

❶ Tóngxuémen hǎo!   Hello, everyone! (Teacher to students)

❷ Qǐng kàn shū.   Please read your book.

❸ Qǐng dà shēng dú.   Please read aloud.

❹ Xiàkè.   The class is over.

---

[1] "∘" here represents the neutral tone.

❧ 第二部分　PART TWO ❧

一、课文 *TEXT*

（一） 🔊 1-02-05

Qǐngwèn, Chén lǎoshī zài ma?
A:　请问，　　陈 老师 在 吗?

Zài. / Bú zài.
B:　在。/ 不 在。　　土　soil/ earth

- -

A:　Excuse me, is Teacher Chen in?
B:　Yes, she is. / No, she isn't.

（二） 🔊 1-02-06

time incrament　later

Zàijiàn!
A:　再见!

Zàijiàn!
B:　再见!

- -

A:　Goodbye.
B:　Goodbye.

Communication activity

In groups of two, act according to the pictures.

（1）

（2）

二、语音 *PHONETICS*

1 语音知识 Knowledge about Phonetics

(1) Initials: z, c, and s

The pronunciation of z is similar to "ds" as in the English word "goods", except that the vocal cords do not vibrate.

The pronunciation of c is similar to "ts" as in the English word "cats" and is aspirated.

When pronouncing s, you put the tip of your tongue close to your teeth and squeeze out your breath. It sounds close to "s" in the English word "sweet".

Note:

The pronunciations of z and zh are unaspirated while c and ch are aspirated.

(2) The final: -i [ɿ]

When pronouncing the syllables zi, ci, and si, the tongue remains in the same position from beginning to end.

2 语音练习 Pronunciation Drills

 1-02-07

1. Read aloud and pay attention to the tones

zī	cī	sī		
qīng	qíng	qǐng	qìng	
wēn	wén	wěn	wèn	qǐngwèn
zuō	zuó	zuǒ	zuò	qǐng zuò
zāi		zǎi	zài	zài ma
jiān		jiǎn	jiàn	zàijiàn

2. Sound discrimination

zài (at) —— cài (vegetable)

zǎo (early) —— zhǎo (to look for)

cí (word) —— chí (late)

sì (four) —— shì (to be)

zū (to rent) —— cū (thick)

zú (foot) —— zhú (bamboo)

cūn (village) —— chūn (spring)

sān (three) —— shān (mountain)

3. Tone discrimination

zì (character) —— zǐ (son)　　　　zuó (yesterday) —— zuò (to sit)

cí (word) —— cǐ (this)　　　　cān (meal) —— cán (silkworm)

sì (four) —— sī (silk)　　　　suí (to follow) —— suì (to break into pieces)

4. Combination of tones

ˇ + ˉ	ˇ + ˊ	ˇ + ˇ	ˇ + ˋ	ˇ + ˚
lǎoshī	yǔyán	kěyǐ	qǐng jìn	wǒmen
Běijīng	lǚxíng	yǔfǎ	kǎoshì	jiějie
(Beijing)	(to travel)	(grammar)	(exam)	(elder sister)

ˋ + ˉ	ˋ + ˊ	ˋ + ˇ	ˋ + ˋ	ˋ + ˚
dì-yī (first)	wàipó	Hànyǔ	guìxìng	mèimei
miànbāo	liànxí	bàozhǐ	zhùyì	kèqi
(bread)	(exercise)	(newspaper)	(to pay attention to)	

5. Practice reading the disyllabic words

sì céng (fourth floor)　　shí céng (tenth floor)　　sùshè (dormitory)　　cèsuǒ (toilet)

míngzi (name)　　Hànzì (Chinese character)　　zuòyè (homework)　　zìjǐ (oneself)

zǎoshang (morning)　　xiàwǔ (afternoon)　　zài jiā (at home)　　zàijiàn

三、课堂用语 CLASSROOM EXPRESSIONS

❶ Tīng wǒ niàn.　　　　　　　Listen to me read aloud.

❷ Wǒ shuō, nǐmen tīng.　　　I'll speak, and you listen.

❸ Qǐng nǐ niàn shēngcí.　　　Please read the new words aloud.

❹ Qǐng nǐ xiě Hànzì.　　　　Please write the Chinese characters.

1-02-08

第三部分　PART THREE

一、课文 TEXT

（一）　1-02-09

Qǐngwèn, xǐshǒujiān zài nǎr?
A:　请问，　洗手间 在 哪儿？

Bù hǎoyìsi, wǒ bù zhīdào.
B:　不好意思，我 不 知道。

Méi guānxi.
A:　没　关系。

A:　Where's the washroom?
B:　Sorry, I don't know.
A:　It's all right.

（二）　1-02-10

Děng yíxià.
A:　等　一下。

Duìbuqǐ, qǐng zài shuō yí biàn.
B:　对不起，请 再 说 一 遍。

Děng yíxià.
A:　等　一下。

A:　Wait a moment.
B:　Excuse me, say it again, please.
A:　Wait a moment.

Communication activity

In groups of two, and based on the sentences given, ask your partner if he or she knows each location in the picture.

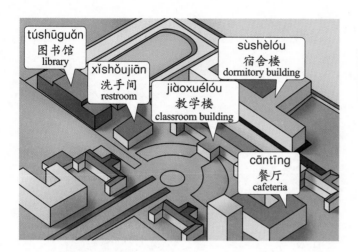

Example

Qǐngwèn……zài nǎr?
A: 请问……　在 哪儿?

Duìbuqǐ, qǐng zài shuō yí biàn.
B: 对不起，请 再 说 一 遍。

二、语音 *PHONETICS*

1 语音知识 Knowledge about Phonetics

(1) The final: er

The final er [-r] is similar to the American English pronunciation of "er" in the word "sister".

Note:

The pronunciation of er will be affected by the tone. When pronouncing the fourth tone, the mouth is noticeably wider, for example "dì-èr ge érzi de ěrduo 第二个儿子的耳朵" (the second son's ears).

(2) The retroflex ending

The final er sometimes is not a syllable by itself, but is merged with the syllable before it, creating a retroflex ending. When writing *pinyin*, add r at the end of the syllable; When writing Chinese characters, add 儿 after the character, e.g., "nǎr 哪儿" (where).

(3) The tone sandhi of "bù 不" (not)

The original tone of "bù 不" is the fourth tone, but when used before a fourth tone, it is changed to the second tone "bú 不".

Example　　bù hē　　　bù máng　　　bù hǎo
　　　　　　bú shì　　　bú yào

2 语音练习 Pronunciation Drills 1-02-11

1. Read aloud and pay attention to the tones

xī	xí	xǐ	xì	
shōu	shóu	shǒu	shòu	
jiān		jiǎn	jiàn	xǐshǒujiān
nā	ná	nǎ	nà	nǎr
zāi		zǎi	zài	zài nǎr
shuō			shuò	
xiā	xiá		xià	yíxià

2. Sound discrimination

zhèr (here) —— zhè (this)   nàr (there) —— nà (that)

nǎr —— nǎ (which)   wánr (to play) —— wán (to finish)

huàr (picture) —— huà (to draw)   gàir (lid) —— gài (to cover)

tiānr (weather) —— tiān (sky)   xìnr (message) —— xìn (letter)

3. Tone discrimination

èr (two) —— ér (son)   èr —— ěr (ear)

huār (flower) —— huàr (picture)   wánr —— wǎnr (bowl)

zǐr (seed) —— zìr (character)   cír (word) —— cìr (thorn)

4. The final "er" and the retroflex ending

èr   érzi (son)

nǚ'ér (daughter)   ěrduo (ear)

zhèr   nàr

nǎr   wánr

5. The variations of the tone of "不 (bù)"

bù gāo	bù hē	bù máng	bù qí	bù kě	bù hǎo
bú dà	bú shì	bú zài	bú kèqi	duìbuqǐ	bù hǎoyìsi

6. Combination of tones

ˉ + ˉ	ˉ + ́	ˉ + ̌	ˉ + ̀	ˉ + ˳
cāntīng (dining hall)	Yīngguó	jīnglǐ (manager)	gāoxìng (happy)	xiānsheng (sir)
fēijī (plane)	shēngcí (new word)	qiānbǐ (pencil)	gōngzuò (work)	qīzi (wife)

ˊ + ˉ   ˊ + ˊ   ˊ + ˇ   ˊ + ˋ   ˊ + ˚

míngtiān (tomorrow) xuéxí (to study) yóuyǒng (to swim) xuéyuàn (institute) shénme (what)

shíjiān (time) huídá (to answer) píjiǔ (beer)   zázhì (magazine) míngzi (name)

7. Practice reading the disyllabic words

nánháir (boy)   nǚháir (girl)   xiǎoháir (child)   yíhuìr (a while)

jiàoshì (classroom) yīyuàn (hospital) cāochǎng (playground) lǐtáng (auditorium)

Fǎguó (France)   Éguó (Russia)   Yīngyǔ (English)   Rìyǔ (Japanese)

三、课堂用语 CLASSROOM EXPRESSIONS

① dì-yī shēng   the first tone   1-02-12

② dì-èr shēng   the second tone

③ dì-sān shēng   the third tone

④ dì-sì shēng   the fourth tone

⑤ qīngshēng   the neutral tone

⑥ Dì jǐ shēng?   Which tone?

⑦ Qǐng zài niàn yí biàn. Please read/say it again.

第四部分 PART FOUR

一、课文 TEXT

（一） 1-02-13

Fúwùyuán, diǎn cài.

A: 服务员，点菜。

Nín yào shénme?

B: 您要什么？

Wǒ yào kǎoyā.

A: 我要烤鸭。

A: Waiter, I want to order the food.
B: What would you like?
A: I'd like some roast duck.

（二） 1-02-14

Nín hǎo, qù nǎr?
A: 您 好，去 哪儿？

Qù gùgōng.
B: 去 故宫。

Qǐng shàng chē.
A: 请 上 车。

A: Hello, where are you going?
B: The Forbidden City.
A: Please get in.

Communication activity

Work in groups of two. Select a scene from the pictures below and act it out in front of the whole class.

（1）

（3）

（2）

（4）

二、语音 *PHONETICS*

1 语音知识 Knowledge about Phonetics

1. Summary of the spelling rules (2): Rules for the omission of syllables

(1) -iu, -ui, -un

$$\text{Initial} + \begin{cases} \text{iou} \\ \text{uei} \\ \text{uen} \end{cases} \longrightarrow \text{Initial} + \begin{cases} \text{iu} \\ \text{ui} \\ \text{un} \end{cases} \quad \begin{array}{l} \text{Example: píjiǔ (beer)} \\ \text{guìxìng (honorable surname)} \\ \text{tǎolùn (to discuss)} \end{array}$$

(2) When i or ü is combined with j, q, or x, the dot or dots must be omitted. For example, "jǐ 几" (how many, how much), "qù 去" (to go). However, when ü follows n or l, the two dots cannot be omitted, such as "nǚ 女" (female) and "lǜ 绿" (green).

2. Brief review of phonetics (2)

(1) Complete table of initials

① There are 21 initials in Modern Standard Chinese, divided into six groups based on the positions of their pronunciations (see the table below). Among them only r, m, n, and l are voiced. The rest are voiceless, i.e., without the vibration of the vocal cords when being pronounced.

Table of Initials

	Unaspirated Stops	Aspirated Stops	Nasals	Fricatives
Labials	b[p]	p[p']	m[m]	f[f]
Blade-Alveolars	d[t]	t[t']	n[n]	l[l]
Velars	g[k]	k[k']		h[x]
Palatals	j[tɕ]	q[tɕ']		x[ɕ]
Blade-Palatals	zh[tʂ]	ch[tʂ']		sh[ʂ]、r[ʐ]
Dental Sibilants	z[ts]	c[ts']		s[s]

② Of the 21 initials, there are six pairs of corresponding aspirated and unaspirated sounds. When pronouncing an aspirated or unaspirated sound, pay close attention to the differences between them because each sound has the function of distinguishing meanings.

A. b —— p　　　　C. g —— k　　　　E. zh —— ch

B. d —— t　　　　D. j —— q　　　　F. z —— c

(2) Complete table of finals

① There are 38 finals in Modern Standard Chinese, divided into four groups based on the shape of the mouth for the vowel in the final (see the table below).

Table of Finals

Finals	Kāikǒuhū 开口呼 (Finals other than those that begin with i, u, or ü)	Qíchǐhū 齐齿呼 (Finals that begin with i)	Hékǒuhū 合口呼 (Finals that begin with u)	Cuōkǒuhū 撮口呼 (Finals that begin with ü)
Single Finals	-i[ʅ]、-i[ɿ]	i[i]	u[u]	ü[y]
	a[A]	ia[iA]	ua[uA]	
	o[o]		uo[uo]	
	e[ɤ]			
	er[ɚ]	ie[iɛ]		üe[yɛ]
Compound Finals	ai[ai]		uai[uai]	
	ei[ei]		uei[uei]	
	ao[ɑu]	iao[iɑu]		
	ou[ou]	iou[iou]		
Finals with a Nasal Consonant or Consonants	an[an]	ian[iɛn]	uan[uan]	üan[yan]
	en[ən]	in[in]	uen[uən]	ün[yn]
	ang[ɑŋ]	iang[iɑŋ]	uang[uɑŋ]	
	eng[əŋ]	ing[iŋ]	ueng[uəŋ]	
			ong[uŋ]	iong[yŋ]

② The letter i represents three different pronunciations: i [i] as in yī, -i [ʅ] as in zhī, and -i [ɿ] as in sī.

③ The letter e represents four different pronunciations: e [ɤ] as in è, e [ɛ] as in yě, e [e] as in mèi, and e [ə] as in wèn.

④ The final ueng itself is a syllable without an initial (spelled as weng), representing the very few Chinese characters that we have not learned.

(3) Complete table of combined initials and finals

In Modern Standard Chinese there are altogether over four hundred meaningful basic syllables. If the four tones are added, there will be over 1,200 syllables. All the syllables that we have studied at this stage of phonetics are found in the table below.

2 语音练习 Pronunciation Drills 1-02-15

1. Read aloud and pay attention to the tones

fū	fú	fǔ	fù	
wū	wú	wǔ	wù	
yuān	yuán	yuǎn	yuàn	fúwùyuán
diān		diǎn	diàn	
cāi	cái	cǎi	cài	diǎn cài
shāng		shǎng	shàng	
chē		chě	chè	shàng chē

2. Sound discrimination

bǎo (full) —— pǎo (to run)　　duì (right) —— tuì　　gū (aunt) —— kū (to cry)

zū (to rent) —— cū (thick)　　zhǎo (to look for) —— chǎo　　jiāng (river) —— qiāng (gun)

jiǔ (nine) —— xiǔ　　sī (silk) —— shī (poem)　　zǐ (son) —— jǐ (self)

sì (four) —— xì (drama)　　guǎn —— juǎn　　guō (pot) —— guā (to scratch)

3. Tone discrimination

wáng (to die) —— wàng (to forget)　　kàn (to look) —— kǎn　　gōng (labor) —— gòng

sān (three) —— sǎn　　shēn —— shèn　　guāi —— guǎi

4. Combination of tones

ˇ + ˉ	ˇ + ˊ	ˇ + ˇ	ˇ + ˋ	ˇ + ˳
yǔyīn (pronunciation)	dǎ qiú	yǔsǎn	qǐngwèn	zěnme (how)
xiǎoshuō (novel)	qǐchuáng (to get up)	fǔdǎo (to coach)	nǔshì (madam)	yǐzi (chair)

ˋ + ˉ	ˋ + ˊ	ˋ + ˇ	ˋ + ˋ	ˋ + ˳
shàngbān (to go to work)	kèwén (text)	wàiyǔ	bàoqiàn	xièxie
qìchē (car)	fùxí (to review)	diànyǐng (movie)	huìhuà (conversation)	dìdi

5. Practice reading the disyllabic words

duànliàn (to do physical training)　　chàng gē (to sing a song)

chī fàn (to have a meal)　　tiàowǔ (to dance)

shàngkè (to have lessons)　　xǐzǎo (to take a bath)

xiàkè (class is over)

shēngcí (new word)

fānyì (to translate)

shuìjiào (to sleep)

liànxí (exercise)

diànnǎo (computer)

6. Read the following classical poem aloud

Shāncūn Yǒnghuái

山村　咏怀

(Sòng) Shào Yōng

（宋）邵　雍

Yí　qù　èr-sān　lǐ,

一 去 二 三 里,

Yāncūn　sì-wǔ　jiā.

烟 村 四 五 家。

Tíngtái　liù-qī　zuò,

亭 台 六 七 座,

Bā-jiǔ-shí　zhī　huā.

八 九 十 枝 花。

Ode to a Mountain Village

By Shao Yong (1011 – 1077 in the Song Dynasty)

Walk one, two, or three miles,

See four or five homes,

Six or seven pavilions,

And eight, nine, or ten flowers.

三、课堂用语 *CLASSROOM EXPRESSIONS*

❶ Zhùyì fāyīn.　　　　　Pay attention to the pronunciation.

❷ Qǐng zhùyì shēngdiào.　Please say attention to the tones.

❸ Yǒu wèntí ma?　　　　Do you have any questions?

❹ Wǒ yǒu wèntí.　　　　I have some questions.

❺ Méiyǒu wèntí.　　　　No questions.

1-02-16

四、汉字 *CHINESE CHARACTERS*

1 汉字知识 Knowledge about Chinese Characters

Compound strokes of Chinese characters (I)

Stroke Form	Name	Example	Way of Writing
乛 [乛]	hénggōu	子 zǐ (son)	Like the 1st stroke of 子

Stroke Form	Name	Example	Way of Writing
フ [⁊]	héngzhé	马 mǎ (horse)	Like the 1st stroke of 马
㇄ [㇄]	shùwān	四 sì (four)	Like the 4th stroke of 四
㇄ [㇄]	shùwāngōu	七 qī (seven)	Like the 2nd stroke of 七
㇉ [㇉]	shùzhézhégōu	马 mǎ (horse)	Like the 2nd stroke of 马
乙 [乙]	héngzhéwāngōu	九 jiǔ (nine)	Like the 2nd stroke of 九
㇊ [㇊]	piědiǎn	女 nǚ (female)	Like the 1st stroke of 女

2　汉字偏旁 Chinese Radicals

Radical	Name	Stroke Order	No. of Strokes	Example	Explanation
口	kǒuzìpáng	丨 冂 口	3	吗 ma (question particle)	Related to "mouth"
女	nǚzìpáng	㇛ 女 女	3	好 hǎo (good) 妈 mā (mom)	Related to "female"

3　认写基本汉字 Learn and Write the Basic Chinese Characters

(1) 四　　丨 冂 冂 四 四　　　　　　　5 strokes
sì　　　four

(2) 五　　一 丅 五 五　　　　　　　　4 strokes
wǔ　　　five

(3) 七　　一 七　　　　　　　　　　　2 strokes
qī　　　seven

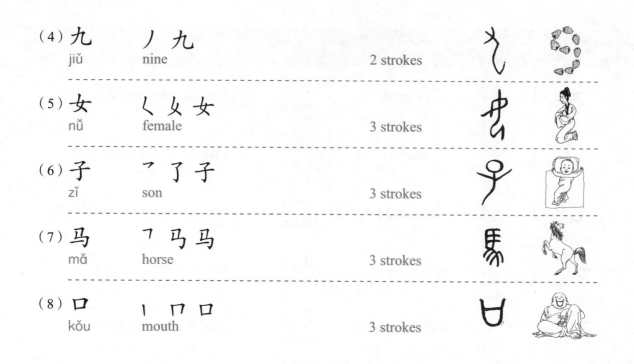

（4）九　　丿九　　　　　　　　　nine　　　2 strokes
jiǔ

（5）女　　く女女　　　　　　　　female　　3 strokes
nǚ

（6）子　　フ了子　　　　　　　　son　　　3 strokes
zǐ

（7）马　　フ马马　　　　　　　　horse　　3 strokes
mǎ

（8）口　　丨口口　　　　　　　　mouth　　3 strokes
kǒu

4 认写课文中的汉字 Learn and Write the Chinese Characters in the Text

（1）好 hǎo

好 → 女 + 子　　　　　　　6 strokes

（2）吗 ma

吗 → 口 + 马　　　　　　　6 strokes

五、文化知识 *CULTURAL KNOWLEDGE*

Chinese Characters and Hànyǔ Pīnyīn

Chinese characters are the oldest kind of script that is still in use in the world today. They use a symbolic writing system to record words or morphemes. The ideographs do not actually represent the sounds. Hence, we usually cannot identify accurately the pronunciation of a character from its shape. This is the biggest difference between Chinese characters and alphabetic writing.

In order to understand the phonetic annotations assigned to Chinese characters, and to help learners to read characters aloud, as well as to make it easy to consult a dictionary, the Chinese government invited specialists to develop the "Hànyǔ Pīnyīn Fāng'àn《汉语拼音方案》" (*Scheme for the Chinese Phonetic Alphabet*) and started to promote the system in 1958. The

"Hànyǔ pīnyīn 汉语拼音" system uses the Latin alphabet that is used internationally and attaches four simple marks to represent the tones. As a tool to transcribe the pronunciations of Chinese characters, "汉语拼音" has been widely used around the world. Its functions are to show learners the sounds of Chinese characters, promote "pǔtōnghuà 普通话" (the Common Speech or Standard Spoken Chinese, known as Mandarin abroad), and to help foreigners to study Chinese. However, "汉语拼音" is not the writing system of the Chinese language. The Chinese still communicate in writing using Chinese characters.

趣味汉语　Fun with Chinese

Move, Try, and Speak – Chinese Gestures for the Numbers

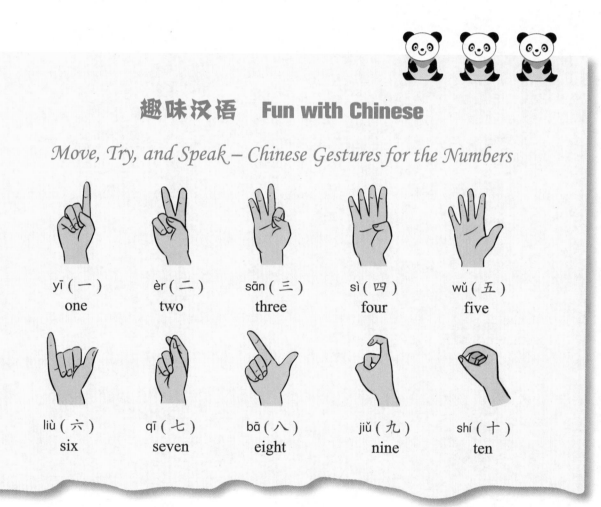

| yī（一）one | èr（二）two | sān（三）three | sì（四）four | wǔ（五）five |
| liù（六）six | qī（七）seven | bā（八）eight | jiǔ（九）nine | shí（十）ten |

《Xīn Shíyòng Hànyǔ Kèběn》 huānyíng nǐ!

《新实用汉语课本》欢迎你！

New Practical Chinese Reader welcomes you!

From now on you and your fellow students will meet the international students Ding Libo, Lin Na, and Ma Dawei. You will study Chinese along with the help of your classroom teacher and a few other Chinese teachers (Teacher Chen and Professor Zhang) and your Chinese friends (the students Song Hua and Wang Xiaoyun as well as the reporter Lu Yuping). The Chinese language is used by the largest number of people in the world. Because this magical language could be completely different from your mother tongue, this may be a challenging yet enjoyable journey.

Let's first meet our friends who will be traveling with us along the way.

人物介绍
Characters in the NPCR Series

马大为
Mǎ Dàwéi
An American student,
22, male

丁力波
Dīng Lìbō
A Canadian student,
21, male. His father's
name is Gǔ Bō and his
mother's name is Dīng Yún.

王小云
Wáng Xiǎoyún
A Chinese student,
20, female

宋华
Sòng Huá
A Chinese student,
20, male

林娜
Lín Nà
A British student,
19, female

陆雨平
Lù Yǔpíng
A Chinese reporter,
33, male

陈老师
Chén lǎoshī
A Chinese teacher,
35, female

张教授
Zhāng jiàoshòu
A Chinese professor,
48, male

1

Nǐ zuìjìn zěnmeyàng

你最近怎么样

How have you been lately

With the foundation of Chinese phonetics and Chinese characters, you can now study Lesson 1. After completing this lesson, you can greet Chinese people in Chinese. You can also ask someone's name in Chinese, and give a brief self-introduction. In addition, using simple sentences, you can ask how your friends have been doing lately, and also reply to the same questions that your friends ask you.

一、热身 WARM-UP

1 思考 Think

Think about the following questions:

(1) In your country, how do friends greet each other?
(2) When you meet someone for the first time, how do you ask the person's name?
(3) In the culture of your country, do you put the surname first or last?

2 活动 Activity

The following names in Chinese are based on transliterations. Please read these names aloud quickly in Chinese and guess their corresponding names in English.

A

Male names

Āndōngní
安东尼

Kèlǐsī
克里斯

Màikè
麦克

Mǎxiū
马修

Dàwèi
大卫

B

Female names

Zhēnnīfó
珍妮佛

Kǎisèlín
凯瑟琳

Sūshān
苏珊

Yīlìshābái
伊丽莎白

Líndá
琳达

二、课文 *TEXT*

（一）  2-01-01

(Ma Dawei meets Song Hua on campus for the first time.)

Mǎ Dàwéi： Nǐ hǎo! ①
马大为： 你 好！

日常打招呼

Daily greetings

Sòng Huá： Nǐ hǎo!
宋华： 你 好！

Mǎ Dàwéi： Wǒ jiào Mǎ Dàwéi. Qǐngwèn, ② nǐ jiào shénme míngzi? ③
马大为： 我 叫 马 大 为。请 问， 你 叫 什 么 名 字？

Sòng Huá： Wǒ xìng Sòng, jiào Sòng Huá.
宋华： 我 姓 宋， 叫 宋 华。

问名字

Asking about one's name

Mǎ Dàwéi： Rènshi nǐ hěn gāoxìng. ④
马大为： 认 识 你 很 高 兴。

Sòng Huá： Rènshi nǐ wǒ yě hěn gāoxìng.
认 识 你 我 也 很 高 兴。

生词 New Words　2-01-02

1. nǐ	你	Pr	you (*singular*)
2. hǎo	好	A	good; well; fine; OK　你好
3. wǒ	我	Pr	I; me
4. jiào	叫	V	to be called; to call
5. qǐngwèn	请问	V	may I ask; excuse me
qǐng	请	V	please; to request; to invite
wèn	问	V	to ask
6. shénme	什么	QPr	what
7. míngzi	名字	N	name　什么名字　叫什么名字
8. xìng	姓	V/N	one's surname is / surname　姓宋　姓马
9. rènshi	认识	V	to know　认识你　认识他　认识马大为
10. hěn	很	Adv	very　很好
11. gāoxìng	高兴	A	happy　很高兴
12. yě	也	Adv	also; too　也很高兴　也认识你
13. Mǎ Dàwéi	马大为	PN	Ma Dawei, name of an American student
14. Sòng Huá	宋华	PN	Song Hua, name of a Chinese student

注释 Notes

① Nǐ hǎo!

Hello!

"Nǐ hǎo! 你好!" (Hello) is a very common greeting in Chinese. Whether between strangers or acquaintances, whether in the morning, at noon, or in the evening, you can use it. The response is also "你好!".

② Qǐngwèn……

May I ask... (Excuse me, ...)

This is a polite way to start asking someone a question.

③ Nǐ jiào shénme míngzi?

What is your name?

This is a common way to ask someone's name, usually by a senior to a junior or between young people.

In Chinese, the surname comes first and the given name comes next. For example, in "Sòng Huá 宋华", "宋" is the surname and "华" is the given name. Most names have three characters, such as "Lù Yǔpíng 陆雨平", in which "陆" is the surname and "雨平" is the given name. When asked "Nǐ jiào shénme míngzi? 你叫什么名字?" (What is your name?), the response is "Wǒ xìng 我姓……, jiào 叫……" (My surname is… and my given name is…) or "Wǒ jiào 我叫……" (My full name is…).

When one addresses a junior or someone around one's age and familiar, whose given name has two characters, one often calls the person by the given name without using the surname. For example, "Lù Yǔpíng 陆雨平" can be called "Yǔpíng 雨平".

④ Rènshi nǐ hěn gāoxìng.

Nice to meet you.

This is often used when meeting someone for the first time.

（二） 2-01-03

(Ding Libo talks with Lin Na in Lin Na's dorm room.)

Dīng Lìbō: Qǐngwèn, Lín Nà zài ma? ①
丁力波：请问， 林娜 在 吗？

Lín Nà: Zài.　Lìbō,　qǐng jìn, ②　qǐng zuò.
林娜：在。力波，请进，　请坐。

Dīng Lìbō: Xièxie.　Nǐ zuìjìn zěnmeyàng? ③
丁力波：谢谢。你最近 怎么样？

问候
Greetings

Lín Nà: Wǒ hěn hǎo.　Nǐ ne? ④
林娜：我 很 好。你 呢？

Dīng Lìbō: Wǒ hěn máng.　Nǐ máng ma?
丁力波：我 很 忙。你 忙 吗？

Lín Nà: Wǒ bú tài máng. Dàwéi hǎo ma?
林娜：我 不 太 忙。大为 好 吗？

问候他人
Greeting others

Dīng Lìbō: Tā yě hěn hǎo.
丁力波：他 也 很 好。

生词 New Words　2-01-04

1.	zài	在	V	to be (here, there); to be (in, on, at)
2.	ma	吗	QPt	*a modal particle used for a question expecting a yes-no answer*　你忙吗 宋华在吗
3.	jìn	进	V	to enter　请进
4.	zuò	坐	V	to sit　请坐
5.	xièxie	谢谢	V	to thank　谢谢你
6.	zuìjìn	最近	Adv	lately; recently
7.	zěnmeyàng	怎么样	QPr	how (is, are); how about　你怎么样 最近怎么样
8.	ne	呢	QPt	*a modal particle used for an elliptical question*　你呢
9.	máng	忙	A	busy　很忙
10.	bù	不	Adv	not; no　不忙 不好 不高兴 不在
11.	tài	太	Adv	too; extremely　不太忙 不太好
12.	tā	他	Pr	he; him
13.	Dīng Lìbō	丁力波	PN	Ding Libo, name of a Canadian student
14.	Lín Nà	林娜	PN	Lin Na, name of a British student

注释 Notes

① Lín Nà zài ma?

Is Lin Na in?

② Qǐng jìn.

Come in, please.
"Qǐng 请 + verb" is a polite way to make a request.

③ Nǐ zuìjìn zěnmeyàng?

How have you been lately?
"……zěnmeyàng 怎么样？" (How is/are…?) is often used to ask about the situation of some-one or something. "Nǐ (zuìjìn) zěnmeyàng? 你（最近）怎么样？" (How have you been (lately)?) is a greeting used between acquaintances or friends. The response could be "hěn hǎo 很好" (very well), "hěn máng 很忙" (very busy), etc.

④ Nǐ ne?

And (how are) you?

三、语言点 LANGUAGE POINTS

1 核心句 Key Sentences

 2-01-05

1. Nǐ zuìjìn zěnmeyàng?

2. Wǒ hěn hǎo. Nǐ ne?

3. Nǐ máng ma?

4. Tā yě hěn hǎo.

5. Nǐ jiào shénme míngzi?

6. Wǒ xìng Sòng, jiào Sòng Huá.

2　语法 Grammar

1. 用"吗"的是非问句　Yes-no questions with "ma 吗"

Adding the modal question particle "吗" at the end of a declarative sentence makes a simple yes-no question. The response is the affirmative or negative form of the declarative sentence without "吗". For example,

Declarative Sentence	Interrogative Sentence
Tā máng. 他 忙。	→	Tā máng ma? 他 忙 吗?
Wǒ jiào Mǎ Dàwéi. 我 叫 马 大为。	→	Nǐ jiào Mǎ Dàwéi ma? 你 叫 马 大为 吗?
Lín Nà zài. 林 娜 在。	→	Lín Nà zài ma? 林 娜 在 吗?

Exercise I　Change the following sentences into questions and then in groups of two, ask each other questions and answer them.

Wǒ hěn hǎo.
（1）我 很 好。→ _____ ?

Wǒ bú tài máng.
（3）我 不太 忙。→ _____ ?

Dīng Lìbō hěn gāoxìng.
（2）丁 力波 很 高兴。→ _____ ?

Lín Nà hěn máng.
（4）林 娜 很 忙。→ _____ ?

Exercise II　Based on the pictures, complete the dialogues using proper words.

Nǐ hǎo ma?
（1）A：你 好 吗?

Nǐ _____ ma?
（2）A：你 _____ 吗?

Tā gāoxìng ma?
（3）A：他 高兴 吗?

Wǒ
B：我 _____ 。

Wǒ hěn máng.
B：我 很 忙。

Tā hěn
B：他 很 _____ 。

2. 形容词谓语句 A sentence with an adjectival predicate

Subject	Predicate	
	Adverb	Adjective
Nǐ 你		hǎo. 好。
Wǒ 我	hěn 很	hǎo. 好。
Dàwéi 大为	yě hěn 也 很	hǎo. 好。
Wǒ 我	bù 不	máng. 忙。

In Chinese an adjective by itself can serve as a predicate, which can be modified by adverbs like "hěn 很" (very) and/or "yě 也" (also; too), etc. such as "Wǒ hěn hǎo. 我很好。" (I am fine), "Dàwéi yě hěn hǎo. 大为也很好。" (Dawei is also fine). The negative form is formed by putting the adverb "bù 不" (not) before the adjective, such as "Wǒ bù máng. 我不忙。" (I am not busy).

Notes:

❶ The adverbs "很", "也", "不" and so on must be put before the adjective they modify.

❷ If a sentence does not have another adverb (e.g., "不", "也", "tài 太", etc.), the adverb "很" is often added. For example, to respond to "Nǐ zuìjìn zěnmeyàng? 你最近怎么样？" (How have you been recently?), the response is not "*Wǒ hǎo. 我好。" (I'm fine) or "*Wǒ máng. 我忙。(I'm busy); usually it is "Wǒ hěn hǎo. 我很好。" (I'm very well) or "Wǒ hěn máng. 我很忙。" (I'm very busy). "很" in this context does not necessarily carry the literal meaning of "very".

❸ When a sentence with an adjectival predicate is changed to a question ending with "吗", "很" is usually removed. For example, "我很好。" (I'm very well) → "Nǐ hǎo ma? 你好吗？" (How are you?). Do not ask "*Nǐ hěn hǎo ma? 你很好吗？".

Exercise I   Complete the dialogues with the words/phrases on the right.

Nǐ máng ma?
（1）A：你 忙 吗？

Wǒ   máng. Nǐ ne?
B：我＿＿＿＿＿忙。你呢？

Wǒ   máng.
A：我＿＿＿＿＿忙。

hěn
很
bú tài
不 太
bù
不

（2）A：马 大为 好 吗?
Mǎ Dàwéi hǎo ma?

B：他 很 好。_____呢?
Tā hěn hǎo.   ne?

A：他 也 很 好。
Tā yě hěn hǎo.

Sòng Huá
宋　华

Dīng Lìbō
丁　力波

Exercise II Following the example, put the words in order to form sentences.

Example 好　　他　　很 → 他 很 好。
hǎo　 tā　 hěn　 Tā hěn hǎo.

（1）我　忙　很 → _____
wǒ　 máng　 hěn

（2）高兴　不　太　他 → _____
gāoxìng　 bù　 tài　 tā

（3）好　你　吗 → _____
hǎo　 nǐ　 ma

3. 副词 "也" 的位置 The position of the adverb "yě 也" (also; too)

The adverb "也" must be put after the subject but before the predicate verb or adjective. For example, "Wǒ yě hěn hǎo. 我也很好。" (I'm also fine), but not "*Yě wǒ hěn hǎo. 也我很好。" or "*Wǒ hěn hǎo yě. 我很好也。" Besides, "也" cannot serve as the predicate on its own, for example, it's not right to say "*wǒ yě 我也".

也 + Verb/Adjective

Subject	Predicate	
	Adverb	Verb/Adjective
Tā 他	yě 也	xìng Sòng. 姓 宋。
Lín Nà 林 娜	yě hěn 也 很	gāoxìng. 高兴。

In a negative sentence, "也" must be put before "不".

也 + 不 + Verb/Adjective

Subject	Predicate	
	Adverb	Verb/Adjective
Tā 他	yě bú 也 不	xìng Sòng. 姓 宋。
Lìbō 力波	yě bù 也 不	máng. 忙。

Exercise I   Complete the dialogues with the words on the right.

（1）A：Dàwéi _____ ma?
大为 _____ 吗？

B：Dàwéi hěn _____, wǒ yě hěn _____。
大为 很 _____, 我 也 很 _____。

（2）A：Lín Nà _____ ma?
林 娜 _____ 吗？

B：Lín Nà bú tài _____, Lìbō yě bú tài _____。
林 娜 不 太 _____, 力 波 也 不 太 _____。

hǎo
好
máng
忙

máng
忙
gāoxìng
高兴

Exercise II   Following the example, put the words in order to form sentences.

Example
máng wǒ bù yě   Wǒ yě bù máng.
忙 我 不 也 → 我 也 不 忙。

（1）wǒ hǎo yě hěn
我 好 也 很 → _____

（2）tā bù yě zài
他 不 也 在 → _____

（3）Dàwéi hǎo ma yě
大为 好 吗 也 → _____

4. 汉语的语序   Word order in Chinese

There are several main characteristics of Chinese grammar. There are no changes, strictly speaking, in terms of personal pronouns, verb tenses, gender, singular or plural case, etc. Grammatically, the word order plays an extremely important role. The word order in Chinese, in general, has the subject at the beginning, which may also be called the topic to be described; the predicate, which describes the subject, follows. For example,

Subject (Topic)	Predicate (Statement)
Wǒ 我	hěn máng. 很　忙。
Tā 他	xìng Sòng. 姓　宋。

四、练习与运用 PRACTICE AND APPLICATION

补充词语 Supplementary Words　2-01-06

1.	kùn	困	A	sleepy	很困　不困　不太困
2.	kě	渴	A	thirsty	很渴　不渴　不太渴
3.	è	饿	A	hungry	很饿　不饿　不太饿
4.	lèi	累	A	tired	很累　不累　不太累
5.	hái xíng	还行		not bad	
6.	mǎmǎhūhū	马马虎虎	A	so-so	
7.	tā	她	Pr	she; her	

1　语音练习 Pronunciation Drills　2-01-07

Listen and read aloud: Add tone marks to the following words and sentences, and then read them aloud.

❶ laoshi　　　　❷ hen ke　　　　❸ qingwen

❹ hen mang　　　❺ bu mang　　　❻ bu e

❼ bu ke　　　　❽ bu gaoxing　　 ❾ Wo bu tai mang.

❿ Renshi ni hen gaoxing.

2 会话练习 Conversation Practice

Pair activity: Create dialogues based on the scenes and the requirements below.

1. Greetings

（1）

（2）

2. Meeting for the first time

（1）

（2）

Qǐngwèn, nǐ jiào shénme míngzi? / Rènshi nǐ hěn gāoxìng.
（请问，你叫 什么 名字？/ 认识你 很 高兴。）

3. Greetings

（1）

（2）

Nǐ hǎo ma?
（你好 吗？）

Nǐ zuìjìn zěnmeyàng?
（你最近 怎么样？）

4. How is he/she?

3 听后复述 Listening and Repeating 2-01-08

Listen to the following dialogues and repeat what you hear.

Nǐ hǎo ma?
（1）A：你 好 吗？

Wǒ hěn hǎo. Nǐ ne?
B：我 很 好。你 呢？

Wǒ yě hěn hǎo.
A：我 也 很 好。

Nǐ zuìjìn máng ma?
（2）A：你 最近 忙 吗？

Wǒ hěn máng. Nǐ ne?
B：我 很 忙。你 呢？

Hái xíng.
A：还 行。

Qǐngwèn, nǐ jiào shénme míngzi?
（3）A：请问，你 叫 什么 名字？

Wǒ xìng Lín, jiào Lín Nà. Nǐ ne?
B：我 姓 林，叫 林 娜。你 呢？

Wǒ jiào Sòng Huá. Rènshi nǐ hěn gāoxìng.
A：我 叫 宋 华。认识 你 很 高兴。

Rènshi nǐ wǒ yě hěn gāoxìng.
B：认识 你 我 也 很 高兴。

4 阅读理解 Reading Comprehension

Tā jiào Mǎ Dàwéi, tā jiào Dīng Lìbō, tā jiào Lín Nà.
他 叫 马 大为，他 叫 丁 力波，她 叫 林 娜。

Dàwéi hěn hǎo, Dīng Lìbō hěn máng, Lín Nà bú tài máng, tā yě hěn hǎo.
大为 很 好，丁 力波 很 忙，林 娜 不 太 忙，她 也 很 好。

Answer the following questions:

Mǎ Dàwéi hǎo ma?
（1）马 大为 好 吗？

Lín Nà zěnmeyàng?
（2）林 娜 怎么样？

Dīng Lìbō máng ma?
（3）丁 力波 忙 吗？

Tā jiào Chéng Lóng, tā jiào Gǒng Lì. Chéng Lóng hěn máng, Gǒng Lì yě hěn máng.
他 叫 成 龙，她 叫 巩俐。成 龙 很 忙，巩俐 也 很 忙。

Yáo Míng zěnmeyàng? Yáo Míng yě hěn máng.
姚 明 怎么样？姚 明 也 很 忙。

Tā jiào shénme míngzi? Tā jiào Mǎ Yún. Mǎ Yún máng ma? Mǎ Yún hěn máng.
他 叫 什么 名字？他 叫 马云。马 云 忙 吗？马 云 很 忙。

Answer the following questions:

Tāmen jiào shénme míngzi?
（1）他们 叫 什么 名字？

Tāmen zěnmeyàng?
（2）他们 怎么样？

5 任务与活动 Task and Activity

Class activity: In groups of three to five, following the form below, ask your group members their names, give simple greetings, and ask them how they are. Then report back to the whole class.

No.	Name	How about...
1.	Háng chān dịp lóng	
2.	Steven	很 困
3.		
4.		
5.		

The following words may be helpful to you:

zěnmeyàng	jiào	rènshi	máng	hǎo
怎么样	叫	认识	忙	好

6 写作练习 Writing Exercise

Make a business card of your own based on the sample below.

陆雨平 Lù Yǔpíng

《北京晚报》记者

电话：138-0695-2371

邮箱：luyuping@bjwb.com

地址：北京市建国门内大街 20 号

五、汉字 CHINESE CHARACTERS

1 汉字知识 Knowledge about Chinese Characters

1. Components of Chinese characters

The structure of modern Chinese characters can be analyzed from three perspectives: strokes, components, and the whole character. For instance, the character "mù 木" (wood) is composed of four strokes: 一, 丨, 丿 and 乀. "木" is a basic character itself, but it is also a component to form a character. For instance, the character "lín 林" (woods; forest) is composed of two "木" components. Some components can stand on their own as independent characters, but others cannot and can only be part of another character. This characteristic is the key to understanding modern Chinese characters. For example, the character "yuàn 院" (courtyard) can be divided into three components: "阝", "宀", and "yuán 元" (first). Only "元" can stand on its own, while "阝" and "宀" cannot. To master the components is crucial to learning Chinese characters well.

2. The interrelationships between strokes in Chinese characters

The interrelationships between strokes in characters have the function of distinguishing meaning. For the same strokes, with different interrelationships, the meanings are different. There are three kinds of interrelationships between strokes. They are:

(1) Close but not touching, e.g.,

bā 八 (eight), ér 儿 (son), èr 二 (two), and xiǎo 小 (small)

(2) Strokes that cross each other, e.g.,

shí 十 (ten), dà 大 (big), jiǔ 九 (nine), and fū 夫 (husband)

(3) Strokes that touch but do not cross, e.g.,

chǎng 厂 (factory), Dīng 丁 (a surname), rén 人 (person), and shān 山 (mountain)

3. Compound strokes of Chinese characters (II)

Stroke Form	Name	Example	Way of Writing
ㄱ [ ]	héngpiě	又 yòu (again)	Like the 1st stroke in 又
ㄥ [ ]	piězhé	么 me (the 2nd character of the word "shénme 什么" (what))	Like the 2nd stroke of 么
ㄴ [ ]	shùtí	以 yǐ (to use; to take)	Like the 1st stroke of 以
⏦ [ ]	shùgōu	你 nǐ (you)	Like the 5th stroke of 你
ㄱ [ ]	héngzhégōu	问 wèn (to ask)	Like the 3rd stroke of 问
ㄥ [ ]	héngzhétí	认 rèn (to recognize)	Like the 2nd stroke of 认
ㄋ [ ]	héngzhézhépiě	近 jìn (near)	Like the 6th stroke of 近

Count the strokes of the following character and practice writing it.

永

yǒng (forever)

2 汉字偏旁 Chinese Radicals

Radical	Name	Stroke Order	No. of Strokes	Example	Explanation
亻	dānrénpáng	ノ 亻	2	你 nǐ (you) 什 shén (what)	Related to "human"
讠	yánzìpáng	、 讠	2	认 rèn (to recognize) 识 shí (to know)	Related to "speech"
木	mùzìpáng	一 十 木 木	4	林 lín (woods; forest) 样 yàng (shape)	Related to "wood"
辶	zǒuzhīdǐ	、 讠 辶	3	进 jìn (to enter) 近 jìn (near)	Related to "walking"

3　认写基本汉字 Learn and Write the Basic Chinese Characters

（1）力　　フ 力
　　lì　　strength　　　　　　　　　2 strokes

（2）生　　丿 ㇒ 亡 牛 生
　　shēng　　to be born　　　　　　5 strokes

（3）言　　丶 二 亠 言 言 言 言
　　yán　　speech　　　　　　　　7 strokes

（4）人　　丿 人
　　rén　　person　　　　　　　　2 strokes

（5）木　　一 十 才 木
　　mù　　wood　　　　　　　　　4 strokes

（6）羊　　丶 丷 丷 羊 羊 羊
　　yáng　　sheep　　　　　　　　6 strokes

（7）井　　一 二 尹 井
　　jǐng　　well (N)　　　　　　　　4 strokes

（8）土　　一 十 土
　　tǔ　　earth　　　　　　　　　3 strokes

4　认写课文中的汉字 Learn and Write the Chinese Characters in the Text

（1）叫 jiào

叫 → 口 + 丩（丩：㇄ 丩）　　　　　　5 strokes

（2）姓 xìng

姓 → 女 + 生（生：丿 ㇒ 亡 牛 生）　　8 strokes

（3）什么 shénme

么 → 丿 + 厶　　　　　　　　　　3 strokes

（4）名字 míngzi

名 ⟶ 夕（夕：ノ ク 夕）+ 口　　　　　　6 strokes

（5）最近 zuìjìn

最 ⟶ 曰（曰：丨 冂 曰 曰）+ 耳（耳：一 厂 丌 丌 耳 耳）+ 又　12 strokes

近 ⟶ 斤（斤：ノ 丆 斤 斤）+ 辶　　　　　7 strokes

（6）认识 rènshi

认 ⟶ 讠 + 人　　　　　　　　　　　　4 strokes

识 ⟶ 讠 + 只（只：丨 冂 口 尸 只）　　　7 strokes

（7）怎么样 zěnmeyàng

样 ⟶ 木 + 羊　　　　　　　　　　　　10 strokes

（8）林 lín

林 ⟶ 木 + 木　　　　　　　　　　　　8 strokes

（9）进 jìn

进 ⟶ 井 + 辶　　　　　　　　　　　　7 strokes

（10）坐 zuò

坐 ⟶ 人 + 人 + 土　　　　　　　　　　7 strokes

六、文化知识　*CULTURAL KNOWLEDGE*

Chinese Characters and Simplified Chinese Characters

Chinese characters are one of the oldest scripts in the world. Usually, one character has one syllable that has a meaning. The total number of characters is extremely large, estimated at over 50,000. However, only 5,000 – 8,000 characters are commonly used, and only more than 3,000 characters are in daily use.

Different from alphabetical writing systems, Chinese characters are ideographic. This ideographic writing system is the only one that is still in use today. Most characters are pictophonetic, with the semantic component indicating the meaning and the phonetic component indicating the sound.

Modern Chinese characters have evolved from ancient pictographic characters, many of which were written in a rather complicated way. In order to write quickly, for over two thousand years, people have been trying hard to simplify the way of writing characters. There are two ways to simplify characters. One is to reduce the number of characters; the other is to reduce the number of strokes. Characters that have been simplified are called "jiǎntǐzì 简体字 / 簡體字" (simple-form characters; simplified characters) and their original unsimplified forms are called "fántǐzì 繁体字 / 繁體字" (complex-form characters; complex characters). The simplified characters are standardized in mainland China today, while unsimplified characters are mostly used in

the publication of classical literature. Compared with unsimplified characters, simplified characters are easy to learn, remember, read, and write. Let's compare the characters below:

mā 妈 / 媽 mom (simplified character / complex character)

mén 门 / 門 door (simplified character / complex character)

七、自我评估 *SELF-EVALUATION*

I can basically do the following things in Chinese:

☐ I can greet people who I know or don't know.

☐ I can ask people their names and introduce myself.

☐ I know how to talk to people who I meet for the first time.

☐ I can greet people who I am familiar with.

趣味汉语 Fun with Chinese

Animal Sounds in Chinese

Do you know how to describe animal sounds in Chinese?

Xiǎo yáng:　Miē miē miē,　nǐmen hǎo,　wǒ shì xiǎo yáng,　wǒ hěn gāoxìng.
1. 小 羊：咩 咩 咩，你们 好，我 是 小 羊，我 很 高兴。

Xiǎo gǒu: Wāng wāng wāng,　nǐmen hǎo,　wǒ shì xiǎo gǒu,　wǒ yě hěn gāoxìng.
2. 小 狗：汪 汪 汪，你们 好，我 是 小 狗，我 也 很 高兴。

Xiǎo mìfēng:　Wēng wēng wēng,　nǐmen hǎo,　wǒ shì xiǎo mìfēng,　wǒ hěn máng.
3. 小 蜜蜂：嗡 嗡 嗡，你们 好，我 是 小 蜜蜂，我 很 忙。

Xiǎo nǎiniú:　Mōu mōu mōu,　nǐmen hǎo,　wǒ shì xiǎo nǎiniú,　wǒ yě hěn máng.
4. 小 奶牛：哞 哞 哞，你们 好，我 是 小 奶牛，我 也 很 忙。

Xiǎo māo: Miāo miāo miāo,　nǐmen hǎo,　wǒ shì xiǎo māo,　wǒ hěn kùn.
5. 小 猫：喵 喵 喵，你们 好，我 是 小 猫，我 很 困。

Xiǎo lù:　Yōu yōu yōu,　nǐmen hǎo,　wǒ shì xiǎo lù,　wǒ yě hěn kùn.
6. 小 鹿：呦 呦 呦，你们 好，我 是 小 鹿，我 也 很 困。

(1) A little lamb: Miē miē miē (baa, baa, baa), hello, everyone. I'm a little lamb. I'm very happy.

(2) A little puppy: Wāng wāng wāng (woof, woof, woof), hello, everyone. I'm a little puppy. I'm very happy too.

(3) A little bee: Wēng wēng wēng (buzz, buzz, buzz), hello, everyone. I'm a little bee. I'm very busy.

(4) A little cow: Mōu mōu mōu (moo, moo, moo), hello, everyone. I'm a little cow. I'm very busy too.

(5) A little kitten: Miāo miāo miāo (meow, meow, meow), hello, everyone. I'm a little kitten. I'm very sleepy.

(6) A little fawn: Yōu yōu yōu (ma-mah, ma-mah, ma-mah), hello, everyone. I'm a little fawn. I'm very sleepy too.

Nǐ shì nǎ guó rén

你是哪国人

Which country do you come from

In this lesson, you will learn how to introduce your friends as well as how to ask others about their nationalities. You will also learn another way to greet people and to ask someone's name in a polite manner. Finally, with Wang Xiaoyun and Ma Dawei, you will stroll through a street selling snacks and refreshments and taste the food that the Chinese like.

一、热身 *WARM-UP*

1 思考 Think

Think about the following questions:

(1) Do you know how to say the name of your country in Chinese?

(2) Can you say the names of other countries in Chinese?

(3) In your country, how do people greet each other? How do they say goodbye?

2 活动 Activity

Among the items below, can you guess which ones Chinese people often eat? Do you know how to say the names of these foods in Chinese?

二、课文 TEXT

（一） 2-02-01

(Ding Libo and Ma Dawei come across Teacher Chen. Teacher Chen and Ma Dawei do not know each other.)

Dīng Lìbō： Lǎoshī, zǎoshang hǎo! ①
丁力波： 老师， 早上 好！

| 问好 |
| Greetings |

Chén lǎoshī： Nǐmen hǎo!
陈老师： 你们 好！

Dīng Lìbō： Zhè shì Mǎ Dàwéi, ② tā shì wǒ péngyou,
丁力波： 这 是 马大为， 他 是 我 朋友，

| 介绍他人 |
| Introducing others |

gāng dào Běijīng. ③
刚 到 北京。

Mǎ Dàwéi： Nín hǎo! ④ Lǎoshī, nín guìxìng?
马大为： 您 好！ 老师，您 贵姓？

| 问姓氏 |
| Asking someone's surname |

Chén lǎoshī：　Wǒ xìng Chén. ⑤　Nǐ shì nǎ guó rén? ⑥
陈老师：　我　姓　陈。　你是哪国人？

问国籍
Asking about one's nationality

Mǎ Dàwéi：　Wǒ shì Měiguórén. ⑦　Wǒ yě xuéxí Hànyǔ. Chén lǎoshī, ⑧
马大为：　我　是　美国人。　我也学习汉语。陈老师，

rènshi nín hěn gāoxìng.
认识您很　高兴。

Chén lǎoshī：　Rènshi nǐ wǒ yě hěn gāoxìng.
陈老师：　认识你我也很　高兴。

告别
Saying goodbye

Mǎ Dàwéi：　Lǎoshī, 　zàijiàn!
马大为：　老师，　再见！

Chén lǎoshī：　Zàijiàn!
陈老师：　再见！

生词 New Words　2-02-02

√	1.	lǎoshī	老师	N	teacher　老师好
√	2.	zǎoshang	早上	N	morning　早上好
		zǎo	早	A	early　很早　你早
	3.	nǐmen	你们	Pr	you (*plural*)　你们好
		men	们	Suf	*plural suffix*　我们　他们
√	4.	zhè	这	Pr	this
√	5.	shì	是	V	to be; is/am/are...　这是宋华
√	6.	péngyou	朋友	N	friend　我朋友　你朋友
√	7.	gāng	刚	Adv	just　刚认识
√	8.	dào	到	V	to reach; to arrive　刚到
	9.	nín	您	Pr	you (*singular, polite form*)　您好
	10.	guìxìng	贵姓	N	one's (honorable) surname　您贵姓

✓ 11.	nǎ	哪	QPr	which
✓ 12.	guó	国	N	country
13.	rén	人	N	person　哪国人
✓ 14.	xuéxí	学习	V	to study; to learn　学习什么
	xué	学	V	to study (usually with an object)
✓ 15.	Hànyǔ	汉语	N	Chinese (usually referring to Mandarin)　学习汉语 刚学汉语
16.	zàijiàn	再见	V	goodbye
17.	Chén	陈	PN	Chen, a surname
18.	Běijīng	北京	PN	Beijing
19.	Měiguó	美国	PN	the United States

注释　Notes

① Zǎoshang hǎo!

Good morning!

This is a greeting used at 8 or 9 a.m. or even earlier. You may say "zǎo 早" (good morning). You may respond in the same way, or you could say "nǐ zǎo 你早" (good morning to you) or "nǐ hǎo 你好" (hello).

② Zhè shì Mǎ Dàwéi.

This is Ma Dawei.

When introducing a person, "Zhè shì 这是……" (This is...) is often used. The pronunciation of "是" is weak.

③ Tā shì wǒ péngyou, gāng dào Běijīng.

He is my friend and just arrived in Beijing.

Examples similar to "wǒ péngyou 我朋友" (my friend) are "wǒ bàba 我爸爸" (my dad) and "nǐ māma 你妈妈" (your mom).

In "gāng dào Běijīng 刚到北京" (just arrived in Beijing), the subject "tā 他" is omitted. In spoken Chinese, when the subject has already appeared or the topic is understood, it is often omitted.

④ Nín hǎo!

Hello!

The respectful form of "nǐ 你" is "nín 您". This polite expression is commonly used to address the elderly or a person of older generation. It may also be used among those of the same generation out of courtesy. People in Beijing are quite fond of using this form of address.

⑤ Nín guìxìng?
Wǒ xìng Chén.

May I have your (honorable) surname?
My surname is Chen.

This is a polite way to ask someone's surname. Note that in response, you cannot use "*Wǒ guìxìng 我贵姓……", but should say "Wǒ xìng 我姓……" (you may add "Wǒ jiào 我叫……"). The word "guì 贵" can only be used along with "nǐ 你" (you, *singular*) or "nín 您" (you, *singular, polite*), but cannot be used with "wǒ 我" (I) or "tā 他/她" (he/she).

⑥ Nǐ shì nǎ guó rén?

Which country do you come from?

⑦ Wǒ shì Měiguórén.

I am American.
The word "rén 人" after the name of a country indicates one's nationality, e.g.,
　　Měiguó 美国 (America) —— Měiguórén 美国人 (American)
The word "rén 人" after a place name indicates one's ancestral place or birthplace, e.g.,
　　Běijīng 北京 (Beijing) —— Běijīngrén 北京人 (someone from Beijing)

⑧ Chén lǎoshī

Teacher Chen

In China, in addition to common relationships between people, one's position – such as a CEO, manager, section chief, engineer, director, teacher, and so on – is often used as a title. The surname is always placed before the title. The most common form of address for a teacher is "surname + lǎoshī 老师 (teacher)", such as "Chén lǎoshī 陈老师" (Teacher Chen) and "Wáng lǎoshī 王老师" (Teacher Wang). In China, it is very impolite for a student to address a teacher by his or her name without adding the word "老师".

（二） 2-02-03

(Wang Xiaoyun takes Ma Dawei to a street selling snacks and refreshments.)

Mǎ Dàwéi： Xiǎoyún, zhè shì shénme?
马大为： 小云， 这是 什么？

指认物品
Identifying items

Wáng Xiǎoyún： Zhè shì diǎnxin.
王小云： 这 是 点心。

Mǎ Dàwéi： Diǎnxin hǎochī ma?
马大为： 点心 好吃 吗？

Wáng Xiǎoyún： Hǎochī. Wǒ bàba shì Shànghǎirén, tā xǐhuan chī diǎnxin
王小云： 好吃。我爸爸是 上海人，他喜欢吃点心

hé mǐfàn. ①
和 米饭。

Mǎ Dàwéi： Běijīngrén xǐhuan chī shénme?
马大为： 北京人 喜欢 吃 什么？

问喜好
Asking about one's
likes

Wáng Xiǎoyún： Wǒ māma shì Běijīngrén, tā xǐhuan chī miàntiáo hé jiǎozi.
王小云： 我 妈妈是 北京人， 她喜欢吃 面条 和饺子。

Mǎ Dàwéi：Zhè shì jiǎozi ma?
马大为：这　是 饺子 吗？

Wáng Xiǎoyún：Zhè bú shì jiǎozi,　　shì bāozi.　　Bāozi dà,　　jiǎozi xiǎo. ②
王小云：这 不 是 饺子，是 包子。包子 大，　饺子 小。

Nǐ kàn,　nà shì jiǎozi.
你 看，那 是 饺子。

Mǎ Dàwéi：Bāozi hǎochī ma?
马大为：包子 好吃 吗？

Wáng Xiǎoyún：Bāozi hé jiǎozi dōu hěn hǎochī.
王小云：包子 和 饺子 都　很 好 吃。

Mǎ Dàwéi：Hǎo, wǒ yào jiǎozi,　yě yào bāozi. ③
马大为：好，我 要 饺子，也 要 包子。

生词 New Words　2-02-04

1.	diǎnxin	点心	N	snacks; dim sum
2.	hǎochī	好吃	A	delicious; tasty　很好吃 不好吃
	chī	吃	V	to eat　吃点心
3.	bàba	爸爸	N	dad; father　我爸爸 你爸爸 爸爸很忙
4.	xǐhuan	喜欢	V	to like　喜欢点心 喜欢吃点心 喜欢学汉语
5.	hé	和	Conj	and　我和你
6.	mǐfàn	米饭	N	(cooked) rice　米饭和点心 喜欢吃米饭
	fàn	饭	N	(cooked) rice; meal　吃饭
7.	māma	妈妈	N	mom; mother　我妈妈 妈妈喜欢
8.	tā	她	Pr	she; her　她朋友 她妈妈
9.	miàntiáo	面条	N	noodles　吃面条 不喜欢吃面条 面条很好吃
10.	jiǎozi	饺子	N	*jiaozi*; dumpling　不吃饺子 喜欢吃饺子 饺子很好吃

11.	bāozi	包子	N	*baozi*; steamed stuffed bun　吃包子　不喜欢吃包子 包子很好吃
12.	dà	大	A	big　大人　大包子　很大
13.	xiǎo	小	A	small　小点心　小饺子　很小
14.	kàn	看	V	to look at; to see　你看　看什么
15.	nà	那	Pr	that　那是面条　那是我爸爸
16.	dōu	都	Adv	all; both　都很好　都很好吃
17.	yào	要	V	to want; would like　要包子　不要饺子　我也要
18.	Shànghǎi	上海	PN	Shanghai
19.	Wáng Xiǎoyún	王小云	PN	Wang Xiaoyun, name of a Chinese student

注释 Notes

① Tā xǐhuan chī diǎnxin hé mǐfàn.

He likes to eat snacks and rice.

The third person "tā" in Chinese has two characters: one is the male "他" (he; him) and the other is the female "她" (she; her).

② Bāozi dà, jiǎozi xiǎo.

Steamed stuffed buns are bigger and dumplings are smaller.

In a sentence with an adjectival predicate, when "hěn 很" is not present before the adjective, it often implies a comparison. In this sentence, the sizes of "bāozi 包子" and "jiǎozi 饺子" are compared.

③ Hǎo, wǒ yào jiǎozi, yě yào bāozi.

OK, I would like *jiaozi* (dumplings) and (would) also (like) *baozi* (steamed stuffed buns).

Here, "hǎo 好" has the meaning of OK. It is often used to express agreement, acceptance as well as the completion of the discussion on a topic.

The word "yào 要" indicates one's desire. When shopping or ordering in a restaurant, you may say "Wǒ yào 我要……" (I want…; I would like…). A shop assistant or restaurant server often asks customers "Nín yào shénme? 您要什么？" (What would you like?)

三、语言点 LANGUAGE POINTS

1 核心句 Key Sentences

2-02-05

1. Zhè shì Mǎ Dàwéi, tā shì wǒ péngyou.
2. Nín guìxìng?
3. Nǐ shì nǎ guó rén?
4. Wǒ māma shì Běijīngrén.
5. Zhè shì shénme?
6. Zhè shì jiǎozi ma?
7. Zhè bú shì jiǎozi, shì bāozi.
8. Nà shì jiǎozi.
9. Bāozi hé jiǎozi dōu hěn hǎochī.

2 语法 Grammar

1. "是" 字句（1） A sentence with "shì 是" (to be) (1)

In a sentence with "是", the verb "是" is used to link two related parts, which can be nouns, pronouns or noun phrases. The negative is formed by adding "bù 不" (not; changed to the 2nd tone bú) before "是". If not particularly emphasized, "是" is usually lightly pronounced.

Subject	Predicate			
	Adverb	是	Noun / Noun Phrase	Particle
Zhè 这		shì 是	Mǎ Dàwéi. 马 大为。	
Nà 那	bú 不	shì 是	jiǎozi. 饺子。	
Tā 他	bú 不	shì 是	Chén lǎoshī. 陈 老师。	
Nǐ 你	yě 也	shì 是	Shànghǎirén 上海人	ma? 吗?

Note:

The negative adverb "不" must be placed before "是".

Exercise I   Based on the example given, turn each statement into a negative sentence and then into a question.

Example Zhè shì jiǎozi.   Zhè bú shì jiǎozi.   Zhè shì jiǎozi ma?
这 是 饺子。 → 这 不 是 饺子。 → 这 是 饺子吗？

Zhè shì miàntiáo.
（1）这 是 面条。   → _____。 → _____？

Nà shì bāozi.
（2）那 是 包子。   → _____。 → _____？

Tā shì Běijīngrén.
（3）他 是 北京人。   → _____。 → _____？

Wǒ shì Shànghǎirén.
（4）我 是 上海人。   → _____。 → _____？

Exercise II   Pattern drill: Complete the dialogues with the words/phrases on the right.

Nà shì shéi?
（1）A：那 是 谁（who）？

Nà shì
B：那 是 _____。

wǒ péngyou
我 朋友
wǒmen lǎoshī
我们 老师
Mǎ Dàwéi
马 大为

Tā shì nǎ guó rén?
（2）A：他 是 哪 国 人？

Tā shì   rén.
B：他 是 _____ 人。

Zhōngguó
中国（China）
Měiguó
美国

2. 用疑问代词的问句（1）：什么、哪   An interrogative sentence using a question pronoun (1): "shénme 什么"（what）or "nǎ 哪"（which）

In Chinese, the word order of an interrogative sentence using a question pronoun is the same as the word order of a declarative sentence.

Declarative Sentence	Interrogative Sentence
Zhè shì jiǎozi. 这 是 饺子。	Zhè shì shénme? → 这 是 什么？

Declarative Sentence	Interrogative Sentence
Běijīngrén xǐhuan chī miàntiáo hé jiǎozi. 北京人　喜欢 吃　面条 和饺子。→	Běijīngrén xǐhuan chī shénme? 北京人　喜欢 吃 什么？
Tā shì Měiguórén. 他是 美国人。 →	Tā shì nǎ guó rén? 他是 哪 国 人？

Exercise I　Change the statements into questions.

Example
Zhè shì bāozi.　　Zhè shì shénme?
这 是 包子。→这 是 什么？

Nà shì mǐfàn.
(1) 那 是 米饭。→ _____ ?

Qiáodān　　　　shì Měiguórén.
(2) 乔丹（Jordan）是 美国人。→ _____ ?

Wáng Xiǎoyún xǐhuan chī mǐfàn.
(3) 王　小云 喜欢 吃 米饭。→ _____ ?

Mǎ Dàwéi xuéxí Hànyǔ.
(4) 马 大为 学习 汉语。→ _____ ?

Exercise II　Complete the dialogues.

(1) A: _____ ?

Zhè shì miàntiáo.
B：这 是 面条。

A: _____ ?

Nà shì diǎnxin.
B：那是 点心。

A: _____ ?

Shànghǎirén xǐhuan chī diǎnxin
B：上海人　喜欢 吃 点心

hé mǐfàn.
和米饭。

(2) A: _____ ?

Tā shì Měiguórén.
B：她是 美国人。

A: _____ ?

Tā xuéxí Hànyǔ.
B：她学习 汉语。

3. 连词 "和" The conjunction "hé 和" (and)

The conjunction "和" usually connects pronouns, nouns, or noun phrases, such as "tā hé tā 她和他" (she and he), "bàba hé māma 爸爸和妈妈" (dad and mom), and "wǒ māma hé nǐ māma 我妈妈和你妈妈" (my mom and your mom). The conjunction "和" cannot connect two sentences and is seldom used to connect two verbs or two adjectives.

Exercise I Complete the sentences by using the words in parentheses.

Example
Bāozi hé jiǎozi dōu hěn hǎochī. bāozi, jiǎozi
包子和饺子都 很 好吃。（包子，饺子）

（1）＿＿＿＿＿＿＿＿
dōu hěn máng. Wáng Xiǎoyún, Sòng Huá
都 很 忙。（王 小云， 宋 华）

（2）＿＿＿＿＿＿＿＿
dōu hěn hǎochī. miàntiáo, diǎnxin
都 很 好吃。（面条，点心）

（3）我 喜欢 吃＿＿＿＿＿＿＿。
Wǒ xǐhuan chī   bāozi, jiǎozi
（包子，饺子）

（4）＿＿＿＿＿＿＿＿
dōu xuéxí Hànyǔ. Lín Nà, Dīng Lìbō
都学习汉语。（林娜，丁力波）

（5）＿＿＿＿＿＿＿＿
zuìjìn zěnmeyàng? nǐ bàba, nǐ māma
最近 怎么样?（你爸爸，你妈妈）

Exercise II Decide whether the sentences below are correct (√) or not (x).

Mǐfàn hé diǎnxin dōu hěn hǎochī.
（1）米饭 和 点心 都 很 好吃。   （   ）

Wǒ shì Měiguórén, hé wǒ xǐhuan chī jiǎozi.
（2）我 是 美国人，和 我 喜欢 吃 饺子。   （   ）

Wǒ hěn hǎo hé bú tài máng.
（3）我 很 好 和 不太 忙。   （   ）

Chén lǎoshī hé Wáng lǎoshī zuìjìn zěnmeyàng?
（4）陈 老师和 王 老师最近 怎么样?   （   ）

Wǒ bàba shì Shànghǎirén, hé wǒ māma shì Běijīngrén.
（5）我 爸爸是 上海人， 和 我 妈妈是 北京人。   （   ）

4. 副词 "都" 的位置　The position of the adverb "dōu 都" (all; both)

Like "yě 也" (also), the adverb "都" must be placed after the subject but before the predicate verb or adjective. For example, "Bāozi hé jiǎozi dōu hěn hǎochī. 包子和饺子都很好吃。" (Both *baozi* and *jiaozi* are very delicious). You must not say "*Dōu bāozi hé jiǎozi hěn hǎochī. 都包子和饺子很好吃。" as it is grammatically incorrect. When "都" and "也" appear in the same sentence, "也" precedes "都", for example, "Wǒ bàba hé wǒ māma yě dōu hěn máng. 我爸爸和我妈妈也都很忙。" (My dad and mom are also very busy).

Subject	Predicate	
	Adverb	Verb/Adjective
Dīng Lìbō hé Mǎ Dàwéi 丁 力波和马大为	dōu hěn 都 很	hǎo. 好。
Wǒ hé Lín Nà 我 和 林娜	dōu bú tài 都 不 太	máng. 忙。
Nǐ bàba hé nǐ māma 你爸爸和你 妈妈	dōu 都	shì Běijīngrén ma? 是 北京人 吗?
Wáng Xiǎoyún hé Sòng Huá 王 小云 和宋 华	yě dōu bù 也都 不	xǐhuan chī miàntiáo. 喜欢 吃 面条。

Exercise I　Change the sentences using "都" following the example.

Example

Wǒ hěn máng.
我 很 忙。

Tā hěn máng.
她 很 忙。

⟹ Wǒ hé tā dōu hěn máng.
我 和 她 都 很 忙。

（1）Lín Nà hěn hǎo.
林 娜 很 好。

Dīng Lìbō hěn hǎo.
丁 力波 很 好。

⟹ _____。

（2）Wǒ bú tài máng.
我 不 太 忙。

Sòng Huá bú tài máng.
宋 华不太 忙。

⟹ _____。

（3）Tā shì Měiguórén.
他 是 美国人。

Mǎ Dàwéi shì Měiguórén.
马 大为 是 美国人。

⟹ _____。

Wǒ māma shì Shànghǎirén.

（4）我 妈妈 是 上海人。 ⟹

Wǒ bàba shì Shànghǎirén.

我 爸爸是 上海人。 _____ 。

Exercise II Following the example, put the words and phrases in order to form sentences.

wǒmen   hǎo   hěn   dōu   Wǒmen dōu hěn hǎo.

Example   我们   好   很   都 → 我们 都 很 好。

     máng   wǒmen   dōu   bù

（1）忙   我们   都   不 → _____

     dōu   bāozi hé jiǎozi   hěn   hǎochī

（2）都   包子和饺子   很   好吃 → _____

     dōu   wǒ péngyou hé wǒ   gāoxìng   hěn

（3）都   我 朋友 和我   高兴   很 → _____

     wǒ bàba hé wǒ māma   dōu   Běijīngrén   shì

（4）我 爸爸和我 妈妈   都   北京人   是 → _____

     diǎnxin   Dīng Lìbō   Mǎ Dàwéi   dōu   xǐhuan chī   hé

（5）点心   丁 力波   马 大为   都   喜欢 吃   和 → _____

_____

四、练习与运用 *PRACTICE AND APPLICATION*

补充词语 Supplementary Words   2-02-06

1.	Zhōngguó	中国	PN	China
2.	Fǎguó	法国	PN	France
3.	Déguó	德国	PN	Germany
4.	Jiānádà	加拿大	PN	Canada
5.	Yīngguó	英国	PN	United Kingdom; England
6.	Àodàlìyà	澳大利亚	PN	Australia
7.	Éluósī	俄罗斯	PN	Russia
8.	Xībānyá	西班牙	PN	Spain
9.	Rìběn	日本	PN	Japan
10.	Hánguó	韩国	PN	South Korea

11.	Tàiguó	泰国	PN	Thailand
12.	Yìndù	印度	PN	India
13.	Āijí	埃及	PN	Egypt
14.	tóngxué	同学	N	classmate; schoolmate; fellow student　同学和老师
15.	miànbāo	面包	N	bread　面包很好吃
16.	hànbǎobāo	汉堡包	N	hamburger　喜欢吃汉堡包
17.	bǐsàbǐng	比萨饼	N	pizza　汉堡包和比萨饼

语音练习 Pronunciation Drills 2-02-07

Listen and read aloud: Add tone marks to the following words and sentences, and then read them aloud.

❶ Meiguo　　　　❷ haochi　　　　❸ mifan

❹ xihuan　　　　❺ jiaozi　　　　❻ women

❼ renshi　　　　❽ pengyou　　　　❾ Qingwen nin guixing?

❿ Ni shi na guo ren?

2　会话练习 Conversation Practice

Pair activity: Create dialogues based on the scenes and the requirements below.

1. Greetings in the morning

（1）

（2）

2. Ask your classmates about their nationality.

　　　　Nǐ shì　　　　　　rén?
A：你是＿＿＿＿＿＿人？

　　　　Wǒ shì　　　　　　rén.
B：我 是＿＿＿＿＿＿人。

        Tā / Tā yě shì   rén ma?

A：他 / 她也是＿＿＿＿＿＿人 吗？

        Tā / Tā bú shì   rén, shì   rén.

B：他 / 她不 是＿＿＿＿＿＿人，是＿＿＿＿＿人。

3. Based on the pictures and sentence patterns given, introduce your friends.

Zhè shì   tā / tā shì   rén.

这 是＿＿＿＿＿＿＿，他 / 她是＿＿＿＿＿＿＿人。

Nà shì   tā / tā shì   rén.

那 是＿＿＿＿＿＿＿，他 / 她是＿＿＿＿＿＿＿人。

4. Based on the pictures and sentence patterns given, talk about food.

        bāozi   hànbǎobāo   jiǎozi   bǐsàbǐng

        包子   汉堡包   饺子   比萨饼

Zhè shì   Nà shì

这 是＿＿＿＿＿＿＿。那 是＿＿＿＿＿＿＿。

Nà shì   ma?

那 是＿＿＿＿＿＿＿吗？

Nà bú shì   nà shì

那 不 是＿＿＿＿＿＿＿，那 是＿＿＿＿＿＿＿。

Wǒ xǐhuan chī   hé

我 喜欢 吃＿＿＿＿＿＿＿和＿＿＿＿＿＿＿。

5. Create dialogues based on the pictures below.

（1）

　　　　 Nǐ　bàba māma zuìjìn zěnmeyàng?
A：你爸爸 妈妈 最近 怎么样?

　　　　 Tāmen　　　　　　　　 Nǐ bàba
B：他们＿＿＿＿＿＿＿。你爸爸

　　　　 māma ne?
　　　　 妈妈 呢?

　　　　 Tāmen
A：他们＿＿＿＿＿＿＿＿＿。

（2）

　　　　 Tā xuéxí shénme?
A：她学习　什么?

　　　　 Tā
B：她＿＿＿＿＿＿＿＿＿＿。

　　　　 Nǐ ne?
A：你 呢?

　　　　 Wǒ yě
B：我 也＿＿＿＿＿＿＿＿＿。

　　　　 Wǒmen
　　　　 我们＿＿＿＿＿＿＿＿＿。

3 听后复述 Listening and Repeating

 2-02-08

Listen to the following dialogues and repeat what you hear.

　　　　 Nín zǎo!
（1）A：您 早!

　　　　 Nín hǎo!
　　　B：您 好!

　　　　 Wǒ xìng Dīng, jiào Dīng Lìbō.
　　　A：我 姓 丁, 叫 丁 力波。

　　　　 Wǒ jiào Sòng Huá.　Rènshi nǐ hěn gāoxìng.
　　　B：我 叫 宋 华。认识 你 很 高兴。

　　　　 Zhè shì wǒ tóngxué, nǐmen rènshi ma?
（2）A：这 是 我 同学, 你们 认识 吗?

　　　　 Nǐ hǎo!　Wǒ jiào Lín Nà. Qǐngwèn, nǐ shì nǎ guó rén?
　　　B：你好! 我 叫 林娜。请问, 你是 哪国人?

Wǒ jiào Mǎ Dàwéi,　wǒ shì Měiguórén.　Nǐ yě shì Měiguórén ma?
C：我　叫　马大为，我　是　美国人。你也是　美国人　吗？

Wǒ bú shì Měiguórén,　wǒ shì Yīngguórén.
B：我　不是　美国人，　我　是　英国人。

Qǐngwèn, nǐ shì Zhōngguórén ma?
（3）A：请问，　你是　中国人　吗？

Wǒ bú shì Zhōngguórén,　wǒ shì Jiānádàrén.
B：我　不是　中国人，　我是加拿大人。

Tāmen ne?
A：他们　呢？

Tāmen yě bú shì Zhōngguórén,　tāmen dōu shì Hánguórén.
B：他们　也不是　中国人，　他们　都　是　韩国人。

4 阅读理解 Reading Comprehension

Ⅰ

Wǒ jiào Dīng Lìbō,　wǒ shì Jiānádàrén.　Zhè shì Mǎ Dàwéi,　tā shì wǒ péngyou,　tā shì Měiguó-
我　叫　丁力波，我是加拿大人。这是马大为，他是我　朋友，他是美国

rén.　Nà shì Lín Nà,　tā yě shì wǒ péngyou, tā shì Yīngguórén.　Wǒ hé Dàwéi、Lín Nà dōu xuéxí
人。那是林娜，她也是我　朋友，她是　英国人。我和大为、林娜　都学习

Hànyǔ.
汉语。

Answer the following questions:

Dīng Lìbō、Mǎ Dàwéi hé Lín Nà dōu shì nǎ guó rén?
（1）丁　力波、马大为和林娜　都是哪国人？

Tāmen dōu xuéxí shénme?
（2）他们　都学习　什么？

Ⅱ

Wǒ xìng Lín, jiào Lín Nà.　Zhè shì Sòng Huá,　tā shì wǒ péngyou. Sòng Huá shì Běijīngrén,
我　姓林，叫林娜。这是　宋　华，他是我　朋友。宋　华是北京人，

xǐhuan chī jiǎozi hé miàntiáo. Wǒ yě xǐhuan chī jiǎozi,　jiǎozi hěn hǎochī.　Nà shì Chén lǎoshī,　tā
喜欢　吃饺子和　面条。我也喜欢　吃饺子，饺子很　好吃。那是　陈　老师，她

shì wǒmen lǎoshī. Chén lǎoshī shì Shànghǎirén, tā xǐhuan chī diǎnxin.
是　我们　老师。陈　老师是　上海人，她喜欢　吃点心。

Answer the following questions:

Sòng Huá shì nǎ guó rén?
（1）宋　华是哪国人？

Sòng Huá xǐhuan chī shénme?
（2）宋　华喜欢吃什么？

Lín Nà xǐhuan chī jiǎozi ma?
（3）林娜喜欢吃饺子吗？

Chén lǎoshī shì Běijīngrén ma?
（4）陈　老师是北京人吗？

Chén lǎoshī xǐhuan chī shénme?
（5）陈　老师喜欢吃什么？

5　任务与活动 Task and Activity

1. Do you know who they are?

Group activity: Can you read aloud their Chinese names? Talk about the names in your group and then report back to the whole class. See which group knows the most.

Kǒngzǐ
孔子
Confucius

Lǐ Bái
李白
Li Bai

Lǔ Xùn
鲁迅
Lu Xun

Shāshìbǐyà
莎士比亚
William Shakespeare

Bèiduōfēn
贝多芬
Ludwig van Beethoven

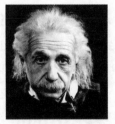

Àiyīnsītǎn
爱因斯坦
Albert Einstein

Tā jiào shénme míngzi? Tā shì nǎ guó rén?
（他叫什么名字？他是哪国人？）

2. Acting

Below is a staple food menu of a Chinese restaurant. Complete the dialogue in groups of two, one acting as a customer from abroad and the other acting as a server.

主食菜谱　　　　　Menu

bāozi
包子

jiǎozi
饺子

miàntiáo
面条

mǐfàn
米饭

Zhè shì shénme?
A：这 是 什么？

B：_____。

Nà shì shénme?
A：那 是 什么？

B：_____。

hǎochī ma?
A：_____好吃 吗？

hé
B：_____和_____

dōu hěn hǎochī.　Nǐ yào shénme?
都 很 好吃。你要 什么？

Wǒ yào
A：我 要_____，

yě yào
也 要_____。

 6 学习活动 Learning Activity

In small groups, summarize the personal pronouns that you have learned and list them in a table. Report back to the whole class.

7 写作练习 Writing Exercise

1. Write a brief paragraph to introduce your friend based on the format below.

Wǒ péngyou xìng　　　　jiào　　　　Tā / Tā shì　　　　rén, tā / tā
我 朋友 姓_____，叫_____。他 / 她 是_____人，他 / 她

xuéxí
学习_____。

2. Based on the following pictures, write a paragraph to introduce the foods you and your parents like respectively.

Zhè shì　　　　nà shì　　　　Wǒ shì　　　rén, wǒ xǐhuan chī　　　　hé
这 是＿＿＿＿，那 是＿＿＿＿。我 是＿＿＿＿人，我 喜欢 吃＿＿＿＿和

　　　　　　hé　　　　hěn hǎochī.
＿＿＿＿，＿＿＿＿和＿＿＿＿很 好吃。

Zhè shì　　　　nà shì　　　　Wǒ bàba shì　　　rén, tā xǐhuan chī
这 是＿＿＿＿，那 是＿＿＿＿。我 爸爸 是＿＿＿＿人，他 喜欢 吃＿＿＿＿

hé　　　　　　hé　　　　hěn hǎochī.
和＿＿＿＿，＿＿＿＿和＿＿＿＿很 好吃。

Zhè shì　　　　nà shì　　　　Wǒ māma shì　　　rén, tā xǐhuan chī
这 是＿＿＿＿，那 是＿＿＿＿。我 妈妈 是＿＿＿＿人，她 喜欢 吃＿＿＿＿

hé　　　　　　hé　　　　hěn hǎochī.
和＿＿＿＿，＿＿＿＿和＿＿＿＿很 好吃。

五、汉字　*CHINESE CHARACTERS*

1　汉字知识 Knowledge about Chinese Characters

The structure of Chinese characters (I)

Chinese characters are divided into one-component characters and compound characters. The basic characters that we have learned are mostly one-component characters, which are composed of a single component, such as "yī 一 (one), rén 人 (person), xiǎo 小 (small), mǎ 马 (horse), nǚ 女 (female), kǒu 口 (mouth)", and so on. Compound characters are composed of two or more components, such as "bà 爸 (dad), mā 妈 (mom), nǐ 你 (you, singular), men 们 (*plural suffix*), nǎ 哪 (which), wèn 问 (to ask)", and so on.

There are a lot of characters that are made of two components. The rules for the sequence of the two components are the same as those for the strokes.

The three basic modes for the two-component compound characters are as follows:

(1) Left-right structure: | 1 | 2 | e.g., mā 妈 (mom)

(2) Top-bottom structure: | 1 | / | 2 | e.g., bà 爸 (dad)

(3) Enclosed structure: | 1 | 2 | e.g., guó 国 (country)

2 汉字偏旁 Chinese Radicals

Radical	Name	Stroke Order	No. of Strokes	Example	Explanation
饣	shízìpáng	ノ 𠃋 饣	3	饭 fàn (meal) 饼 bǐng (round flat pastry) 饿 è (hungry)	Related to "food"
囗	guózìkuàng	丨 冂 囗	3	国 guó (country) 困 kùn (trapped)	Related to "limits" or "boundary"

3 认写基本汉字 Learn and Write the Basic Chinese Characters

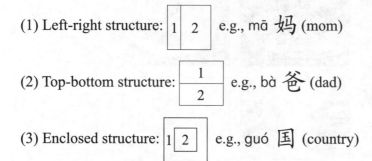

（1）匕　　ノ 匕
bǐ　　　a type of ancient spoon; dagger　　2 strokes

（2）又　　フ 又
yòu　　　again　　2 strokes

（3）贝　　丨 冂 贝 贝
bèi　　　shell　　4 strokes

（4）玉　　一 二 干 王 玉
yù　　　jade　　5 strokes

(5) 见　　丨 冂 贝 见　　　　　　to see　　　　4 strokes

jiàn

(6) 米　　丶 丶 丷 斗 半 米 米　　(uncooked) rice　　6 strokes

mǐ

(7) 目　　丨 冂 月 目 目　　　　eye　　　　5 strokes

mù

(8) 心　　丶 心 心 心　　　　　heart　　　4 strokes

xīn

(9) 上　　丨 卜 上　　　　　　up　　　　3 strokes

shàng

(10) 云　　一 二 云 云　　　　cloud　　　4 strokes

yún

(11) 王　　一 二 干 王　　　　king; a surname　　4 strokes

wáng

---

4 认写课文中的汉字 Learn and Write the Chinese Characters in the Text

(1) 老师 lǎoshī

老 → 耂（耂: 一 + 十 土 耂）+ 匕　　　　6 strokes

(2) 朋友 péngyou

友 → 𠂇（𠂇: 一 𠂇）+ 又　　　　4 strokes

(3) 贵姓 guìxìng

贵 → 虫（虫: 丶 丷 口 口 中 虫）+ 贝　　9 strokes

(4) 国 guó

国 → 囗 + 玉　　　　8 strokes

（5）米饭 mǐfàn

饭 —→ 饣 + 反　　　　　　　　　　　　7 strokes

（6）看 kàn

看 —→ 手（手：一 二 三 手）+ 目　　　9 strokes

六、文化知识　*CULTURAL KNOWLEDGE*

Types of Chinese Dictionaries

In China today, the most common "zìdiǎn 字典" (character dictionary) is the "Xīnhuá Zìdiǎn 《新华字典》" (*Xinhua Dictionary*), with over 13,000 Chinese characters. The most common "cídiǎn 词典" (word dictionary) is the "Xiàndài Hànyǔ Cídiǎn 《现代汉语词典》" (*Modern Chinese Dictionary*), with over 69,000 word entries. The most comprehensive dictionaries are the "Cíhǎi 《辞海》" (*Cihai Encyclopedia*) and the "Cíyuán 《辞源》" (*Ciyuan Encyclopedia*), etc. There are also dictionaries specially compiled for foreign learners of Chinese language and culture.

There are various types of indexes in a Chinese dictionary. The first is arranged in alphabetical order, i.e., "Hànyǔ pīnyīn 汉语拼音". The second is arranged according to the number of strokes, from one, two, three, to the largest number of strokes. The third is arranged according to the radicals.

In our present information age, there are also many electronic dictionaries, for example, the "Bǎidù Bǎikē 百度百科" (*Baidu Encyclopedia*) is an open and easy-to-search online encyclopedia. It is a platform that provides knowledge in Chinese in all fields and mobilizes the strength of the Internet users to communicate and to share information. If you want to know the natural environment of giant pandas, search for "dàxióngmāo 大熊猫" (giant panda) via "Bǎidù 百度(www.baidu.com)". Input the three characters "大熊猫", and you can see the pictures and texts about them.

七、自我评估　*SELF-EVALUATION*

I can basically do the following things in Chinese:

☐ I can greet people in the morning.

☐ I can ask someone's surname in a polite manner.

☐ I can ask about another person's nationality.

☐ I can say goodbye to someone.

☐ I can introduce my friend to someone.

☐ I can identify objects.

趣味汉语　**Fun with Chinese**

Body Language That the Chinese Often Use for Greetings

wēixiào

微笑

to smile

diǎntóu

点头

to nod

zhāoshǒu

招手

to wave; to beckon

wòshǒu

握手

to shake hands

bàoquán

抱拳

to cup two hands together in front
of one's chest as a sign of respect

jūgōng

鞠躬

to bow

3

Nǐmen jiā yǒu jǐ kǒu rén

你们家有几口人

How many people are there in your family

Family is one of the intimate topics that the Chinese often like to talk about when they meet friends. When you are with a Chinese friend, in addition to greetings, if you can talk about each other's families, it will definitely bring both of you closer. Let's first listen to the conversation between Lin Na and Wang Xiaoyun. Then, following Lin Na and Song Hua, you'll visit a Chinese family as a guest to see how they talk about family in Chinese.

一、热身 *WARM-UP*

1 思考 Think

Think about the following questions:

(1) Do you have an elder brother, a younger brother, an elder sister, or a younger sister?
(2) In your country, do you often ask others about their age?
(3) In your country, how do people entertain guests?

2 活动 Activity

Look at the pictures, and match them with the words. (Find the meanings of the words in the vocabulary lists in this lesson.)

（1）_____

（2）_____

（3）_____

（4）_____

a. 钢琴   b. 医生   c. 咖啡   d. 狗

二、课文 *TEXT*

（一）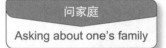 2-03-01

(Lin Na and Wang Xiaoyun are looking at a picture.)

Lín Nà：Nǐmen jiā yǒu jǐ kǒu rén? ①
林娜：你们 家有几口人？

> 问家庭
> Asking about one's family

Wáng Xiǎoyún：Wǒmen jiā yǒu sì kǒu rén.　Nǐ kàn,　zhè shì wǒmen jiā de
王小云：我们 家有四口人。你看，这是我们家的

zhàopiàn.
照片。

Lín Nà：Nǐ bàba māma zuò shénme gōngzuò? ②
林娜：你爸爸妈妈做 什么 工作？

> 问职业
> Asking about one's profession

Wáng Xiǎoyún：Wǒ bàba shì yīshēng,　māma shì lǎoshī.
王小云：我爸爸是 医生，妈妈是老师。

Lín Nà：Zhè shì nǐ dìdi ma?
林娜：这 是你弟弟吗？

Wáng Xiǎoyún: Zhè bú shì wǒ dìdi, zhè shì wǒ gēge. Lín Nà, nǐmen jiā
王小云：这 不是我弟弟，这是我哥哥。林娜，你们家

yǒu jǐ kǒu rén?
有几口人？

Lín Nà: Wǒmen jiā yígòng yǒu liù kǒu rén: māma、 yí ge gēge、
林娜：我们 家一共有六口人：妈妈、一个哥哥、

liǎng ge jiějie hé wǒ, hái yǒu Bèibei.
两 个姐姐和我，还有贝贝。

Wáng Xiǎoyún: Bèibei shì shéi? Shì nǐ mèimei ma?
王小云：贝贝是谁？是你妹妹吗？

Lín Nà: Wǒ méi yǒu mèimei. Bèibei shì wǒ de xiǎo gǒu.
林娜：我 没有妹妹。贝贝是我的小狗。

Wáng Xiǎoyún: Xiǎo gǒu yě shì yì kǒu rén ma?
王小云：小 狗也是一口人吗？

生词 New Words 2-03-02

1.	jiā	家	N	family; home 我们家 你们家
2.	yǒu	有	V	to have; there is/are 有朋友 有点心
3.	jǐ	几	QPr	how many
4.	kǒu	口	M	*a measure word mainly for the number of people in a family* 几口人 六口人
5.	de	的	StPt	*a possessive or modifying particle* 我的饺子 爸爸的米饭 他的名字 老师的姓
6.	zhàopiàn	照片	N	picture; photo 看照片 有照片 妈妈的照片
7.	zuò	做	V	to do; to make 做点心 做面条
8.	gōngzuò	工作	V/N	to work / work; job 她不工作 做工作 有工作
9.	yīshēng	医生	N	doctor 爸爸是医生

10.	dìdi	弟弟	N	younger brother　我弟弟　弟弟的老师
11.	gēge	哥哥	N	elder brother　她哥哥　有哥哥
12.	yígòng	一共	Adv	altogether　一共几口人
13.	gè	个	M	*a measure word for general use*　一个人　一个包子 几个朋友
14.	liǎng	两	Nu	two　两个老师　两口人　两个饺子
15.	jiějie	姐姐	N	elder sister　两个姐姐　我姐姐　姐姐的朋友
16.	hái	还	Adv	in addition　还有米饭　还做饺子　还吃点心
17.	shéi	谁	QPr	who; whom　还有谁　他是谁　谁的照片
18.	mèimei	妹妹	N	younger sister　我妹妹　姐姐和妹妹　一个妹妹
19.	méi	没	Adv	not　没有　没有朋友　没有人
20.	gǒu	狗	N	dog　小狗　我的小狗
21.	Bèibei	贝贝	PN	Beibei, a name

注释　Notes

① Nǐmen jiā yǒu jǐ kǒu rén?

How many people are there in your family?

When a personal pronoun modifies a place, an organization, or a workplace, in spoken Chinese, one often uses the plural form of the pronoun. For example, "nǐmen jiā 你们家" (your family), "wǒmen xuéxiào 我们学校" (our school), and "wǒmen guójiā 我们国家" (our country).

② Nǐ bàba māma zuò shénme gōngzuò?

What kind of work do your father and mother do?

The expression "zuò shénme gōngzuò 做什么工作" can be used to ask about someone's profession. For example, "Nǐ zuò shénme gōngzuò? 你做什么工作？" (What kind of work do you do?) and "Nǐ bàba zuò shénme gōngzuò? 你爸爸做什么工作？" (What kind of work does your father do?) In the response, one uses the verb "shì 是" (to be) plus one's profession, such as "Wǒ shì lǎoshī. 我是老师。" (I am a teacher) or "Wǒ bàba shì yīshēng. 我爸爸是医生。" (My father is a doctor).

（二）  2-03-03

(On the weekend, Lin Na and Song Hua go to Lu Yuping's home to have fun.)

Lù Yǔpíng: Nǐmen hǎo! Qǐng jìn!
陆雨平： 你们 好！ 请 进！

Lín Nà: Nín hǎo! Nǐmen jiā zhēn piàoliang! ①
林娜： 您 好！ 你们家 真 漂亮！

Lù Yǔpíng: Xièxie. Qǐng zuò. Nǐmen hē shénme? Wǒmen jiā yǒu chá
陆雨平： 谢谢。 请 坐。 你们 喝 什么？ 我们 家有 茶

hé kāfēi.
和 咖啡。

招待客人
Entertaining guests

Sòng Huá: Wǒ hē kāfēi.
宋华： 我 喝咖啡。

Lín Nà: Wǒ yào chá.
林娜： 我 要 茶。

(Song Hua is looking at a picture on the wall.)

Sòng Huá: Zhè zhāng zhàopiàn zhēn piàoliang! Zhè shì nǐ nǚ'ér ma?
宋华： 这 张 照片 真 漂亮！ 这 是 你女儿 吗？

Lù Yǔpíng：Shì. Zhè shì wǒ nǚ'ér.
陆雨平：是。这是我女儿。

Sòng Huá：Nǐ nǚ'ér jīnnián jǐ suì? ②
宋华：你女儿今年几岁？

问年龄 (1)
Asking about one's age (1)

Lù Yǔpíng：Wǔ suì.　Jīntiān tā yǒu gāngqínkè, ③　bú zài jiā.
陆雨平：五 岁。今天她有 钢琴课，　不在家。

Lín Nà：Zhōngguó de háizi zhēn máng!
林娜：中国　的孩子真　忙！

Lù Yǔpíng：Shì a. ④　Wǎnshang tā hái yǒu Yīngyǔkè.
陆雨平：是啊。　晚上　她还有英语课。

生词 New Words　🔊 2-03-04

1.	zhēn	真	Adv/A	really / real　真好 真忙 真高兴
2.	piàoliang	漂亮	A	beautiful; pretty　真漂亮 很漂亮
3.	hē	喝	V	to drink　喝什么
4.	chá	茶	N	tea　喝茶 喜欢喝茶 茶很好
5.	kāfēi	咖啡	N	coffee　喝咖啡 喜欢喝咖啡
6.	zhāng	张	M	*a measure word for flat objects*　一张照片
7.	nǚ'ér	女儿	N	daughter　我女儿 女儿很漂亮
	nǚ	女	A	female
8.	jīnnián	今年	N	this year　今年很忙
	nián	年	N	year　2016 年 2020 年
9.	suì	岁	M	year (of age)　五岁 九岁 几岁
10.	jīntiān	今天	N	today
	tiān	天	N	day　一天 两天
11.	gāngqín	钢琴	N	piano　学钢琴

✓12.	kè	课	N	class; lesson; course	钢琴课 汉语课 没有课
13.	háizi	孩子	N	child	中国孩子 美国孩子 一个孩子
14.	a	啊	MdPt	*attached to a verb, adjective, or the end of a sentence as a sign of confirmation*	
✓15.	wǎnshang	晚上	N	evening	晚上工作 晚上有课
	wǎn	晚	A	late	很晚 不晚
16.	Yīngyǔ	英语	N	English (language)	学习英语 英语课
✓17.	Zhōngguó	中国	PN	China	
18.	Lù Yǔpíng	陆雨平	PN	Lu Yuping, name of a Chinese reporter	

注释 Notes

① Nǐmen jiā zhēn piàoliang!

> Your home is really beautiful!
> The word "zhēn 真" (really) followed by an adjective often expresses an exclamation.

② Nǐ nǚ'ér jīnnián jǐ suì?

> How old is your daughter this year?
> The expression "Jīnnián jǐ suì? 今年几岁？" (How old... this year?) is often used to ask a child's age. Note: It is not used to ask an adult's age.

③ Jīntiān tā yǒu gāngqínkè.

> Today she has a piano lesson.
> A noun that comes directly before another noun acts as a modifier, e.g., "Měiguórén 美国人" (American people), "gāngqínkè 钢琴课" (piano lesson) and "Yīngyǔkè 英语课" (English lesson).

④ Shì a.

> Yes.
> The modal particle "a 啊" is attached to "shì 是" as a sign of confirmation.

三、语言点 LANGUAGE POINTS

1 核心句 Key Sentences

2-03-05

1. Nǐmen jiā yǒu jǐ kǒu rén?

2. Wǒmen jiā yígòng yǒu liù kǒu rén.

3. Wǒ méi yǒu mèimei.

4. Bèibei shì shéi?

5. Zhè shì wǒmen jiā de zhàopiàn.

6. Zhè zhāng zhàopiàn zhēn piàoliang!

7. Nǐ bàba māma zuò shénme gōngzuò?

8. Nǐ nǚ'ér jīnnián jǐ suì?

9. Wǎnshang tā hái yǒu Yīngyǔkè.

2 语法 Grammar

1. "有"字句　A sentence with "yǒu 有" (to have)

A sentence with the verb "有" in the predicate usually expresses possession. The negative is formed by putting "méi 没" before "有". Note: Do not use "bù 不" before "有".

Subject	Predicate		
	（没）有	Object	Particle
Wǒ 我	yǒu 有	yí ge gēge. 一个哥哥。	
Wǒmen jiā 我们家	yǒu 有	sì kǒu rén. 四口人。	
Tā 她	méi yǒu 没有	mèimei. 妹妹。	
Dīng Lìbō 丁力波	méi yǒu 没有	kāfēi. 咖啡。	
Tā nǚ'ér 他女儿	jīntiān yǒu 今天 有	Yīngyǔkè 英语课	ma? 吗?
Nǐmen jiā 你们家	yǒu 有	xiǎo gǒu 小狗	ma? 吗?

If the subject of a sentence with "有" begins with an organization, a place, or a location, the sentence is similar to the English sentence pattern "There is/are…".

Exercise I   Substitute the underlined parts and complete the dialogues.

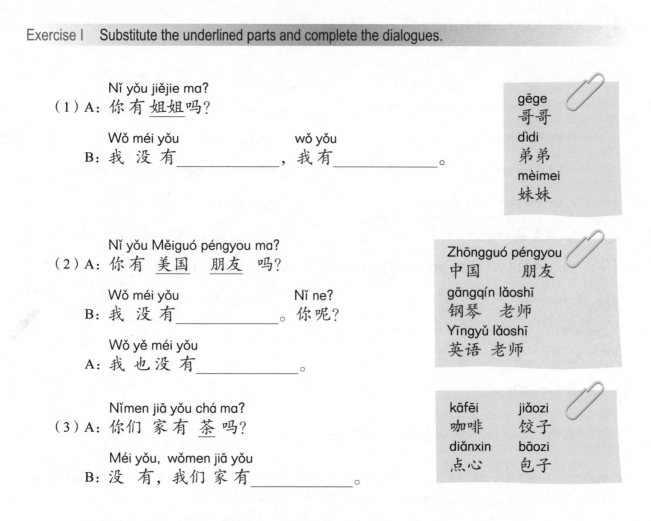

Nǐ yǒu jiějie ma?
（1）A：你有 <u>姐姐</u> 吗？

Wǒ méi yǒu   wǒ yǒu
B：我 没 有＿＿＿＿＿＿，我 有＿＿＿＿＿＿。

gēge
哥哥
dìdi
弟弟
mèimei
妹妹

Nǐ yǒu Měiguó péngyou ma?
（2）A：你 有 <u>美国</u> <u>朋友</u> 吗？

Wǒ méi yǒu   Nǐ ne?
B：我 没 有＿＿＿＿＿＿。你 呢？

Wǒ yě méi yǒu
A：我 也 没 有＿＿＿＿＿＿。

Zhōngguó péngyou
中国   朋友
gāngqín lǎoshī
钢琴 老师
Yīngyǔ lǎoshī
英语 老师

Nǐmen jiā yǒu chá ma?
（3）A：你们 家有 <u>茶</u> 吗？

Méi yǒu, wǒmen jiā yǒu
B：没 有，我们 家有＿＿＿＿＿＿。

kāfēi   jiǎozi
咖啡   饺子
diǎnxin   bāozi
点心   包子

Exercise II   Following the example, change the sentence pattern.

Wǒ yǒu gēge.   Wǒ méi yǒu gēge.   Nǐ yǒu gēge ma?
Example   我 有哥哥。 → 我 没 有哥哥。 → 你 有哥哥 吗？

Tāmen yǒu háizi.
（1）他们 有孩子。   → ＿＿＿＿＿＿。 → ＿＿＿＿＿＿？

Xiǎoyún wǎnshang yǒu Yīngyǔkè.
（2）小云 晚上 有 英语课。 → ＿＿＿＿＿＿。 → ＿＿＿＿＿＿？

Wǒmen jiā yǒu xiǎo gǒu.
（3）我们 家有 小 狗。   → ＿＿＿＿＿＿。 → ＿＿＿＿＿＿？

Lín Nà jiā yǒu Bèibei de zhàopiàn.
（4）林娜家有 贝贝的 照片。 → ＿＿＿＿＿＿。 → ＿＿＿＿＿＿？

2. 表领属关系的定语　A modifier expressing possession

In Chinese, a modifier, also known as an attributive, is always placed before the word it modifies. When a pronoun or a noun is used as a modifier to express possession, the structural particle "de 的" is usually required.

Noun (Phrase) / Pronoun	+	的	+	Noun
wǒ 我		de 的		gōngzuò 工作
wǒmen jiā 我们 家		de 的		zhàopiàn 照片
Lù Yǔpíng 陆 雨平		de 的		nǚ'ér 女儿

When a personal pronoun modifies a relative or the name of a workplace that is very close to the person, "的" may be omitted. For example, "wǒ māma 我妈妈" (my mom), "nǐ nǚ'ér 你女儿" (your daughter), "tāmen jiā 他们家" (their home/family).

Exercise I　Substitute the underlined parts and complete the dialogues.

Zhè shì shéi de kāfēi?
（1）A：这 是 谁 的 咖啡？

Zhè shì wǒ de kāfēi.
B：这 是 我的 咖啡。

nín de
您的
dìdi　de
弟弟 的
tāmen de
他们 的

Nǐ yǒu Bèibei de zhàopiàn ma?
（2）A：你 有 贝贝的 照片 吗？

Wǒ méi yǒu Bèibei de zhàopiàn.
B：我 没有 贝贝的 照片。

Lín Nà de
林 娜 的
tā nǚ'ér de
他 女儿的
lǎoshī de
老师 的

Shéi shì yīshēng?
（3）A：谁 是 医生？

Wǒ māma shì yīshēng.
B：我 妈妈 是 医生。

tā bàba
他爸爸
tā gēge
她哥哥
wǒ dìdi
我弟弟

Exercise II   Complete the sentences using the words in parentheses.

Example
 Zhè shì　wǒ de gǒu.　　　 de　gǒu　wǒ
 这 是 ＿我的狗＿ 。（的　狗　我）

 Tā bú shì　　　　　　　　　　　　 mèimei　Wáng Xiǎoyún de
（1）她不是＿＿＿＿＿＿＿＿＿＿＿＿。（妹妹　王　小云　的）

 Nǐ shì　　　　　　　　　 ma?　péngyou　de　Lín Nà
（2）你是＿＿＿＿＿＿＿＿＿吗？（朋友　的　林娜）

 Wǒ xǐhuan　　　　　　　　 míngzi　de　nǐ
（3）我 喜欢＿＿＿＿＿＿＿＿＿。（名字　的　你）

 Nà shì　　　　　　　　　 zhàopiàn　de　wǒmen jiā
（4）那是＿＿＿＿＿＿＿＿。（照片　的　我们　家）

3. 数量词做定语　A numeral-measure-word compound as a modifier

In modern Chinese, a numeral alone usually cannot modify a noun, but should be combined with a measure word. A noun usually has its own particular measure word.

Numeral	+	Measure Word	+	Noun
liù 六		kǒu 口		rén 人
liǎng 两		ge 个		jiějie 姐姐
yí 一		ge 个		péngyou 朋友
sān 三		zhāng 张		zhàopiàn 照片

The measure word "个" is commonly used before nouns referring to people, things, workplaces, etc. It is read in the neutral tone. The measure word "张" is usually used before objects with a flat surface such as paper, pictures, and business cards. The measure word "口" is used to express the number of people in a family. For example, "wǔ kǒu rén 五口人" (five family members). In other cases, "个" should be used. For example, "Wǒmen bān yǒu shí ge rén. 我们班有十个人。" (There are 10 people in our class). One cannot say "*Wǒmen bān yǒu shí kǒu rén. 我们班有十口人。"

Note:

When the demonstrative pronoun "zhè 这" (this) or "nà 那" (that) is used as a modifier, there should also be a measure word before the modified noun. For example,

Demonstrative Pronoun	+	Measure Word	+	Noun
zhè 这		zhāng 张		zhàopiàn 照片
nà 那		ge 个		péngyou 朋友

Exercise I　Substitute the underlined parts and complete the dialogues.

（1）A：Nǐmen jiā yǒu jǐ kǒu rén?
你们 家有几口人?

　　B：Wǒmen jiā yǒu liù kǒu rén.
我们 家有 六口人。

sān kǒu rén
三 口人
wǔ kǒu rén
五 口人
qī kǒu rén
七 口 人

（2）A：Tāmen yǒu jǐ ge háizi?
他们 有几个孩子?

　　B：Tāmen yǒu yí ge háizi.
他们 有一个孩子。

liǎng ge háizi
两 个孩子
sān ge háizi
三 个孩子
sì ge háizi
四个孩子

（3）A：Nǐ yǒu jǐ zhāng zhàopiàn?
你有几张 照片?

　　B：Wǒ yǒu liù zhāng zhàopiàn.
我有六张 照片。

bā zhāng zhàopiàn
八 张 照片
jiǔ zhāng zhàopiàn
九 张 照片
shí zhāng zhàopiàn
十 张 照片

Exercise II　Complete the sentences with the numbers given.

（1）Wǒ yǒu　　　　　Bèibei de zhàopiàn.
我 有＿＿＿＿贝贝的 照片。（1）

（2）Wáng Xiǎoyún jiā yǒu　　　　　rén.
王 小云 家有＿＿＿＿人。（4）

（3）Tā yǒu　　　　　gēge.
她有＿＿＿＿哥哥。（2）

（4）Mǎ Dàwéi yǒu　　　　　Zhōngguó péngyou.
马 大为 有＿＿＿＿中国 朋友。（3）

Exercise III Substitute the underlined parts and complete the dialogues.

Zhè zhāng zhàopiàn zěnmeyàng?
A：这 张 照片 怎么样？

Zhè zhāng zhàopiàn hěn piàoliang.
B：这 张 照片 很 漂亮。

háizi ge	máng
孩子（个）	忙
lǎoshī ge	piàoliang
老师（个）	漂亮
bāozi ge	hǎochī
包子（个）	好吃
gōngzuò ge	hǎo
工作（个）	好

4. 用疑问代词的问句（2）：谁、几　An interrogative sentence using a question pronoun (2): "shéi 谁" (who) or "jǐ 几" (how many)

In an interrogative sentence using "谁" or "几", the word order is the same as that in a declarative sentence. You only need to use the question word "谁" or "几" to replace what you do not know and want to ask. The question word "谁" is used to ask about people, while "几" is used to ask about a number under 10.

Declarative Sentence		Interrogative Sentence
Nà shì wǒ gēge. 那 是 我 哥哥。	→	Nà shì shéi? 那 是 谁？
Wáng Xiǎoyún xǐhuan chī diǎnxin. 王 小云 喜欢 吃 点心。	→	Shéi xǐhuan chī diǎnxin? 谁 喜欢 吃 点心？
Zhè shì Lín Nà de zhàopiàn. 这 是 林娜 的 照片。	→	Zhè shì shéi de zhàopiàn? 这 是 谁 的 照片？
Wǒmen jiā yǒu sì kǒu rén. 我们 家 有 四 口 人。	→	Nǐmen jiā yǒu jǐ kǒu rén? 你们 家 有 几 口 人？
Tā jīnnián wǔ suì. 她 今年 五 岁。	→	Tā jīnnián jǐ suì? 她 今年 几 岁？

Exercise I Following the example, change each statement into a question by using the question pronoun in parentheses.

Tā shì wǒ mèimei. shéi Tā shì shéi?
Example 她是我 妹妹。（谁）→她是 谁？

Wǒmen jiā yígòng yǒu liù kǒu rén. jǐ Nǐmen jiā yígòng yǒu jǐ kǒu rén?
我们 家一共 有六口人。（几）→你们家一共 有几口人？

Mǎ Dàwéi xǐhuan hē chá.　shéi

（1）马 大为 喜欢 喝茶。(谁)　→ _____

Zhè shì wǒ de xiǎo gǒu.　shéi

（2）这 是 我的 小 狗。(谁)　→ _____

Lín Nà yǒu liǎng ge jiějie.　jǐ

（3）林 娜 有 两 个 姐姐。(几)　→ _____

Tā yǒu sān zhāng zhàopiàn.　jǐ

（4）他 有 三 张 照片。(几)　→ _____

Exercise II　Fill in the blanks with "谁" or "几".

shì nǐ nǚ'ér?

（1）_____是 你 女儿?

Nǐ yǒu　　　ge háizi?

（2）你 有_____个 孩子?

Nǐ de lǎoshī shì

（3）你 的 老师 是_____?

Bèibei　　　suì?

（4）贝贝_____岁?

Zhè shì　　　de chá?

（5）这 是_____的 茶?

5. 还（1）：表示补充、追加　The adverb "hái 还" (1): Indicating "in addition"

One use of "还" is to make an additional remark. For example, "Wǒ yǒu liǎng ge jiějie, hái yǒu yí ge gēge. 我有两个姐姐，还有一个哥哥。" (I have two elder sisters and an elder brother).

Exercise I　Substitute the underlined parts and complete the dialogues.

Nǐ yǒu gēge ma?

（1）A：你 有 哥哥 吗?

Wǒ yǒu yí ge gēge,　hái yǒu liǎng ge dìdi.

　　B：我 有一个 哥哥，还 有 两 个 弟弟。

jiějie
姐姐
mèimei
妹妹

Nǐ yào shénme?

（2）A：你 要 什么?

Wǒ yào kāfēi,　hái yào diǎnxin.

　　B：我 要 咖啡，还 要 点心。

miànbāo
面包
hànbǎobāo
汉堡包
bǐsàbǐng
比萨饼

Nǐ rènshi shéi?
（3）A：你认识 谁？

Wǒ rènshi Mǎ Dàwéi, hái rènshi Lín Nà.
B：我 认识 马大为，还认识 林娜。

Dīng Lìbō
丁 力波
Chén lǎoshī
陈 老师
tā gēge
他哥哥

Jīntiān nǐ yǒu kè ma?
（4）A：今天 你有 课吗？

Jīntiān wǒ yǒu Hànyǔkè, hái yǒu Yīngyǔkè.
B：今天 我有 汉语课，还有 英语课。

gāngqínkè
钢琴课
Fǎyǔkè
法语课（French lesson）
Xībānyáyǔkè
西班牙语课（Spanish lesson）

Exercise II   Complete the sentences using the words in parentheses.

Tā xǐhuan chī bāozi,   miàntiáo xǐhuan chī hái
（1）他喜欢 吃包子，_____。（面条 喜欢 吃 还）

Tāmen jiā yǒu sì kǒu rén,   xiǎo gǒu hái yǒu
（2）他们 家有四口 人，_____。（小 狗 还 有）

Wǒ xuéxí Hànyǔ,   Yīngyǔ xuéxí hái
（3）我 学习 汉语，_____。（英语 学习 还）

Wǒ yǒu yí ge Měiguó péngyou,   yǒu hái yí ge Zhōngguó péngyou
（4）我 有一个 美国 朋友，_____。（有 还 一个 中国 朋友）

四、练习与运用 PRACTICE AND APPLICATION

补充词语 Supplementary Words 2-03-06

1.	lùshī	律师	N	lawyer
2.	jìzhě	记者	N	reporter
3.	fúwùyuán	服务员	N	waiter; waitress; server
4.	jīnglǐ	经理	N	manager
5.	gōngchéngshī	工程师	N	engineer
6.	xuésheng	学生	N	student

7.	shāngrén	商人	N	business person
8.	xiānsheng	先生	N	Mr.; sir; gentleman; husband　王先生　陆雨平先生
9.	tàitai	太太	N	Mrs.; madam; wife　陈太太　他太太
10.	nánpéngyou	男朋友	N	boyfriend　她男朋友　我姐姐的男朋友
11.	nǚpéngyou	女朋友	N	girlfriend　我女朋友　马大为的女朋友
12.	chéngzhī	橙汁	N	orange juice　喜欢橙汁
13.	kělè	可乐	N	Coke; cola　不喝可乐
14.	niúnǎi	牛奶	N	milk　没有牛奶
15.	dòujiāng	豆浆	N	soyabean milk　喜欢喝豆浆
16.	shuǐ	水	N	water
17.	bēi	杯	N	cup; glass; mug　一杯水　一杯咖啡　一杯茶
18.	shuài	帅	A	handsome

1 语音练习 Pronunciation Drills 2-03-07

Listen and read aloud: Add tone marks to the following words and sentences, and then read them aloud.

❶ yigong　　　❷ yi kou　　　❸ yi ge

❹ he cha　　　❺ haizi　　　❻ wanshang

❼ piaoliang　　❽ shenme　　❾ Nimen jia you ji kou ren?

❿ Zhe zhang zhaopian zhen piaoliang!

2 会话练习 Conversation Practice

Pair activity: Create dialogues based on the scenes and the requirements below.

1. Talking about one's family

（1）

Tāmen jiā yǒu jǐ kǒu rén?　Tāmen shì shéi?
他们　家　有　几口　人？　他们　是　谁？

Tāmen jiā yǒu jǐ ge　háizi?
他们　家　有　几个　孩子？

（2）Based on the actual situation, ask each other questions and respond.

2. Asking about one's profession

（1）

Example

Tā zuò shénme gōngzuò?
A：她做 什么 工作？

Tā shì lǜshī.
B：她是 律师。

（2）Based on the actual situation, ask each other questions and respond.

Nǐ bàba zuò shénme gōngzuò?
❶ 你爸爸做 什么 工作？

Nǐ māma zuò shénme gōngzuò?
❷ 你妈妈 做 什么 工作？

Nǐ yǒu gēge (jiějie、 dìdi、 mèimei) ma?
❸ 你有 哥哥（姐姐、弟弟、妹妹）吗？

Tā / Tā zuò shénme gōngzuò?
❹ 他/她做 什么 工作？

Nǐ xǐhuan shénme gōngzuò?
❺ 你喜欢 什么 工作？

3. Entertaining guests

（1）

（2）

The following words may be helpful to you:

nǐ hǎo	qǐng	nǐmen jiā	dà	piàoliang			
（1）你好	请	你们家	大	漂亮			

nǐ hē	wǒmen jiā yǒu	wǒ yào	chá	kāfēi	diǎnxin	qǐng
（2）你喝	我们 家有	我要	茶	咖啡	点心	请

4. Asking about one's age

Tā / Tā jīnnián jǐ suì?

他 / 她 今年 几岁?

3 听后复述 Listening and Repeating　　2-03-08

Listen to the following dialogues and repeat what you hear.

（1）
A：Zhè zhāng zhàopiàn shì shéi? Shì nǐ
这 张 照片 是 谁? 是 你
gēge ma? Zhēn shuài!
哥哥 吗? 真 帅!

B：Shì wǒ nánpéngyou.
是 我 男朋友。

（2）
A：Nǐ tàitai zuò shénme gōngzuò?
你 太太 做 什么 工作?

B：Tā shì lùshī. Nǐ nǚpéngyou ne?
她 是 律师。 你 女朋友 呢?

A：Tā hé wǒ dōu shì Hànyǔ lǎoshī.
她 和 我 都 是 汉语 老师。

（3）
A：Tāmen yǒu jǐ ge háizi?
他们 有几个孩子?

B：Tāmen yǒu liǎng ge háizi, dōu hěn
他们 有 两 个孩子, 都 很
piàoliang.
漂亮。

A：Zhège háizi jīnnián jǐ suì?
这个 孩子 今年几岁?

B：Tā jīnnián qī suì.
他 今年 七岁。

（4）
A：Nín yào shénme?
您 要 什么?

B：Wǒ yào liǎng ge bāozi, yì bēi niúnǎi.
我 要 两 个包子, 一杯牛奶。

4 阅读理解 Reading Comprehension

Wáng Xiǎoyún jiā yǒu sì kǒu rén. Tā bàba shì yīshēng, māma shì lǎoshī. Tā hái yǒu yí ge
王 小云 家有四口人。她爸爸是 医生, 妈妈 是 老师。她还有一个
gēge. Zhè shì tāmen jiā de zhàopiàn. Lín Nà jiā yígòng yǒu wǔ kǒu rén, māma、 yí ge gēge、liǎng
哥哥。这是她们家的 照片。林娜家一共有五口人, 妈妈、一个哥哥、两

ge jiějie hé tā,　hái yǒu Bèibei. Bèibei shì tā de xiǎo gǒu.
个 姐姐 和 她，还 有 贝贝。贝贝 是 她的 小　狗。

Lù Yǔpíng jiā yǒu sān kǒu rén.　Tā yǒu yí ge nǚ'ér,　jīnnián wǔ suì.　Tā nǚ'ér hěn máng, jīntiān
陆 雨平 家 有 三 口 人。他 有 一个 女儿，今年 五岁。他 女儿 很　忙，今天

yǒu gāngqínkè, hái yǒu Yīngyǔkè.
有 钢琴课，还 有 英语课。

Answer the following questions:

Wáng Xiǎoyún jiā yǒu jǐ kǒu rén?
（1）王 　小云 家 有 几 口 人？

Bèibei shì Lín Nà jiā de rén ma?
（2）贝贝 是 林娜 家 的 人 吗？

Lù Yǔpíng de nǚ'ér zěnmeyàng?
（3）陆 雨平 的 女儿 怎么样？

Dàjiā hǎo! Wǒ xìng Mǎ,　jiào Mǎ Dàwéi,　shì Měiguórén. Wǒmen jiā yígòng yǒu wǔ kǒu rén,
大家 好！我 姓 马，叫 马 大为，是 美国人。 我们 家 一共 有 五 口 人，

bàba、　māma、　gēge hé wǒ,　hái yǒu Yuēhàn.　　Yuēhàn shì wǒ de gǒu, jīnnián liǎng suì.　Wǒ
爸爸、妈妈、哥哥 和 我，还 有 约翰（John）。约翰 是 我的 狗，今年 两 岁。我

bàba shì lǜshī,　wǒ māma shì gōngchéngshī, wǒ gēge shì jīnglǐ. Wǒ de lǎoshī shì Chén lǎoshī,
爸爸 是 律师，我 妈妈 是　 工程师，我 哥哥 是 经理。我 的 老师 是 陈 老师，

wǒmen dōu hěn xǐhuan tā.　Wǒ yǒu sān ge Zhōngguó péngyou, Wáng Xiǎoyún、Sòng Huá hé Lù Yǔpíng.
我们 都 很 喜欢她。我 有 三个 中国　 朋友，王 　小云、宋 华 和 陆 雨平。

Answer the following questions:

Mǎ Dàwéi shì nǎ guó rén?
（1）马 大为 是 哪 国 人？

Mǎ Dàwéi yǒu jiějie ma?
（2）马 大为 有 姐姐 吗？

Yuēhàn jīnnián jǐ suì?
（3）约翰　 今年 几岁？

Mǎ Dàwéi de bàba zuò shénme gōngzuò? Tā māma ne?
（4）马 大为 的爸爸 做 什么　 工作？ 他 妈妈 呢？

Chén lǎoshī shì shéi?
（5）陈 老师 是 谁？

Mǎ Dàwéi yǒu jǐ ge Zhōngguó péngyou? Tāmen dōu shì shéi?
（6）马 大为 有 几个 中国　 朋友？ 他们 都 是 谁？

5 任务与活动 Task and Activity

1. Conduct a survey in your class and complete the table below.

Questions	Answers
Shéi jiā yǒu liù kǒu rén / wǔ kǒu rén / sì kǒu rén / sān kǒu rén? 谁 家有 六口人 / 五口人 / 四口人 / 三口人?	
Shéi yǒu gēge / dìdi / jiějie / mèimei? 谁 有 哥哥 / 弟弟 / 姐姐 / 妹妹?	
Shéi jiā yǒu xiǎo gǒu? 谁 家有 小 狗?	
Shéi de māma shì lǎoshī? 谁 的 妈妈 是 老师?	
Shéi xǐhuan hē chá? 谁 喜欢 喝 茶?	
Shéi xǐhuan tán　　　　gāngqín? 谁 喜欢 弹（to play）钢琴?	

2. According to the guidelines below, interview a classmate. Write down what you find out and report it to the class.

Guidelines for your interview:

Nǐ jiào shénme míngzi?　Nǐ shì nǎ guó rén?
（1）你 叫 什么 名字? 你 是 哪 国 人?

Nǐmen jiā yǒu jǐ kǒu rén?　Tāmen zuò shénme gōngzuò?
（2）你们 家 有 几口人? 他们 做 什么 工作?

Nǐ zuò shénme gōngzuò?　Nǐ xǐhuan zuò shénme gōngzuò?
（3）你 做 什么 工作? 你 喜欢 做 什么 工作?

Nǐ xǐhuan chī shénme?　Nǐ xǐhuan hē shénme?
（4）你 喜欢 吃 什么? 你 喜欢 喝 什么?

Nǐ yǒu jǐ ge hǎo péngyou?
（5）你 有 几 个 好 朋友?

（6）……

6 写作练习 Writing Exercise

Following the example, introduce a friend of yours.

Example

Tā jiào Sòng Huá, tā shì Zhōngguórén. Tāmen jiā yǒu sān kǒu rén, bàba,
他叫 宋 华，他是 中国人。他们家有 三 口 人，爸爸、

māma hé tā. Tā bàba shì yīshēng, māma shì lǎoshī. Tā shì xuésheng. Tā xǐhuan chī
妈妈 和他。他爸爸是 医生，妈妈是 老师。他是 学生。他喜欢 吃

jiǎozi.
饺子。

五、汉字 *CHINESE CHARACTERS*

1 汉字知识 Knowledge about Chinese Characters

The structure of Chinese characters (II)

Common left-right structure:

(1) Left-right, equal: | 1 | 2 | e.g., péng 朋 (friend)

(2) Left small, right big: | 1 | 2 | e.g., tā 他 (he; him)

(3) Left big, right small: | 1 | 2 | e.g., nà 那 (that)

2 汉字偏旁 Chinese Radicals

Radical	Name	Stroke Order	No. of Strokes	Example	Explanation
艹	cǎozìtóu	一 十 艹	3	茶 chá (tea) 英 yīng (blossom; England)	Related to "grass"
宀	bǎogàitóu	丶 宀 宀	3	家 jiā (family; home) 字 zì (originally a child in the house; script; character)	Related to "house"

3 认写基本汉字 Learn and Write the Basic Chinese Characters

(1) 工　一 丁 工
gōng　work　3 strokes

(2) 弓　フ コ 弓
gōng　bow　3 strokes

(3) 山　丨 凵 山
shān　mountain　3 strokes

(4) 儿　丿 儿
ér　son　2 strokes

(5) 天　一 二 干 天
tiān　day; sky　4 strokes

(6) 中　丶 冂 口 中
zhōng　middle　4 strokes

4 认写课文中的汉字 Learn and Write the Chinese Characters in the Text

(1) 家 jiā

家 → 宀 + 豕（豕：一 ㇇ 了 豕 豸 豕 豕）　10 strokes

(2) 有 yǒu

有 → 𠂇 + 月　6 strokes

(3) 狗 gǒu

狗 → 犭（犭：丿 犭 犭）+ 句（句：丿 勹 勹 句 句）　8 strokes

(4) 张 zhāng

张 → 弓 + 长（长：丿 二 ㇏ 长）　7 strokes

（5）茶 chá

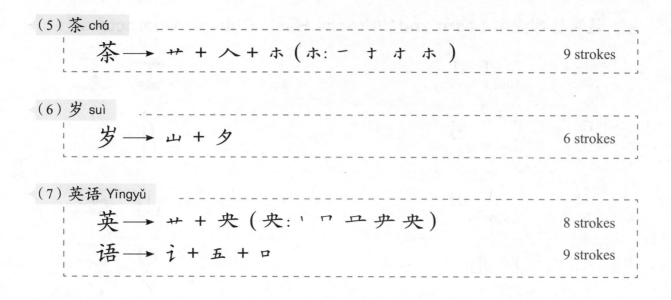

茶 → 艹 + 人 + 朩 (朩: 一 十 オ 朩)   9 strokes

（6）岁 suì

岁 → 山 + 夕   6 strokes

（7）英语 Yīngyǔ

英 → 艹 + 央 (央: 丶 冂 口 央 央)   8 strokes

语 → 讠 + 五 + 口   9 strokes

六、文化知识 *CULTURAL KNOWLEDGE*

Forms of Address for Family Members and Relatives

The forms of address for family members and relatives in Chinese are more complex than in English. The heart of a family is composed of "bàba 爸爸", "māma 妈妈", "érzi 儿子", and "nǚ'ér 女儿". These terms of address are very similar to the English words "father", "mother", "son", and "daughter". Other terms of address in Chinese are, however, more complicated than in English. There are two basic principles in Chinese. First, the paternal and maternal relatives must be addressed differently. Second, the person's seniority in the generational hierarchy is invariably taken into consideration.

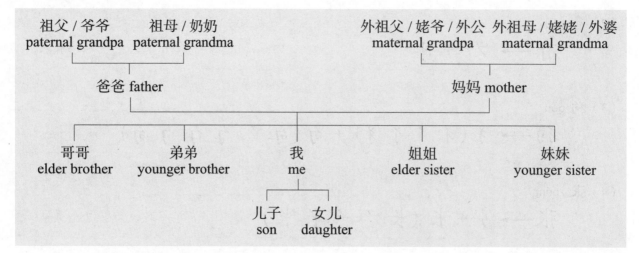

For parents' parents, the English words are "grandfather" and "grandmother", whereas the Chinese indicate more clearly whether they are on the paternal or maternal side. The parents of one's father are "zǔfù 祖父" and "zǔmǔ 祖母" or "yéye 爷爷" and "nǎinai 奶奶". The parents of one's mother are "wàizǔfù 外祖父" and "wàizǔmǔ 外祖母" or "wàigōng 外公" and "wàipó 外婆" or "lǎoye 姥爷" and "lǎolao 姥姥".

How do siblings refer to each other? In English "brother" and "sister" are used, but in Chinese the age of each sibling must be distinguished. The boy older than oneself is addressed as "gēge 哥哥" and the boy younger than oneself is addressed as "dìdi 弟弟". The girl older than oneself is called "jiějie 姐姐" and the girl younger than oneself is referred to as "mèimei 妹妹".

七、自我评估　*SELF-EVALUATION*

I can basically do the following things in Chinese:

☐ I can talk about my family.

☐ I can ask about other people's professions.

☐ I can entertain guests.

☐ I can ask children their age.

趣味汉语　**Fun with Chinese**

Read the Two Classical Poems Aloud

I

Jìng Yè Sī
静 夜 思

(Táng)　Lǐ Bái
（唐）李 白

Chuáng qián　míngyuè　guāng,
床　前　明　月　光，

Yí　shì　dì　shang　shuāng.
疑　是　地　上　霜。

Jǔ　tóu　wàng　míngyuè,
举　头　望　明　月，

Dī　tóu　sī　gùxiāng.
低　头　思　故　乡。

Thoughts on a Quiet Night

by Li Bai (701 – 762 in the Tang Dynasty)

The moon shines beside my bed.

Is it frost upon the ground?

Raising my head, I look at the moon.

Lowering my head, I think of home.

II

Dēng Guànquè Lóu
登　鹳雀　楼

（Táng）Wáng Zhīhuàn
（唐）　王　之涣

Báirì　　yī　shān　jìn,
白　日　依　山　尽，

Huáng Hé　rù　hǎi　liú.
黄　河　入　海　流。

Yù　qióng qiān　lǐ　mù,
欲　穷　千　里　目，

Gèng shàng　yì　céng　lóu.
更　上　一　层　楼。

On the Stork Tower

by Wang Zhihuan (688 – 742 in the Tang Dynasty)

The bright sun sets on the mountain;

The Yellow River flows into the sea.

To enjoy a grander sight,

Climb to a greater height.

Nǐ míngtiān jǐ diǎn yǒu kè

你明天几点有课

What time do you have class tomorrow

What time do you go to class? What time do you see your friends? What time does the movie begin? Every day we face these questions related to time. If you go to China, it becomes important that you learn to tell time in Chinese. In this lesson, we will learn how to express time in Chinese and how to count from 11 to 100. Let's take up the challenges of time and numbers!

一、热身 *WARM-UP*

1 思考 Think

Think about the following questions:

(1) Do you have any classes tomorrow? What time do you have class?

(2) How many class hours do you have each week? Which course do you like best?

(3) What's your major? Is your major interesting?

2 活动 Activity

Guess the meanings of the time words below and choose the correct picture for each word.

（1）八点_____ （3）十点十分_____

（2）两点_____ （4）三点半_____

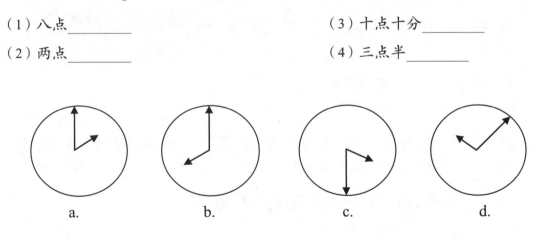

a.　　　　b.　　　　c.　　　　d.

二、课文 TEXT

（一）  2-04-01

(Song Hua would like to make a date with Lin Na to watch a movie.)

宋华： 林娜，你明天做什么？
Sòng Huá: Lín Nà, nǐ míngtiān zuò shénme?

林娜： 我明天有很多课，^① 特别忙。
Lín Nà: Wǒ míngtiān yǒu hěn duō kè, tèbié máng.

> 谈学习（1）
> Talking about studying (1)

宋华： 你明天几点有课？
Sòng Huá: Nǐ míngtiān jǐ diǎn yǒu kè?

林娜： 我明天上午八点半有语法课，十点四十有汉字
Lín Nà: Wǒ míngtiān shàngwǔ bā diǎn bàn yǒu yǔfǎkè, shí diǎn sìshí yǒu Hànzì-

课，下午两点一刻还有口语课。^②
kè, xiàwǔ liǎng diǎn yí kè hái yǒu kǒuyǔkè.

宋华： 你累不累？
Sòng Huá: Nǐ lèi bu lèi?

林娜：不累。对了，你明天晚上有没有时间？③
Lín Nà: Bú lèi. Duìle, nǐ míngtiān wǎnshang yǒu méi yǒu shíjiān?

宋华：有时间，有时间。明天晚上有一
Sòng Huá: Yǒu shíjiān, yǒu shíjiān. Míngtiān wǎnshang yǒu yí

约会
Making a date

个好电影，你看不看？我们一起去吧。④
ge hǎo diànyǐng, nǐ kàn bu kàn? Wǒmen yìqǐ qù ba.

林娜：是不是《再见》？
Lín Nà: Shì bu shì 《Zàijiàn》?

宋华：是啊。我们一起去吧。
Sòng Huá: Shì a. Wǒmen yìqǐ qù ba.

林娜：恐怕不行。⑤ 我们一起练习口语吧。
Lín Nà: Kǒngpà bù xíng. Wǒmen yìqǐ liànxí kǒuyǔ ba.

生词 New Words　🔊 2-04-02

1.	明天	míngtiān	N	tomorrow　明天早上　明天晚上
2.	多	duō	A/Adv	many; much; more　很多课　很多人
3.	特别	tèbié	Adv	especially　特别多　特别忙
4.	点（钟）	diǎn (zhōng)	M	o'clock　九点（钟）两点（钟）
5.	上午	shàngwǔ	N	morning; before noon　今天上午　明天上午
	上	shàng	N	above; preceding; previous
6.	半	bàn	Nu	half　八点半　半个
7.	语法	yǔfǎ	N	grammar　学习语法　语法课
8.	汉字	Hànzì	N	Chinese character　学习汉字　汉字课
9.	下午	xiàwǔ	N	afternoon　今天下午　明天下午　下午没有课
	下	xià	N	below; next; latter
10.	刻	kè	M	quarter (of an hour)　两点一刻　七点三刻
11.	口语	kǒuyǔ	N	spoken language　汉语口语　口语课
12.	累	lèi	A	tired; exhausted　很累　真累　特别累

13.	对了	duìle	V	*(an expression to change the subject of a conversation or to remind the listener of a new subject)* by the way; well, yes
	对	duì	A	right; correct
14.	时间	shíjiān	N	time　有时间　没有时间　有没有时间
15.	电影	diànyǐng	N	movie　看电影
16.	一起	yìqǐ	Adv	together　一起学习　一起工作　一起看电影
17.	去	qù	V	to go　一起去　去上海　刚去美国　去他们家
18.	吧	ba	MdPt	*a modal particle used at the end of a sentence to indicate consultation, suggestion, request, etc.*　一起去吧　坐吧
19.	恐怕	kǒngpà	Adv	*(indicating an estimation)* I'm afraid that...
20.	行	xíng	V	to be OK　不行
21.	练习	liànxí	V/N	to practice / exercise　练习口语　练习汉字　做练习

注释 Notes

① 我明天有很多课。

Tomorrow I have many classes.

When the adjective "duō 多" (many; much) is used as a modifier, you must place an adverb like "hěn 很" (literally "very") before it. Say "hěn duō kè 很多课" (many classes) or "hěn duō péngyou 很多朋友" (many friends), but do not say "* 多课" or "* 多朋友". The particle "de 的" after "很多" is usually omitted.

② 下午两点一刻还有口语课。

I have Spoken Chinese class at 2:15 in the afternoon.

When the number "2" is combined with a measure word, use "liǎng 两" instead of "èr 二". For example, "liǎng ge jiějie 两个姐姐" (two elder sisters), "liǎng zhāng zhàopiàn 两张照片" (two photos), "liǎng diǎn yí kè 两点一刻" (two fifteen). You should not say "*二个姐姐", "*二张照片", or "* 二点一刻". When the number "2" is used alone, e.g., in "yī 一, èr 二, sān 三…" (one, two, three…) or appears in a larger number, even if there is a measure word after "2", still use "二", such as "shí'èr 十二" (twelve), "èrshí'èr 二十二" (twenty-two), "èrshíliù ge nǚshēng 二十六个女生" (twenty-six female students), "shí'èr ge nánshēng 十二个男生" (twelve male students), "shí'èr diǎn 十二点" (twelve o'clock), and so on.

③ 对了，你明天晚上有没有时间？

By the way, do you have time tomorrow evening?

"duìle 对了" (by the way; well, yes) is often used in colloquial speech to express a spontaneous idea or thought, to change the subject of a conversation, or to remind the listener of a new subject.

④ 我们一起去吧。

Let's go together.

The modal particle "ba 吧" is often used at the end of a statement to soften the tone. It makes a suggestion or a request, gives advice or an order, or asks for a discussion.

⑤ 恐怕不行。

I'm afraid not.

"Kǒngpà bù xíng. 恐怕不行。" is an expression used to decline a suggestion gracefully.

（二） 2-04-03

(Ma Dawei and Wang Xiaoyun are chatting in a coffee shop.)

王小云：现在几点？
Wáng Xiǎoyún: Xiànzài jǐ diǎn?

问时间（1）
Asking about time (1)

马大为：差五分七点。
Mǎ Dàwéi: Chà wǔ fēn qī diǎn.

王小云： 七点半我回学校，我们班有活动。①
Wáng Xiǎoyún: Qī diǎn bàn wǒ huí xuéxiào, wǒmen bān yǒu huódòng.

马大为： 听说你们班的女生多，男生少。
Mǎ Dàwéi: Tīngshuō nǐmen bān de nǚshēng duō, nánshēng shǎo.

王小云： 对。我们班只有四个男生。
Wáng Xiǎoyún: Duì. Wǒmen bān zhǐ yǒu sì ge nánshēng.

马大为： 你们班一共有多少人？②
Mǎ Dàwéi: Nǐmen bān yígòng yǒu duōshao rén?

王小云： 我们班一共有三十个人，有二十六个女生。
Wáng Xiǎoyún: Wǒmen bān yígòng yǒu sānshí ge rén, yǒu èrshíliù ge nǚshēng.

马大为： 你们班真有意思。
Mǎ Dàwéi: Nǐmen bān zhēn yǒu yìsi.

王小云： 你们班呢？你们班的女生多不多？
Wáng Xiǎoyún: Nǐmen bān ne? Nǐmen bān de nǚshēng duō bu duō?

马大为： 不多。我们班一共有十八个学生。十二个男
Mǎ Dàwéi: Bù duō. Wǒmen bān yígòng yǒu shíbā ge xuésheng. Shí'èr ge nán-

生，六个女生。
shēng, liù ge nǚshēng.

王小云： 你们班也很有意思。
Wáng Xiǎoyún: Nǐmen bān yě hěn yǒu yìsi.

马大为： 你来我们班吧，我去你们班。
Mǎ Dàwéi: Nǐ lái wǒmen bān ba, wǒ qù nǐmen bān.

王小云： 你来我们班吗？你学习什么专业？
Wáng Xiǎoyún: Nǐ lái wǒmen bān ma? Nǐ xuéxí shénme zhuānyè?

马大为： 我学英语。
Mǎ Dàwéi: Wǒ xué Yīngyǔ.

问专业

Asking about one's major

王小云： 我呢？
Wáng Xiǎoyún: Wǒ ne?

马大为： 你去学汉语。
Mǎ Dàwéi: Nǐ qù xué Hànyǔ.

王小云： 好主意！
Wáng Xiǎoyún: Hǎo zhǔyi!

生词 New Words 2-04-04

1.	现在	xiànzài	N	now	现在几点 现在去
2.	差	chà	V	to be short of; to lack	
3.	分	fēn	M	minute	差五分八点 十点十分
4.	回	huí	V	to return	回家 回国
5.	学校	xuéxiào	N	school	回学校 我们学校
6.	班	bān	N	class	我们班 你们班
7.	活动	huódòng	N	activity; event	有活动 我们班的活动
8.	听说	tīngshuō	V	to be told; to hear of	刚听说 听说这个电影很好
	听	tīng	V	to listen	听汉语 练习听
	说	shuō	V	to say; to speak	说汉语 不说英语
9.	女生	nǚshēng	N	female student	六个女生 女生多 你们班的女生
10.	男生	nánshēng	N	male student	十二个男生 男生多 我们班的男生
	男	nán	A	male	男老师 男孩子
11.	少	shǎo	A	few; little	很少 不少 男生少
12.	只	zhǐ	Adv	only	只有一个人 只说汉语 只喜欢妈妈
13.	多少	duōshao	QPr	how many; how much	多少人 多少个汉字 多少张照片
14.	有意思	yǒu yìsi		interesting	很有意思 没有意思
	意思	yìsi	N	meaning	这个汉字的意思 什么意思
15.	学生	xuésheng	N	student	中国学生 很多学生 女学生
16.	来	lái	V	to come	来中国 刚来北京 来学校 明天晚上来
17.	专业	zhuānyè	N	major (subject)	什么专业 汉语专业 多少个专业
18.	主意	zhǔyi	N	idea	好主意 有主意

注释 Notes

① 七点半我回学校，我们班有活动。

I will return to school at seven thirty. Our class has an event.

The word "huódòng 活动" (activity; event) usually refers to something that two or more people participate in together, such as a meeting, an evening event, a date, etc.

② 你们班一共有多少人？

How many people are there in your class?

The two question pronouns "jǐ 几" (how many) and "duōshao 多少" (how many; how much) are both used to ask about numbers. "几" is often used to ask about a small number under 10. A measure word must be placed between "几" and the noun, such as "jǐ kǒu rén 几口人" (how many family members). "多少" can be used to ask about any number; it can be followed by a measure word or not. For example, for "how many pictures", you can say "duōshao zhāng zhàopiàn 多少张照片" or "duōshao zhàopiàn 多少照片".

三、语言点 LANGUAGE POINTS

1 核心句 Key Sentences 🔊 2-04-05

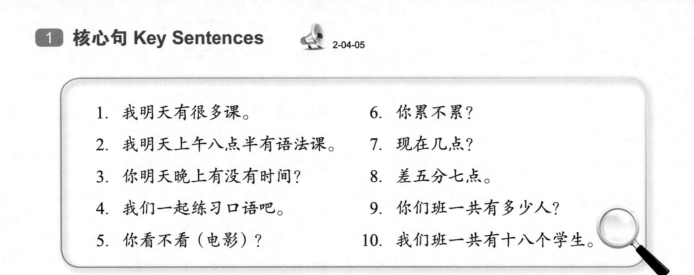

1. 我明天有很多课。
2. 我明天上午八点半有语法课。
3. 你明天晚上有没有时间？
4. 我们一起练习口语吧。
5. 你看不看（电影）？
6. 你累不累？
7. 现在几点？
8. 差五分七点。
9. 你们班一共有多少人？
10. 我们班一共有十八个学生。

2 语法 Grammar

1. 11 ～ 100 的称数法　Numbers from 11 to 100

11 十一	12 十二	13 十三	……	19 十九	20 二十
21 二十一	22 二十二	23 二十三	……	29 二十九	30 三十
31 三十一	32 三十二	33 三十三	……	39 三十九	40 四十
⋮	⋮	⋮		⋮	⋮
81 八十一	82 八十二	83 八十三	……	89 八十九	90 九十
91 九十一	92 九十二	93 九十三	……	99 九十九	100 一百

When asking a question with the number "shí 十" (ten) or a larger number, use the question word "duōshao 多少". The measure word after "多少" is often omitted. For example,

Nǐmen bān yǒu duōshao (ge) xuésheng?
A: 你们　班　有　多少（个）学生？ How many students are there in your class?

Wǒmen bān yǒu sānshí ge xuésheng.
B: 我们　班　有　三十　个　学生。 There are 30 students in our class.

Exercise I　Read the following numbers aloud.

这是多少？这是_____。

① 15	② 26	③ 30	④ 41	⑤ 53
⑥ 64	⑦ 77	⑧ 80	⑨ 99	⑩ 100

Exercise II　Write down the numbers you hear.　2-04-06

（1）_____　　（2）_____　　（3）_____　　（4）_____　　（5）_____

（6）_____　　（7）_____　　（8）_____　　（9）_____　　（10）_____

2. 钟点读法　How to tell time

These words are used to tell time in Chinese: "diǎn (zhōng) 点（钟）" (o'clock), "kè 刻" (quarter), and "fēn 分" (minute). For example, "bā diǎn èrshíwǔ fēn 八点二十五分" (eight twenty-five). In Chinese time is told in the following ways:

2:00	两点（钟）("钟" is often omitted.）
2:05	两点零（líng, zero）五分 （When "分" is used with a number less than 10, "零" is added before them.）
2:10	两点十分
2:12	两点十二（分） （When "分" is used with a number more than 10, "分" may be omitted.）
2:15	两点一刻 or 两点十五（分）
2:30	两点半 or 两点三十（分）
2:45	两点四十五（分）or 差一刻三点
2:55	两点五十五（分）or 差五分三点

Exercise I　What time is it?

> ① 1:20　　② 3:15　　③ 4:30　　④ 5:10
> ⑤ 7:05　　⑥ 11:45　　⑦ 12:00　　⑧ 8:55

Exercise II　Write down the time you hear.　🔊 2-04-07

（1）_____　（2）_____　（3）_____　（4）_____

（5）_____　（6）_____　（7）_____　（8）_____

3. 表时间的词语做状语　A time word as an adverbial

A time word, such as "xiànzài 现在" (now), "jīntiān 今天" (today), "xiàwǔ 下午" (afternoon) and so on, can function as an adverbial to indicate the time of an action or a state of being. An adverbial of time can be placed before or immediately after the subject. In other words:

(1) after the subject and before the verb or adjective (see the first table below), or

(2) before the subject to emphasize the time (see the second table below).

Subject + Time Word + Verb plus Object / Adjective

Subject	Predicate	
	Time Word	Verb plus Object / Adjective
我	明天	有很多课。
林娜	今天下午三点半	练习口语。
你	明天晚上	有时间吗？
力波	今天	不忙。

Time Word + Subject + Verb plus Object / Adjective

Time Word	Subject	Predicate
		Verb plus Object / Adjective
七点半	我们班	有活动。
明天晚上	你	做什么？
下午四点	我	还有口语课。
今天	马大为	很累。

Notes：

❶ An adverbial of time can never be placed after the predicate. For example, one cannot say "*Wǒ yǒu kè jīntiān. 我有课今天。"

❷ If there is more than one time word in an adverbial, the larger unit of time should be put before the smaller one. For example, "jīntiān xiàwǔ 今天下午" (this afternoon) and "míngtiān shàngwǔ bā diǎn bàn 明天上午八点半" (at 8:30 tomorrow morning).

Exercise I　Substitute the underlined parts and complete the sentences.

（1）我<u>明天</u>有课。

今天
九点半
现在

（2）<u>今天上午</u>他很忙。

今天下午
今天晚上
明天上午

（3）我们<u>明天上午八点</u>练习口语。

今天上午十点
今天晚上七点一刻
明天下午四点十分

Exercise II　Complete the sentences with the words given.

（1）他们喝咖啡（下午　今天）→ _____

（2）我们看电影吧（晚上　明天）→ _____

（3）我有语法课（八点　上午　明天）→ _____

（4）你有时间吗（今天　六点半　晚上）→ _____

4. 正反疑问句　A/An verb/adjective-not-verb/adjective question

The affirmative and the negative of the predicate in a sentence can be juxtaposed to form a question as well. In other words, a verb or an adjective plus "not" plus the same verb or adjective can also form a question.

Verb/Adjective ＋不／没＋ Verb/Adjective ＋ Object

Subject	Predicate		
	Verb/Adjective	不／没 Verb/Adjective	Object
林娜	累	不 累?	
他	明天 来	不 来?	
你	要	不 要	咖啡?

Subject	Predicate		
	Verb/Adjective	不 / 没 Verb/Adjective	Object
宋华	有	没 有	时间？
他妈妈	是	不 是	老师？

A response to this type of question may be a complete sentence (affirmative or negative) or a sentence with its subject or object omitted. For example, the responses to the questions above are:

（1）（林娜）很累。/（林娜）不累。

（2）（他明天）来。/（他明天）不来。

（3）（我）要（咖啡）。/（我）不要（咖啡）。

（4）（宋华）有（时间）。/（宋华）没有（时间）。

To answer a "shì bu shì 是不是" question as shown in the last example in the table above, one may say "shì 是" (affirmative answer) or "bú shì 不是" (negative answer). For example,

（5）（他妈妈）是（老师）。/ 是，他妈妈是老师。

（他妈妈）不是（老师）。/ 不是，他妈妈不是老师。

Exercise I   Substitute the underlined parts and complete the dialogues.

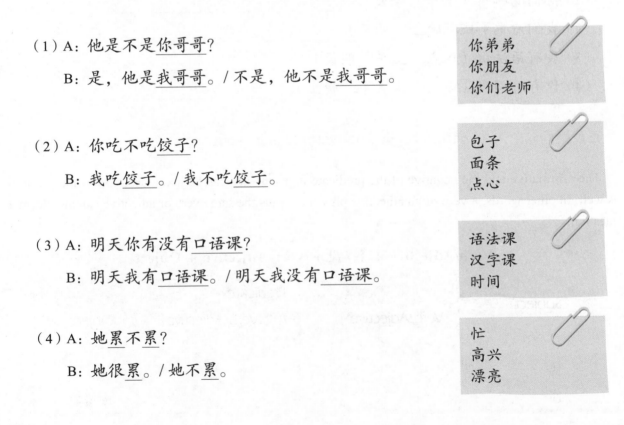

（1）A：他是不是你哥哥？

　　B：是，他是我哥哥。/ 不是，他不是我哥哥。

你弟弟
你朋友
你们老师

（2）A：你吃不吃饺子？

　　B：我吃饺子。/ 我不吃饺子。

包子
面条
点心

（3）A：明天你有没有口语课？

　　B：明天我有口语课。/ 明天我没有口语课。

语法课
汉字课
时间

（4）A：她累不累？

　　B：她很累。/ 她不累。

忙
高兴
漂亮

Exercise II　Following the example, change the "吗" question to the verb/adjective-not-verb/adjective question and also respond.

Example　你有时间吗？→ 你有没有时间？→ 我有时间。→ 我没有时间。

（1）你认识马大为吗？　→ ＿＿＿＿＿＿＿？→ ＿＿＿＿＿。→ ＿＿＿＿＿。

（2）他是中国人吗？　→ ＿＿＿＿＿＿＿？→ ＿＿＿＿＿。→ ＿＿＿＿＿。

（3）明天你的课多吗？　→ ＿＿＿＿＿＿＿？→ ＿＿＿＿＿。→ ＿＿＿＿＿。

（4）你忙吗？　→ ＿＿＿＿＿＿＿？→ ＿＿＿＿＿。→ ＿＿＿＿＿。

5. 动词谓语句　A sentence with a verbal predicate

In a sentence with a verbal predicate, the verb is the main part of the predicate, including "shì 是" (to be) and "yǒu 有" (to have; there is/are), which we have learned. The sentence structure is usually "Subject + Verb + Object" (SVO). The negative is formed by placing "bù 不" (not) before the verb. For a sentence with "有" as the verb, the negative is formed by placing "méi 没" (not) before the verb.

We have already learned many sentences with a verbal predicate.

Subject	Predicate			
	Time Word / Adverb	Verb	Object	Particle
马大为		是	美国人。	
林娜		喝	茶。	
你		来	我们班。	
他朋友	不	姓	陈。	
女儿	不	在	家。	
她	今天	没 有	时间。	
马大为和丁力波	都	学习	汉语。	
你	明天	做	什么？	
她爸爸		喜欢	吃点心。	
你		要	咖啡	吗？
我们	一起	练习	口语	吧。

Exercise I   Substitute the underlined parts and complete the dialogues.

（1）A：你今天做什么？

B：我今天学习汉语。

学习语法
练习钢琴
回学校

（2）A：我们明天做什么？

B：我们一起看电影吧。

喝茶
练习口语
去陆雨平家

（3）A：他在不在家？

B：他在家。

喝咖啡
吃饺子
说汉语

（4）A：今天下午你有没有课？

B：我没有课。

有时间
有活动
有口语课

Exercise II   Choose an appropriate verb for each sentence.

学习   去   要   叫   看   回

（1）我姓王，我_____王小云。

（2）我_____英语专业。

（3）我喜欢_____电影。

（4）我不_____家。

（5）你_____米饭吗？

（6）我明天_____上海。

6. 用"呢"构成的省略问句   An elliptical question ending with "ne 呢"

Putting "呢" after a pronoun or a noun (phrase) will form an elliptical question. The content must already be clearly expressed before you can ask the question ending with "呢".

Pronoun / Noun (Phrase) + 呢 ?

我很好。你呢？   （你呢？   ＝你好吗？）

王小云学英语专业。马大为呢？   （马大为呢？＝马大为学什么专业？）

我们班有二十六个女生。你们班呢？（你们班呢？＝你们班有多少个女生？）

Exercise I　Substitute the underlined parts and complete the dialogues.

（1）A：王小云是中国人。<u>马大为</u>呢？

　　　B：<u>他是美国人</u>。

| 丁力波
加拿大人 | 林娜
英国人 | 宋华
中国人 |

（2）A：我们家有四口人。<u>你们家呢？</u>

　　　B：<u>我们家有三口人</u>。

| 林娜家
五口 | 王小云家
四口 |

（3）A：你现在忙不忙？

　　　B：很忙。

　　　A：<u>今天下午</u>呢？

　　　B：也很忙。

今天晚上
明天上午

（4）A：你<u>八点</u>有课吗？

　　　B：没有课。

　　　A：<u>九点</u>呢？

　　　B：<u>九点有口语课</u>。

十点四十
十一点半
两点一刻

Exercise II　Following the example, rewrite the underlined sentences.

Example　　　A：我有两个姐姐。<u>你有几个姐姐？</u> →（你呢？）

　　　　　　　B：我有一个姐姐。

（1）A：我喝咖啡。<u>你们喝什么？</u>　→（　　　　　　　）

　　　B：我们喝茶。

（2）A：你今天晚上有没有时间？

　　　B：我今天晚上没有时间。

　　　A：<u>你明天晚上有没有时间？</u>　→（　　　　　　　）

　　　B：也没有时间。

（3）A：你们班有多少个男生？

　　　B：我们班有四个男生。

　　　A：<u>你们班有多少个女生？</u>　　→（　　　　　　　）

　　　B：有二十六个女生。

四、练习与运用 PRACTICE AND APPLICATION

补充词语 Supplementary Words　2-04-08

1. 起床	qǐchuáng	VO	to get up　几点起床
2. 早饭	zǎofàn	N	breakfast　吃早饭 做早饭
3. 午饭	wǔfàn	N	lunch　吃午饭 做午饭
4. 运动	yùndòng	N/V	sports; exercise / to do physical exercise 喜欢运动 做运动
5. 打球	dǎ qiú	V O	to play ball　去打球 喜欢打球
6. 跑步	pǎobù	VO	to run; to jog　去跑步 喜欢跑步
7. 电视	diànshì	N	television; TV　看电视
8. 晚饭	wǎnfàn	N	supper; dinner　吃晚饭 做晚饭
9. 睡觉	shuìjiào	VO	to sleep; to go to bed　几点睡觉 去睡觉
10. 听力	tīnglì	N	listening　汉语听力 练习听力
11. 文学	wénxué	N	literature　文学课 学习文学
12. 历史	lìshǐ	N	history　历史课 学习历史
13. 语言	yǔyán	N	language　学习语言 说什么语（言）
14. 经济	jīngjì	N	economics; economy　经济课 学习经济
15. 文化	wénhuà	N	culture　文化课 学习文化 中国文化
16. 容易	róngyì	A	easy　很容易 不容易
17. 难	nán	A	difficult　很难 不难

1 语音练习 Pronunciation Drills　　2-04-09

Listen and read aloud: Add tone marks to the following words and sentences, and then read them aloud.

❶ yufa　　　　　❷ dianying　　　　❸ kouyu

❹ yiding　　　　❺ yiqi　　　　　　❻ lianxi

❼ shijian　　　　❽ bu xing　　　　❾ Ni mingtian ji dian you ke?

❿ Wo ba dian ban you yufake.

2 会话练习 Conversation Practice

Pair activity: Create dialogues based on the scenes and the requirements below.

1. Asking about the time

（1）Based on the information in the chart, ask each other questions and respond.

林娜的一天		
上午	7:00	起床
	8:00	吃早饭
	8:30	有语法课
	10:40	有汉字课
中午	12:00	吃午饭
下午	14:00	有口语课
	16:15	运动
	18:00	吃晚饭
晚上	19:00	练习口语
	21:00	看电视
	22:30	睡觉

Example

A：林娜几点起床？

B：她七点起床。

A：林娜几点＿＿＿＿＿＿＿＿？

B：她＿＿＿＿＿＿＿＿。

（2）Based on the actual situation, ask each other questions and respond.

❶ 现在几点？

❷ 你今天几点有课？

❸ 你几点起床？几点睡觉？

❹ 你几点吃晚饭？

❺ 你今天下午四点做什么？晚上七点呢？

2. Making a date

Based on the scenes in the pictures, complete the dialogues.

（1）

A：你明天下午＿＿＿＿＿＿＿＿＿＿＿＿＿？

B：没有课。什么事？

A：明天下午的电影很好，＿＿＿＿＿＿＿？

B：＿＿＿＿＿＿＿＿＿＿＿＿＿＿。

（2）

A：你现在＿＿＿＿＿＿＿＿＿＿＿＿＿？

B：我很忙。

A：＿＿＿＿＿＿＿＿＿＿＿＿＿？

B：我今天下午也很忙。

A：明天你有没有时间？我们一起去跑步吧。

B：＿＿＿＿＿＿＿＿＿＿＿＿。

3. Talking about studying

Based on the actual situation, complete the dialogues.

（1）A：你的课多不多？

B：＿＿＿＿＿＿＿＿＿＿＿＿＿。

A：你喜欢什么课？

B：＿＿＿＿＿＿＿＿＿＿＿＿。

（2）A：你今天有没有汉语课？

B：＿＿＿＿＿＿＿＿＿＿＿＿＿。

A：你们班一共有多少学生？

B：＿＿＿＿个女生，＿＿＿＿个男生。

（3）A：你＿＿＿＿＿＿＿＿＿＿专业？

B：我＿＿＿＿＿＿＿＿＿＿＿＿。

A：你的专业有意思吗？

B：＿＿＿＿＿＿＿＿＿＿＿＿。

3 听后复述 Listening and Repeating　2-04-10

Listen to the following dialogues and repeat what you hear.

（1）A：现在几点？

　　B：差十分五点。

　　A：你几点回家？

　　B：我五点半回家。

（2）A：你明天忙不忙？

　　B：明天上午、下午我都很忙。

　　　晚上我有时间。

　　A：我们一起去看电影吧。

（3）A：你学习什么专业？

　　B：我学习汉语。

　　A：你们有什么课？

　　B：我们有口语课、语法课、听
　　　力课和汉字课，还有中国文
　　　学课和中国经济课。

（4）A：你们班大不大？

　　B：我们班不大，一共只有十八
　　　个学生。

　　A：我们班很大，有三十五个人。

4 阅读理解 Reading Comprehension

　　林娜明天有很多课。她上午八点半有语法课，十点四十有汉字课，下午两点一刻还有口语课。她不觉得累。明天晚上她和宋华一起练习口语。

　　今天晚上七点半王小云的班有活动。他们班一共有三十个人，有二十六个女生，四个男生。马大为觉得王小云的班很有意思。马大为他们班的女生少，男生多。他们班一共有十八个学生，只有六个女生。王小云说马大为的班也很有意思。

Answer the following questions:

　（1）林娜明天晚上做什么？

　（2）王小云的班有多少个学生？马大为的班呢？

我是一个学生，今年二十一岁。我学习英语专业。

今天我很忙。我有很多课：上午八点有语法课，十点半有口语课，下午两点还有钢琴课。今天晚上七点我们班有活动。我们班的学生一起吃晚饭。我们班很有意思，一共有二十四个学生，只有一个男生。那个男生是谁？对，是我。

Answer the following questions:

（1）"我"学习什么专业？

（2）"我"今天忙不忙？

（3）"我"今天几点有钢琴课？

（4）今天晚上七点"我"做什么？

（5）"我们"班有多少个女生？

（6）"我"是不是女生？

5 任务与活动 Task and Activity

1. You would like to ask a classmate to go with you to an event, e.g., to watch a movie, to drink coffee, to go to a friend's home, to study, etc. First find someone who is willing to participate in this activity with you. Then set up a time with the person for the activity. Finally report to the class about your activity and the time.

You may use the following expressions:

（1）你明天有没有时间？

（2）你今天下午做什么？

（3）我们一起看电影吧。

（4）我去马大为家，你去不去？

（5）我们几点去？

（6）你明天下午有没有课？

2. Complete the following schedule based on the actual situation and then work with your classmates to ask each other questions and respond.

日程表 Schedule

年	月（month）	日（day）
时间	地点（Place）	做什么（What to do）
06:30		
08:00		

年	月（month）	日（day）
时间	地点（Place）	做什么（What to do）
10:00		
12:00		
14:00		
18:00		
20:00		
22:00		
23:00		

6　写作练习 Writing Exercise

Following the example, report a day in your life in writing.

Example

我的一天

　　明天我很长。我七点起床。上午八点半有语法课，十一点和朋友练习口语。中午十二点吃午饭。我下午没有课。我四点运动，六点半吃晚饭。明天晚上我和朋友一起看电影，十二点睡觉。

五、汉字 CHINESE CHARACTERS

1　汉字知识 Knowledge about Chinese Characters

The structure of Chinese characters (III)

Common top-bottom structure:

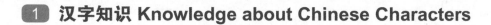

(1) Top-bottom, equal:
1
2
e.g., nán 男 (male)

(2) Top big, bottom small:

1
2

e.g., diǎn 点 (point)

(3) Top small, bottom big:

1
2

e.g., jiā 家 (family; home)

2 汉字偏旁 Chinese Radicals

Radical	Name	Stroke Order	No. of Strokes	Example	Explanation
刂	立刀旁	丨 刂	2	刻 kè (to carve) 别 bié (to part)	Related to "knife"
日	日字旁	丨 冂 日 日	4	明 míng (bright) 时 shí (time) 晚 wǎn (late)	Related to "sun"

3 认写基本汉字 Learn and Write the Basic Chinese Characters

（1）日　　丨 冂 月 日
rì　　　sun　　　　　　4 strokes

（2）月　　丿 刀 月 月
yuè　　　moon　　　　　4 strokes

（3）牛　　丿 丿 乜 牛
niú　　　cow　　　　　　4 strokes

（4）半　　丶 丶丶 丷 半
bàn　　　half　　　　　5 strokes

（5）下　　一 丁 下
xià　　　down　　　　　3 strokes

（6）寸　　一 十 寸
cùn　　　inch　　　　　3 strokes

（7）电　丶 冂 冂 曰 电　electricity　5 strokes
diàn

（8）刀　フ 刀　knife　2 strokes
dāo

（9）田　丨 冂 冂 用 田　farmland　5 strokes
tián

（10）立　丶 二 六 产 立　to stand　5 strokes
lì

4 认写课文中的汉字 Learn and Write the Chinese Characters in the Text

（1）明天 míngtiān

明 → 日 + 月（月：丿 冂 月 月）　8 strokes

（2）特别 tèbié

特 → 牛 + 土 + 寸　10 strokes

别 → 口 + 力 + 刂　7 strokes

（3）时间 shíjiān

时 → 日 + 寸　7 strokes

（4）分 fēn

分 → 八 + 刀　4 strokes

（5）男 nán

男 → 田 + 力　7 strokes

（6）有意思 yǒu yìsi

意 → 立 + 曰 + 心　13 strokes

（7）刻 kè

刻 → 亥（亥：` 一 亠 子 亥 亥）＋ 刂
8 strokes

六、文化知识 *CULTURAL KNOWLEDGE*

The Educational System of China

The educational system of China consists of primary, secondary, and tertiary education. China has a nine-year compulsory educational system, including six years of elementary school and three years of middle school. At present, the nine-year compulsory education has been implemented in most parts of China. "Project Hope", which is a well-known public service in China, helps build primary schools in poor areas and helps poor students.

Elementary education means six years of schooling. Chinese children usually enter a primary school at the age of six. Primary schooling makes education interesting as well as lays a solid foundation for children's future development.

Secondary education means going to secondary school, including three years of junior high school and three years of senior high school. After graduating from junior high school, some students enter senior high schools, other students enter vocational secondary schools, and the period of study for both types of schools is three years. After graduating, students may continue their studies at a higher educational level or seek employment.

Higher education includes four years of undergraduate studies (some programs such as medicine and architecture require five years), two or three years to earn a master's degree, and three years for a doctoral degree. Like most countries in the world, the degree system in China is divided into the bachelor's, the master's, and the doctorate. In order to meet the needs of a fast changing society, today the universities in China are dedicated to training high quality and multidisciplinary talent.

七、自我评估 *SELF-EVALUATION*

I can basically do the following things in Chinese:

☐ I can say numbers up to 100.

☐ I can say any time of the day.

☐ I can schedule and say my study plans for a day.

☐ I can set up a simple appointment.

☐ I can ask other people about their language courses and majors.

趣味汉语　**Fun with Chinese**

Guess the Meanings of the Chinese Characters

(1)　日 + 月 → 明 (　　　　)
rì　　yuè　　míng

(2)　木 + 林 → 森 (　　　　)
mù　　lín　　sēn

(3)　小 + 土 → 尘 (　　　　)
xiǎo　　tǔ　　chén

(4)　口 + 鸟 → 鸣 (　　　　)
kǒu　　niǎo　　míng

(5)　人 + 从 → 众 (　　　　)
rén　　cóng　　zhòng

5

Zhù nǐ shēngrì kuàilè

祝 你 生 日 快 乐

Happy birthday to you

In this lesson you will learn how the Chinese celebrate their birthdays as well as ask about the age of others. In addition, you will learn how to express the year, month, day, and the day of the week. You will also learn about the 12 animals in the Chinese zodiac.

一、热身 WARM-UP

1 思考 Think

Think about the following questions:

(1) In your country, how do people usually celebrate their birthdays?

(2) On their birthday, what kind of greeting would you give to children, people of your age and people older than you? Do you greet each person the same way?

(3) Do you know how are the seven days of the week described in Chinese?

2 活动 Activity

First look at the picture. Then fill in each blank with the most suitable number. Finally listen to the teacher read the numbers and check your answer.

2015年10月

24

星期六
乙未（羊）年九月十二

_____年_____月_____日，星期_____

How do you say the year, month, and day in your language? Is the word order the same as in Chinese?

二、课文 *TEXT*

（一）　 2-05-01

王小云：林娜，星期日你有时间吗？
Wáng Xiǎoyún: Lín Nà,　　Xīngqīrì　nǐ yǒu shíjiān ma?

林娜：什么事儿？
Lín Nà: Shénme　shìr?

王小云：这个星期日是我朋友的生日。我们有一个生日
Wáng Xiǎoyún: Zhège　Xīngqīrì　shì wǒ péngyou de shēngrì.　Wǒmen yǒu yí ge shēngrì

聚会，大家一起唱歌、跳舞，你参加不参加？
jùhuì,　　dàjiā　yìqǐ chàng gē、　tiàowǔ,　nǐ cānjiā bu cānjiā?

林娜：这个星期日几号？
Lín Nà: Zhège　Xīngqīrì　jǐ hào?

王小云：十月二十七号。
Wáng Xiǎoyún: Shí yuè　èrshíqī　hào.

说日期
Talking about the date

林娜： 真 不好意思。①
Lín Nà: Zhēn bù hǎoyìsi.

> 表歉意
>
> Expressing an apology

这一天也是我哥哥的生日， 他也有个生日聚会。
Zhè yì tiān yě shì wǒ gēge de shēngrì, tā yě yǒu ge shēngrì jùhuì.

王小云： 真可惜！
Wáng Xiǎoyún: Zhēn kěxī!

> 表遗憾
>
> Expressing regret

你送你哥哥什么礼物？
Nǐ sòng nǐ gēge shénme lǐwù?

林娜： 我送他一个生日蛋糕。 你送朋友什么礼物？
Lín Nà: Wǒ sòng tā yí ge shēngrì dàngāo. Nǐ sòng péngyou shénme lǐwù?

王小云： 两盒巧克力。 你哥哥今年多大？②
Wáng Xiǎoyún: Liǎng hé qiǎokèlì. Nǐ gēge jīnnián duō dà?

> 问年龄（2）
>
> Asking about one's age (2)

林娜： 他一九八八年出生， 今年二十七岁。
Lín Nà: Tā yī jiǔ bā bā nián chūshēng, jīnnián èrshíqī suì.

王小云： 真的？我朋友也二十七岁， 属龙。③ 他也是英国人。
Wáng Xiǎoyún: Zhēn de? Wǒ péngyou yě èrshíqī suì, shǔ lóng. Tā yě shì Yīngguórén.

林娜： 你朋友叫什么名字？
Lín Nà: Nǐ péngyou jiào shénme míngzi?

王小云： 他的中文名字叫林强。④
Wáng Xiǎoyún: Tā de Zhōngwén míngzi jiào Lín Qiáng.

林娜： 他就是我哥哥！
Lín Nà: Tā jiù shì wǒ gēge!

生词 New Words 2-05-02

✓	1. 星期日	Xīngqīrì	N	Sunday
	星期	xīngqī	N	week　星期一　星期几　一个星期
✓	2. 事儿	shìr	N	matter; thing　什么事儿　有事儿吗　好事儿

✓	3.	生日	shēngrì	N	birthday　他的生日　二十岁生日
		日	rì	N	day　一月一日
✓	4.	聚会	jùhuì	N	get-together; party　生日聚会　有一个聚会
✓	5.	大家	dàjiā	Pr	everyone　大家好　我们大家　大家一起去
✓	6.	唱歌	chàng gē	V O	to sing (a song)　喜欢唱歌
		唱	chàng	V	to sing　唱中国歌　唱生日歌
		歌	gē	N	song
✓	7.	跳舞	tiàowǔ	VO	to dance　不喜欢跳舞　跳个舞
		跳	tiào	V	to jump
		舞	wǔ	N	dance
✓	8.	参加	cānjiā	V	to participate; to attend　参加生日聚会　参加活动
	9.	号	hào	N	day of the month; date; size　15 号　325 号　小号　大号
	10.	月	yuè	N	month　十二个月　十二月　二月四日　八月二十二号
✓	11.	不好意思	bù hǎoyìsi	IE	(to be) sorry; to feel embarrassed
	12.	可惜	kěxī	A	it's a pity　很可惜
✓	13.	送	sòng	V	to give (as a gift); to deliver　送饺子　送照片
✓	14.	礼物	lǐwù	N	gift; present　生日礼物　送礼物
	15.	蛋糕	dàngāo	N	cake　一个蛋糕　吃蛋糕　送蛋糕　生日蛋糕
✓	16.	盒	hé	N	box　一盒点心　一盒咖啡　一盒茶
	17.	巧克力	qiǎokèlì	N	chocolate　送一盒巧克力　吃巧克力
	18.	多大	duō dà	IE	how old　他今年多大
	19.	出生	chūshēng	V	to be born　1988 年出生
	20.	属	shǔ	V	to be born in the year of (one of the 12 animals in the Chinese zodiac)　属狗　属什么
	21.	龙	lóng	N	dragon　属龙　龙年
	22.	中文	Zhōngwén	N	Chinese (language)　说中文　学中文　中文名字
✓	23.	就	jiù	Adv	exactly　就是他　就是我哥哥　就在今天
	24.	英国	Yīngguó	PN	United Kingdom; England
	25.	林强	Lín Qiáng	PN	Lin Qiang, name of a British student, Lin Na's elder brother

注释 Notes

① 真不好意思。

I'm really sorry.

"bù hǎoyìsi 不好意思" originally means "to feel embarrassed" or "to feel bad". It could also mean "to find it embarrassing to do something". For example, "bù hǎoyìsi shuō 不好意思说" (to feel embarrassed to say something) and "bù hǎoyìsi wèn 不好意思问" (to feel embarrassed to ask). In colloquial Chinese, it can be used as a light apology. For a relatively serious apology, people often say "duìbuqǐ 对不起" (sorry).

② 你哥哥今年多大?

How old is your elder brother?

Here "duō 多" is an adverb, followed by an adjective, which is used to raise a question. "dà 大" here refers to one's age. To ask about an adult's age in Chinese, one should use "duō dà 多大" (how old) or "duō dà suìshu 多大岁数" (how old is one's age). The question "jǐ suì 几岁" can only be used to ask the age of a child.

③ 我朋友也二十七岁，属龙。

My friend is also 27 years old, born in the year of the Dragon.

The Chinese use dragon, horse, dog and altogether 12 animals to indicate one's year of birth. These 12 animals make up the 12-year cycle of the Chinese lunar calendar. For example, the years 1988, 2000, and 2012 are the years of the Dragon. Generally speaking, people born in these years all belong to the Dragon. The years 1990, 2002, and 2014 are the years of the Horse. In general, people born in these years all belong to the Horse.

④ 他的中文名字叫林强。

His Chinese name is Lin Qiang.

Western names may be translated into two or three Chinese characters according to the sound or the meaning of the name. For example, the Chinese name for David March could be "Mǎ Dàwéi 马大为", and Natalie Lynn could be translated as "Lín Nà 林娜". A person with the surname of "White" could be translated as "Bái 白", and a girl with the given name of "Amy" could be translated as "Àiměi 爱美" (love beauty).

Both "Hànyǔ 汉语" and "Zhōngwén 中文" refer to the Chinese language. In general, they may be used interchangeably. "中文" refers to the Chinese language and script, the Han language in particular. "汉语" refers to the spoken language of the Han nationality in China.

（二） 2-05-03

(At Lin Qiang's birthday party at his residence)

林强: 你们好，欢迎，欢迎！
Lín Qiáng: Nǐmen hǎo, huānyíng, huānyíng!

王小云: 生日快乐！这是你的生日礼物。
Wáng Xiǎoyún: Shēngrì kuàilè! Zhè shì nǐ de shēngrì lǐwù.

林强: 谢谢你们，小云、宋华。
Lín Qiáng: Xièxie nǐmen, Xiǎoyún、Sòng Huá.

王小云: 不客气。①
Wáng Xiǎoyún: Bú kèqi.

林强: 你们来，我特别高兴。
Lín Qiáng: Nǐmen lái, wǒ tèbié gāoxìng.

(Lin Qiang goes to open the door on hearing the sound of knocking.)

林娜: 哥哥，祝你生日快乐！②
Lín Nà: Gēge, zhù nǐ shēngrì kuàilè!

| 祝贺生日 |
| Congratulating someone on his / her birthday |

林强： 谢谢！我来介绍一下，③ 这是……
Lín Qiáng: Xièxie! Wǒ lái jièshào yíxià, zhè shì……

王小云： 你好，林娜！
Wáng Xiǎoyún: Nǐ hǎo, Lín Nà!

林强： 小云，你认识我妹妹？
Lín Qiáng: Xiǎoyún, nǐ rènshi wǒ mèimei?

王小云： 是啊，林娜是我和宋华的好朋友。她常常 教
Wáng Xiǎoyún: Shì a, Lín Nà shì wǒ hé Sòng Huá de hǎo péngyou. Tā chángcháng jiāo

我们英语。
wǒmen Yīngyǔ.

林娜： 小云和宋华教我说汉语、写汉字，小云昨天还
Lín Nà: Xiǎoyún hé Sòng Huá jiāo wǒ shuō Hànyǔ、 xiě Hànzì, Xiǎoyún zuótiān hái

教我做寿面④。一会儿大家吃寿面。
jiāo wǒ zuò shòumiàn. Yíhuìr dàjiā chī shòumiàn.

宋华： 来，咱们⑤ 干杯！
Sòng Huá: Lái, zánmen gānbēi!

大家： 干杯！祝林强生日快乐！
Dàjiā: Gānbēi! Zhù Lín Qiáng shēngrì kuàilè!

生词 New Words 2-05-04

1.	欢迎	huānyíng	V	to welcome 欢迎你 欢迎大家
2.	快乐	kuàilè	A	happy 生日快乐 很快乐
3.	不客气	bú kèqi	IE	you are welcome
	客气	kèqi	A	polite 很客气
4.	祝	zhù	V	to wish 祝你生日快乐
5.	介绍	jièshào	V	to introduce 介绍朋友 介绍老师
6.	一下	yíxià	Nu-M	*used after a verb to indicate a short or informal action* 认识一下 看一下 问一下
7.	常常	chángcháng	Adv	often 常常说中文

	常	cháng	Adv	often	
✓ 8.	教	jiāo	V	to teach	教汉语　教钢琴　教我
✓ 9.	写	xiě	V	to write	写汉字　写名字
✓ 10.	昨天	zuótiān	N	yesterday	昨天下午　昨天晚上八点
11.	寿面	shòumiàn	N	(birthday) longevity noodles	吃寿面　做寿面
✓ 12.	一会儿	yíhuìr	Nu-M	in a little while	
13.	咱们	zánmen	Pr	we; us	
14.	干杯	gānbēi	VO	to drink a toast; cheers; bottoms up	咱们干杯

注释　Notes

① 不客气。

You are welcome.

This expression is used in response to someone's gratitude or appreciation. You may also respond with "bú xiè 不谢" (Don't mention it).

② 祝你生日快乐！

Happy Birthday to you!

This is a common way to wish others a happy birthday. "Zhù nǐ 祝你……" (Wish you…) is an expression used for a holiday or just to send the best wishes to the other person before the event happens. For example, "Zhù nǐ xīnnián kuàilè! 祝你新年快乐！" (Happy New Year to you!) and "Zhù nǐ gōngzuò shùnlì! 祝你工作顺利！" (Wish you success at work!) On the other hand, the expression "zhùhè 祝贺" is used for something congratulatory that has already happened. For example, if a person has graduated or gotten married, etc., the expression "zhùhè nǐ 祝贺你" (congratulations (to you)) is often used.

③ 我来介绍一下。

Let me introduce.

When "yíxià 一下" is used after a verb, it often indicates a brief action or an attempt. It can soften the tone of the expression so that it sounds less formal. For example, "rènshi yíxià 认识一下" (to get to know someone or something) and "nǐ kàn yíxià 你看一下" (to take a quick look).

④ 寿面

(birthday) longevity noodles

It is a Chinese custom to eat "chángshòumiàn 长寿面" (longevity noodles) to celebrate one's birthday. The length of the noodles symbolizes longevity. "shòutáo 寿桃" (peach-shaped birthday pastry) is also used to celebrate the birthday of the elderly. Nowadays people often eat cake for a birthday celebration.

⑤ 咱们

    we; us

When the speaker uses "zánmen 咱们", the listener is definitely included; "wǒmen 我们" may or may not include the listener.

三、语言点 *LANGUAGE POINTS*

1 核心句 Key Sentences 🔊 2-05-05

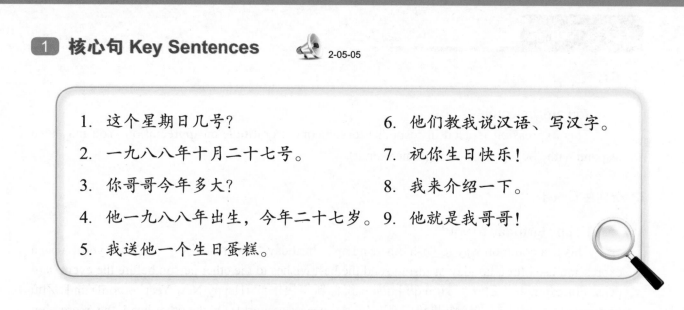

1. 这个星期日几号？
2. 一九八八年十月二十七号。
3. 你哥哥今年多大？
4. 他一九八八年出生，今年二十七岁。
5. 我送他一个生日蛋糕。
6. 他们教我说汉语、写汉字。
7. 祝你生日快乐！
8. 我来介绍一下。
9. 他就是我哥哥！

2 语法 Grammar

1. 年、月、日和星期的读法 Expressing the date and days of the week

In Chinese, the four figures making up the name of a year are read out as four separate digits, with "nián 年" at the end. For example, "一九九八年" is read out as "yī jiǔ jiǔ bā nián" (1998).

一九八八年	yī jiǔ bā bā nián	(1988)
二〇〇〇年	èr líng líng líng nián	(2000)
二〇〇二年	èr líng líng èr nián	(2002)
二〇二〇年	èr líng èr líng nián	(2020)

The numbers making up the name of a month are read out with "yuè 月" at the end. For example,

一月 Yī yuè	January	七月 Qī yuè	July
二月 Èr yuè	February	八月 Bā yuè	August
三月 Sān yuè	March	九月 Jiǔ yuè	September
四月 Sì yuè	April	十月 Shí yuè	October
五月 Wǔ yuè	May	十一月 Shíyī yuè	November
六月 Liù yuè	June	十二月 Shí'èr yuè	December

The way to express a date, from the first to the thirty-first day of the month, is to say a number and then add "hào 号" in the spoken form or "rì 日" in the written form. For example,

(二月)　六号	(Èr yuè) liù hào	(February) 6th
(十月)　十二号	(Shí yuè) shí'èr hào	(October) 12th
(十一月)　二十二日	(Shíyī yuè) èrshí'èr rì	(November) 22nd
(十二月)　三十一日	(Shí'èr yuè) sānshíyī rì	(December) 31st

If it is a date in the current month, one can simply say "号" without "月" (month). For example, "Zhège Xīngqīrì jǐ hào? 这个星期日几号?" (What's the date this Sunday?)

The names for the days of the week begin with the word "xīngqī 星期" followed by the numbers one through six, meaning Monday to Saturday. In China, the week starts on Monday and ends on Sunday, which is called "Xīngqīrì 星期日" or "Xīngqītiān 星期天". Saturday and Sunday are days off and are called "zhōumò 周末" (weekend).

星期一 Xīngqīyī	Monday	星期五 Xīngqīwǔ	Friday
星期二 Xīngqī'èr	Tuesday	星期六 Xīngqīliù	Saturday
星期三 Xīngqīsān	Wednesday	星期日 Xīngqīrì	Sunday
星期四 Xīngqīsì	Thursday	星期天 Xīngqītiān	Sunday

The order of the date and the time are expressed as follows:

年 +	月 +	日 +	星期 +	上午 / 下午 / 晚上 +	钟点
(year +	month +	day +	day of the week +	morning/afternoon/evening +	hour)
二〇一五年	十二月	二十五日	星期五	晚上	八点二十五
2015 年	12 月	25 日	星期五	晚上	8:25

(8:25 p.m., Friday, December 25, 2015)

Exercise I Substitute the underlined parts and complete the dialogue.

A：今天（几月）几号？

B：今天五月八号。

A：明天星期几？

B：明天星期六。

Exercise II Complete the dialogue based on the information given.

A：这个星期_____几号？

B：_____月_____号。

A：这一天他们做什么？

B：他们_____。

星期四 六月二十五日	星期日 七月十九日	星期五 十一月十三日
有口语课	去朋友家	参加聚会

2. 名词谓语句 A sentence with a nominal predicate

Nouns, noun phrases and numeral-measure-word compounds can act as the predicate of a sentence without the verb "shì 是" (to be). This kind of sentence is specially used in spoken language to express age, time, and so on. It is also used to express price or birthplace.

Subject + Numeral-Measure-Word

Subject	Predicate	
	Adverbial	Numeral-Measure-Word
你女儿	今年	几岁？
林强	今年	多大？
他	今年	二十岁。
现在		几点？
现在		差五分十点。
今天		几号？
这个星期日		十月二十七号。

The negative form of a sentence with a nominal predicate uses "bú shì 不是".

Jīntiān bú shì wǔ hào.

Example 今天 不是 五 号。Today is not the 5th day (of the month).

Tā bú shì sānshí'èr suì.

她 不 是 三 十 二 岁。She is not 32 years old.

Exercise I Substitute the underlined parts and complete the dialogue.

A：你哥哥今年多大？

B：_____。

A：他 / 她的生日是哪天？

B：_____。

姐姐
弟弟
妹妹
朋友

Exercise II Ask a question based on the answer given.

A：_____？ B：我今年 19 岁。

A：_____？ B：明天星期四。

A：_____？ B：11 月 5 号。

3. 双宾语动词谓语句（1）：送、教 A sentence with a two-object verbal predicate (1): "sòng 送" (to give as a gift) or "jiāo 教" (to teach)

Verbs like "sòng 送" (to give as a gift), "jiāo 教" (to teach) and so on can take two objects. The first object refers to people and the second object refers to things.

送 / 教 + Pronoun/Noun (Person) + Noun / Noun Phrase (Thing)

Subject	Predicate		
	Verb	Object₁	Object₂
林娜	送	她哥哥	一个大蛋糕。
她	教	我	英语。
他们	教	林娜	说汉语。

Notes:

❶ A verb or a verb phrase may act as the object of a verb, such as "Lǎoshī jiāo wǒ xiě. 老师教我写。" (The teacher taught me how to write), "Xiǎoyún jiāo wǒ zuò shòumiàn. 小云教我做寿面。" (Xiaoyun taught me how to make longevity noodles), and "Tā xǐhuan chī miàntiáo. 她喜欢吃面条。" (She likes to eat noodles).

❷ In Chinese, not all verbs can take two objects.

Exercise I Substitute the underlined parts and complete the dialogues.

（1）A：她送朋友什么？

　　B：她送朋友<u>一个大蛋糕</u>。

　　　　　　　　　　　　　　　　两盒巧克力
　　　　　　　　　　　　　　　　五张照片
　　　　　　　　　　　　　　　　一盒好吃的点心

（2）A：王老师教他们什么？

　　B：王老师教他们<u>汉字</u>。

　　　　　　　　　　　　　　　　唱歌　跳舞　钢琴

Exercise II Complete the sentences with the words given.

（1）她是我的中文老师，_____。（中文　我　教　她）

（2）我喜欢吃点心，_____。（做点心　我的中国朋友　我　教）

（3）明天是王小云的生日，_____？（送　马大为　礼物　她　什么）

4.“就”（1）：表示强调　The adverb “jiù 就” (1): Expressing emphasis

The adverb “就” placed before a verb emphasizes what follows. For example, “Tā jiù shì wǒ gēge. 他就是我哥哥。” (He is my elder brother), “Zhè jiù shì shòumiàn. 这就是寿面。” (These are longevity noodles).

Exercise I Put “就” in the right positions.

（1）我_____来介绍_____一下，这_____是陈老师。

（2）A：那是谁？

　　B：_____那_____是_____马大为。

Exercise II Answer the questions using “就”.

（1）A：请问，马大为在吗？

　　B：我_____。

（2）A：你有你女儿的照片吗？

　　B：这_____。

5. 疑问语调句　A sentence with a rising tone

A statement with a rising tone, without a "ma 吗" ending, may also form a question. In writing, a question mark must be added at the end of the sentence. This type of question often expresses uncertainty or disbelief.

Example
> Nǐ rènshi wǒ mèimei?
> 你认识 我 妹妹？　You know my younger sister?
>
> Nǐ lái wǒmen bān?
> 你来 我们 班？　You are coming to our class?
>
> Nǐ xuéxí Yīngyǔ?
> 你学习 英语？　You are studying English?

6. 语法小结（1）: 主语、谓语、宾语、定语和状语　Summary of grammar (1): Subject, predicate, object, modifier, and adverbial

A Chinese sentence can generally be divided into a subject and a predicate.

The main component of a subject is often a noun or a pronoun. The main component of a predicate is often a verb or an adjective. The subject is usually placed before the predicate. For example,

Subject	Predicate
我	是学生。
林娜	不看电影。
饺子	很好吃。

In a conversation, the subject is often omitted.

Example
> Nǐ míngtiān wǎnshang yǒu méi yǒu shíjiān?
> A：你 明天　晚上　有 没 有 时间？　Do you have time tomorrow evening?
>
> (Wǒ) yǒu shíjiān.
> B：（我）有 时间。 Yes, I do.

If the context is clear, the predicate may also be omitted.

Example
> Nǐ zuìjìn zěnmeyàng?
> A：你最近 怎么样？　How have you been lately?
>
> Wǒ hěn hǎo. Nǐ ne?
> B：我 很 好。你呢？ Pretty good. What about you?

The object is part of the predicate and is usually placed after the verb. In general, the object is a noun or a pronoun, and could also be a verb or a verb phrase. Some verbs may take two objects. For example,

Subject	Predicate	
	Verb	Object
他	是	美国人。
我	认识	他。
我	喜欢	吃面条。
陈老师	教	我汉语。

A modifier primarily modifies a noun. A noun, pronoun, adjective, numeral-measure-word compound, and so on can all act as a modifier, which must be placed before the noun it modifies.

An adverbial primarily modifies a verb or an adjective. An adverb, adjective, noun, and a prepositional construction can all act as an adverbial. An adverbial must be placed before the verb or the adjective it modifies. For example,

Subject	Predicate	
	Adverbial	Verb/Adjective
我们	都很	忙。
他	星期天	去学校。
我朋友	在学校	写汉字。

四、练习与运用 PRACTICE AND APPLICATION

补充词语 Supplementary Words 🔊 2-05-06

1.	前天	qiántiān	N	the day before yesterday　前天下午
2.	后天	hòutiān	N	the day after tomorrow　后天晚上
3.	上星期一	shàng Xīngqīyī		last Monday; Monday last week　上星期一下午
4.	下星期一	xià Xīngqīyī		next Monday; Monday next week　下星期一一起活动
5.	上个月	shàng ge yuè		last month
6.	下个月	xià ge yuè		next month
7.	音乐会	yīnyuèhuì	N	concert　听音乐会
8.	老鼠	lǎoshǔ	N	rat; mouse

9.	牛	niú	N	cow; ox
10.	老虎	lǎohǔ	N	tiger
11.	蛇	shé	N	snake
12.	马	mǎ	N	horse
13.	羊	yáng	N	sheep; goat
14.	猴	hóu	N	monkey
15.	鸡	jī	N	chicken; rooster

 语音练习 Pronunciation Drills 2-05-07

Listen and read aloud: Add tone marks to the following words and sentences, and then read them aloud.

❶ canjia   ❷ shengri   ❸ chang ge

❹ qiaokeli   ❺ bu keqi   ❻ Xingqiri

❼ bu haoyisi   ❽ jieshao yixia

❾ Zhu ni shengri kuaile!

❿ Tamen jiao wo shuo Hanyu, xie Hanzi.

 会话练习 Conversation Practice

Pair activity: Create dialogues based on the scenes and the requirements below.

1. Talking about the dates

Read aloud these dates and also search online what happened in China on each of these days.

1911 年 10 月 10 日　　1949 年 10 月 1 日　　1997 年 7 月 1 日

1999 年 12 月 20 日　　　　2008 年 8 月 8 日　　　　2013 年 12 月 15 日

（1）A：这是哪一天？

　　B：这是＿＿＿＿＿＿＿＿＿＿＿。

（2）A：你们的国庆节是哪一天？

　　B：我们的国庆节是＿＿＿＿＿＿＿＿＿＿。

2. Apologizing

Look at the pictures and complete the dialogues (using "bù hǎoyìsi 不好意思").

（1）

A：这个星期四晚上有音乐会，你

　去不去？

B：＿＿＿＿＿＿＿＿＿＿＿＿＿＿。

（2）

A：我要一杯茶。

B：＿＿＿＿＿＿，我们有＿＿＿＿，

　没有＿＿＿＿＿。

3. Expressing regret

Create dialogues based on the scenes below (using "zhēn kěxī 真可惜").

Scene 1: You (A) have invited a few friends to dinner, but B has a class in the evening and cannot come.

A：＿＿＿＿＿＿＿＿＿＿＿＿＿＿＿＿＿＿。（我们一起）

B：＿＿＿＿＿＿＿＿＿＿＿＿＿＿＿＿。（恐怕不行）

A：＿＿＿＿＿＿＿＿＿＿＿＿＿！

Scene 2: You (B) went to Teacher Zhang's home; a friend (A) asked you what you thought about her daughter. That day, the daughter had a piano lesson and was not at home. What would you say?

A: _____? (怎么样)

B: _____。(不在家)

A: _____!

4. Asking about one's age

Ask your classmate beside you two questions about the age of his or her family members. Then make dialogues.

（1）A：他今年多大？

B：他 1994 年出生，

今年_____。

（2）我今年_____岁，

属_____。

shǔ 鼠	1984 1996 2008	niú 牛	1985 1997 2009	hǔ 虎	1974 1986 1998	tù 兔	1975 1987 1999
lóng 龙	1976 1988 2000	shé 蛇	1977 1989 2001	mǎ 马	1978 1990 2002	yáng 羊	1979 1991 2003
hóu 猴	1980 1992 2004	jī 鸡	1981 1993 2005	gǒu 狗	1982 1994 2006	zhū 猪	1983 1995 2007

3 听后复述 Listening and Repeating 2-05-08

Listen to the following dialogues and repeat what you hear.

（1）A：你的生日是几月几号？

B：我的生日是 8 月 23 号。

A：今天 21 号，后天就是你

的生日。祝你生日快乐！

B：谢谢！

（2）A：你今年多大？

B：我今年 25 岁，属马。你属

什么？

A：我也属马。我不是 25 岁，

我今年 37。

（3）A：下星期六是我的生日。晚上
有个小聚会，欢迎你参加。

B：下星期六几号？

A：7 月 8 号。

B：真不好意思。下星期六我们
班有活动。

A：真可惜！

（4）A：她是谁？

B：她是我们的汉语老师。

A：她教你们什么课？

B：她教我们口语课。

4 阅读理解 Reading Comprehension

I

今天是林强 27 岁的生日。他 1988 年出生，属龙。林娜、王小云和宋华都参加他的生日聚会。林娜送他一个大蛋糕，王小云送他两盒巧克力。他们一起干杯，还吃寿面，祝贺林强的生日。

Answer the following questions:

（1）林强今年多大？

（2）谁参加林强的生日聚会？

（3）朋友们送林强什么生日礼物？

II

这是我们班的汉语老师。她姓张，叫张美华，英文名字叫爱美。她今年 30 岁，属牛。下个月 8 号是她的生日。张老师很漂亮。她喜欢看电影，也喜欢吃巧克力和蛋糕。她爱人（àiren, spouse）是医生。他们有一个小女儿，今年两岁，特别漂亮。张老师教我们口语课和汉字课，也教我们唱中国歌，跳中国舞。她是个好老师，我们都很喜欢她。

Answer the following questions:

（1）张老师是哪年出生的？

（2）张老师喜欢做什么？

（3）张老师的女儿属什么？

（4）张老师教"我们"什么课？

（5）张老师怎么样？

5 任务与活动 Task and Activity

1. I want to know more about you.

Class activity: Ask three to five classmates about their age and birthday and take notes. Then report your findings back to the class.

姓名 (Full Name)	年龄 (Age)	属相 (Zodiac Sign)	生日
1. 林强	27	龙	1988 年 10 月 27 日
2.			
3.			
4.			
5.			

2. Happy Birthday!

Small group activity: In groups of three to five, choose one person and pretend it is the person's birthday today, and you are going to a birthday party. Based on the information above, prepare a skit, including how to choose a birthday gift for the party, and wishing the birthday celebrant a happy birthday during the conversation.

The following words may be helpful to you:

> 送　喜欢　参加　去　可惜　蛋糕　巧克力　咖啡
> 寿面　能（néng, can）希望（xīwàng, to hope）生日快乐

6 写作练习 Writing Exercise

Today is the birthday of your good friend. A few friends will give him a surprise birthday party in the dorm. Unfortunately you have a Chinese culture class this evening and cannot participate. You write him a birthday card, explaining why you cannot attend the party, and send him your birthday wishes.

The following words may be helpful to you:

> 送　喜欢　参加　去　可惜　蛋糕　巧克力
> 咖啡　寿面　晚上　文化课　生日快乐

五、汉字 *CHINESE CHARACTERS*

1 汉字知识 Knowledge about Chinese Characters

The structure of Chinese characters (IV)

Common enclosure structure:

(1) Four-sided enclosure: □ e.g., guó 国 (country) and huí 回 (to return)

(2) Three-sided enclosure: □ □ e.g., jiān 间 (between) and yī 医 (medical)

(3) Two-sided enclosure: □ □ □ e.g., jìn 进 (to enter),

yǒu 友 (friend), and xí 习 (to study)

2 汉字偏旁 Chinese Radicals

Radical	Name	Stroke Order	No. of Strokes	Example	Explanation
礻	示字旁	丶 ㇇ 礻 礻	4	礼 lǐ (gift) 祝 zhù (to wish)	Related to "deity" or "pray"
忄	竖心旁	丶 ㆉ 忄	3	快 kuài (quick) 忙 máng (busy) 惜 xī (to cherish)	Related to "mental activities"
月	月字旁	丿 刀 月 月	4	朋 péng (friend) 期 qī (period of time)	Related to "time" or "date"

3 认写基本汉字 Learn and Write the Basic Chinese Characters

（1）其　　一 十 廿 甘 甘 其 其 其

qí　　　　he, his; she, her; it, its; they, their　　8 strokes

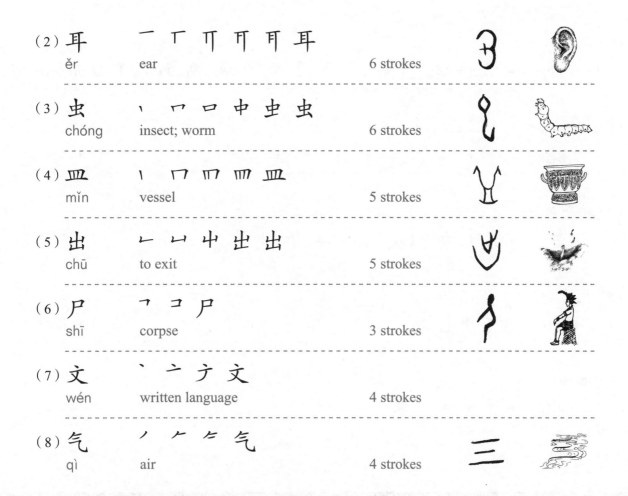

（2）耳　一　丆　丌　丌　耳　耳
ěr　　ear　　　　　　　　　　6 strokes

（3）虫　丶　口　口　中　虫　虫
chóng　insect; worm　　　　　6 strokes

（4）皿　丨　冂　冂　皿　皿
mǐn　　vessel　　　　　　　　5 strokes

（5）出　乚　屮　中　出　出
chū　　to exit　　　　　　　5 strokes

（6）尸　フ　コ　尸
shī　　corpse　　　　　　　　3 strokes

（7）文　丶　一　𠂇　文
wén　　written language　　　4 strokes

（8）气　丿　𠂉　气　气
qì　　air　　　　　　　　　4 strokes

4　认写课文中的汉字 Learn and Write the Chinese Characters in the Text

（1）星期 xīngqī

　　期 ⟶ 其 + 月　　　　　　　　　　　　　12 strokes

（2）聚会 jùhuì

　　聚 ⟶ 耳 + 又 + 乑（乑：一　丆　仒　亍　亦　乑）　14 strokes

（3）蛋糕 dàngāo

　　蛋 ⟶ 疋（疋：一　丆　下　疋　疋）+ 虫　11 strokes

（4）盒 hé

　　盒 ⟶ 合（合：丿　人　人　仐　合　合）+ 皿　11 strokes

（5）属 shǔ

属 → 尸 + 禹 （禹: 丿 𠂉 𠃌 𠃌 𠃌 禹 禹 禹） 12 strokes

（6）可惜 kěxī

惜 → 忄 + 卄 （卄: 一 卄 卄 卄） + 日 11 strokes

（7）快乐 kuàilè

快 → 忄 + 夬 （夬: 𠃌 ユ 𠂈 夬） 7 strokes

（8）礼物 lǐwù

礼 → 礻 + 乚 5 strokes

（9）祝 zhù

祝 → 礻 + 口 + 儿 9 strokes

六、文化知识　*CULTURAL KNOWLEDGE*

The Chinese Zodiac

In the Chinese "shǔxiàng 属相" or "shēngxiào 生肖" (zodiac), which animal do you belong to? In China, each of the 12 zodiac animals represents the year in which one was born. The order is

"shǔ 鼠" (Rat), "niú 牛" (Ox), "hǔ 虎" (Tiger), "tù 兔" (Rabbit), "lóng 龙" (Dragon), "shé 蛇" (Snake), "mǎ 马" (Horse), "yáng 羊" (Goat), "hóu 猴" (Monkey), "jī 鸡" (Rooster), "gǒu 狗" (Dog), and "zhū 猪" (Pig). A new cycle begins every 12 years. The Chinese often talk about the 12 animals of the zodiac and often mention that so-and-so was born in the year of the Ox, the Dragon, the Horse, the Dog, etc. when speaking of one's birthday.

All these animals are full of symbolic meaning. For example, the Ox represents diligence, the Tiger represents courage, the Rabbit represents tenderness, the Dragon represents soaring high, the Horse represents strength, the Monkey represents cleverness, and so on. Some people have a preference for certain animals of the zodiac. The most popular animals are the

Tiger, the Dragon, the Horse, and the Monkey. Therefore, the birth rates in different zodiac years are uneven.

　　Do you feel that the 12 animals of the Chinese zodiac are interesting? Go online and see which animal you belong to based on the Chinese lunar calendar.

七、自我评估　*SELF-EVALUATION*

I can basically do the following things in Chinese:

☐ I can talk about the date in Chinese.

☐ I can ask about other people's age and birthday in Chinese.

☐ I can apologize in Chinese.

☐ I can express regret in Chinese.

☐ I can wish other people a happy birthday in Chinese.

趣味汉语　Fun with Chinese

Write the following *pinyin* in Chinese characters and tell the meanings.

　　Nǐ hǎo ma?

　　Mā nǐ hǎo!

　　Nǐ mā hǎo.

6

Túshūguǎn zài shítáng běibian

图书馆在食堂北边

The library is to the north of the cafeteria

Do you have a good sense of direction? If you get lost, what would you do? After studying this lesson, you will not have to worry about getting lost in China. You will learn to talk about and ask for directions in Chinese.

一、热身 *WARM-UP*

1 思考 Think

Think about the following questions:

(1) In your country, when people give directions, do they use "left and right" or "north, south, east, and west"?

(2) If you go to a new school to study, which buildings would you first want to locate? The library? The cafeteria? The dormitory? The classroom building? Or the office building?

(3) Have you ever heard of the word "hútòng 胡同"? What does that mean?

2 活动 Activity

Walk through the labyrinth by using the directions "dōng 东", "nán 南", "xī 西", and "běi 北".

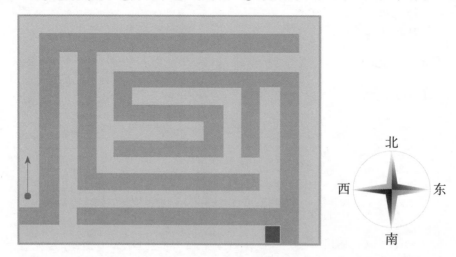

Guess what the four Chinese characters "dōng 东", "nán 南", "xī 西", and "běi 北" mean?

二、课文 *TEXT*

（一） 🔊 2-06-01

新同学： **你好，请问食堂在哪儿？**
Xīn tóngxué: Nǐ hǎo, qǐngwèn shítáng zài nǎr?

丁力波： **食堂在校门右边。你是新同学吗？**①
Dīng Lìbō: Shítáng zài xiàomén yòubian. Nǐ shì xīn tóngxué ma?

新同学： **是啊。我上午刚到学校。**
Xīn tóngxué: Shì a. Wǒ shàngwǔ gāng dào xuéxiào.

丁力波： **你跟我来，这儿有学校的地图，我给你介绍**
Dīng Lìbō: Nǐ gēn wǒ lái, zhèr yǒu xuéxiào de dìtú, wǒ gěi nǐ jièshào

一下，好吗？
yíxià, hǎo ma?

新同学： **好，谢谢你。**
Xīn tóngxué: Hǎo, xièxie nǐ.

丁力波： **不客气。你看，食堂旁边是办公楼。**
Dīng Lìbō: Bú kèqi. Nǐ kàn, shítáng pángbiān shì bàngōnglóu.

新同学： 办公楼不太大。图书馆大不大？
Xīn tóngxué: Bàngōnglóu bú tài dà.　Túshūguǎn dà bu dà?

丁力波： 图书馆很大，在食堂北边。图书馆西边是体育馆。
Dīng Lìbō: Túshūguǎn hěn dà,　zài shítáng běibian.　Túshūguǎn xībian shì tǐyùguǎn.

新同学： 学校里边有银行吗？
Xīn tóngxué: Xuéxiào lǐbian yǒu yínháng ma?

丁力波： 有。银行在图书馆东边。
Dīng Lìbō: Yǒu.　Yínháng zài túshūguǎn dōngbian.

新同学： 我们的宿舍楼在这儿，对吗？②
Xīn tóngxué: Wǒmen de sùshèlóu zài zhèr,　duì ma?

丁力波： 对。右边的楼是新同学的宿舍楼。
Dīng Lìbō: Duì.　Yòubian de lóu shì xīn tóngxué de sùshèlóu.

新同学： 教学楼在哪儿？
Xīn tóngxué: Jiàoxuélóu zài nǎr?

丁力波： 教学楼在食堂东边。
Dīng Lìbō: Jiàoxuélóu zài shítáng dōngbian.

新同学： 我先看一下教学楼吧。
Xīn tóngxué: Wǒ xiān kàn yíxià jiàoxuélóu ba.

丁力波： 好的。再见！③
Dīng Lìbō: Hǎo de.　Zàijiàn!

新同学： 谢谢你，再见！
Xīn tóngxué: Xièxie nǐ,　zàijiàn!

生词 New Words　🔊 2-06-02

1. 新	xīn	A	new	新老师　新年
2. 同学	tóngxué	N	classmate; schoolmate	我的同学　新同学
3. 食堂	shítáng	N	cafeteria; dining hall	学校的食堂　去食堂
4. 哪儿	nǎr	QPr	where	在哪儿　去哪儿

5.	校门	xiàomén	N	school gate; campus entrance
	门	mén	N	door; gate; entrance　大门
6.	右边	yòubian	N	right (side)　右边的同学　在校门右边
	右	yòu	N	right
	边	bian	Suf	side
7.	跟	gēn	Prep	with　跟老师学　跟我来
8.	这儿	zhèr	Pr	here　来这儿　在这儿
9.	地图	dìtú	N	map　学校的地图　北京地图　看地图
10.	给	gěi	Prep	to; for　给你介绍一下　给我们唱歌　给我们上课
11.	旁边	pángbiān	N	side; beside　旁边的同学　在食堂旁边
12.	办公楼	bàngōnglóu	N	office building; administration building 学校的办公楼　去办公楼
	办公	bàngōng	VO	to handle official business; to work (usu. in an office) 今天不办公
	楼	lóu	N	building　二楼　在五楼　楼上　楼下
13.	图书馆	túshūguǎn	N	library　去图书馆　有图书馆　图书馆右边
	书	shū	N	book　看书
14.	北边	běibian	N	north (side)　北边的办公楼　在学校北边
	北	běi	N	north　北门　北校门
15.	西边	xībian	N	west (side)　西边的食堂　在图书馆西边
	西	xī	N	west　西门　西校门
16.	体育馆	tǐyùguǎn	N	gym; stadium　去体育馆　北京体育馆　体育馆的北边
	体育	tǐyù	N	physical education; physical training　体育课　学体育
17.	里边	lǐbian	N	in; inside　在里边　图书馆里边
	里	lǐ	N	in; inside　图书馆里　学校里　班里　家里　楼里
18.	银行	yínháng	N	bank　去银行　在银行　有银行　中国银行　银行里
19.	东边	dōngbian	N	east (side)　东边的体育馆　在校门东边
	东	dōng	N	east　东门　东校门
20.	宿舍	sùshè	N	dormitory　回宿舍　去宿舍　学生宿舍　女生宿舍 宿舍里
21.	教学	jiàoxué	N	teaching and learning　教学楼　汉语教学
22.	先	xiān	Adv	first; before　先去　先看　先说　先做　先学　先问 先认识

注释 Notes

① 你是新同学吗？

Are you a new student?

Students studying in the same course or the same school are called "tóngxué 同学" (classmate; schoolmate; fellow student). For example, "Tā shì wǒ tóngxué. 他是我同学。" (He is my classmate) and "Zhè shì Sòng Huá tóngxué. 这是宋华同学。" (This is student Song Hua / This is my school-mate Song Hua). Teachers and other people call students "同学" such as "tóngxuémen 同学们" instead of "xuéshengmen 学生们" (students).

② 我们的宿舍楼在这儿，对吗？

Our dormitory building is here, isn't it?

On the campus of most Chinese universities, there are usually student dormitories, cafeterias, minimarts, a bank, a post office, a clinic or hospital, a laundromat, and other facilities for the convenience of students.

③ 好的。再见！

OK. Bye!

"hǎo de 好的" expresses the meaning of agreeing with the suggestion made by another person.

（二） 2-06-03

(Song Hua, a young Beijing man, would like to help Lin Na understand the "hútòng 胡同" in Beijing. On her way to Song Hua's home, Lin Na got lost and in a panic phoned Song Hua for help.)

林娜：宋 华，你家在哪儿？
Lín Nà：Sòng Huá,　nǐ jiā zài nǎr?

宋华：别着急，林小姐。①
Sòng Huá：Bié zháojí,　Lín xiǎojiě.

劝慰
Consoling someone

你现在在什么地方？
Nǐ xiànzài zài shénme dìfang?

林娜：我也不知道。对了，我在一个超市前边。
Lín Nà：Wǒ yě bù zhīdào.　Duìle,　wǒ zài yí ge chāoshì qiánbian.

宋华：对面有没有一个饭馆？
Sòng Huá：Duìmiàn yǒu méi yǒu yí ge fànguǎn?

林娜：有。有一个很大的饭馆。
Lín Nà：Yǒu.　Yǒu yí ge hěn dà de fànguǎn.

宋华：你先过马路。饭馆后边有一条胡同。②
Sòng Huá：Nǐ xiān guò mǎlù.　Fànguǎn hòubian yǒu yì tiáo hútòng.

表达未听清
Expressing not hearing clearly or understanding

林娜：等一下，你说什么？
Lín Nà：Děng yíxià,　nǐ shuō shénme?

宋华：饭馆后边有一条胡同，对吗？
Sòng Huá：Fànguǎn hòubian yǒu yì tiáo hútòng,　duì ma?

林娜："什么叫"胡同"？
Lín Nà：Shénme jiào　"hútòng"?

问不懂的词
Asking about words you don't understand

宋华：就是小街道。
Sòng Huá：Jiù shì xiǎo jiēdào.

林娜：对，这儿有一条胡同。
Lín Nà：Duì,　zhèr yǒu yì tiáo hútòng.

宋华：我家就在这条胡同里，是35号。
Sòng Huá：Wǒ jiā jiù zài zhè tiáo hútòng li,　shì 35 hào.

林娜：好的，谢谢你。这条街真小。
Lín Nà：Hǎo de,　xièxie nǐ. Zhè tiáo jiē zhēn xiǎo.

宋华：这就是老北京的胡同。
Sòng Huá：Zhè jiù shì lǎo Běijīng de hútòng.

生词 New Words
2-06-04

1.	别	bié	Adv	don't 别客气 别看 别去
2.	着急	zháojí	A	worried; anxious 别着急 很着急 不着急
3.	小姐	xiǎojiě	N	Miss; young lady 林小姐 王小姐
4.	地方	dìfang	N	place; region 一个地方 在什么地方 是什么地方
5.	知道	zhīdào	V	to know 不知道 我知道
6.	超市	chāoshì	N	supermarket 一个超市 去超市 小超市 超市里
7.	前边	qiánbian	N	front; in front of 前边的同学 在超市前边
	前	qián	N	front 图书馆前 门前
8.	对面	duìmiàn	N	opposite; across (from) 对面的大楼 在我家对面
9.	饭馆	fànguǎn	N	restaurant 去饭馆 饭馆里
10.	过	guò	V	to cross; to pass
11.	马路	mǎlù	N	road; street 马路的对面 过马路
	路	lù	N	road; way; path 大路 小路
12.	后边	hòubian	N	back; behind; rear 超市后边 在饭馆后边
	后	hòu	N	back 后门
13.	条	tiáo	M	(*a measure word for something long, narrow or thin, like rivers, dragons, trousers, etc.*) strip; long narrow piece 一条马路 一条龙 一条狗
14.	胡同	hútòng	N	*hutong*; alley 北京的胡同 一条胡同
15.	等	děng	V	to wait 等人 等他们 等一下 等一会儿
16.	街道	jiēdào	N	street 一条街道 街道的对面
	街	jiē	N	street 大街 小街 街上
17.	老	lǎo	A	old 老人 老北京 老上海

注释 Notes

① 别着急，林小姐。

Don't worry, Miss Lin.
The adverb "bié 别" placed before a verb or an adjective (别 + verb/adjective) means to dissuade or to forbid. Here Song Hua is addressing Lin Na as Miss Lin in a joking way in order to make her feel relaxed.

② 饭馆后边有一条胡同。

There is a *hutong* behind the restaurant.

A *hutong* is an alley on a side street between a group of "sìhéyuàn 四合院" (a compound with houses around a square courtyard). As a cosmopolitan city of over 20 million people and at a time when many modern buildings are being built, Beijing has witnessed a lot of changes and has also kept some of these traditional residential areas. Currently, there are still over 1,000 *hutongs*, which reflect the style of old Beijing.

三、语言点　LANGUAGE POINTS

1 核心句 Key Sentences

2-06-05

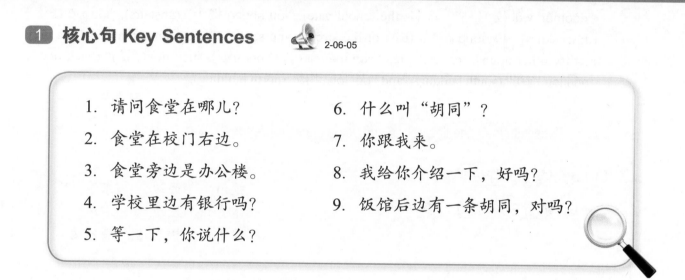

1. 请问食堂在哪儿？

2. 食堂在校门右边。

3. 食堂旁边是办公楼。

4. 学校里边有银行吗？

5. 等一下，你说什么？

6. 什么叫"胡同"？

7. 你跟我来。

8. 我给你介绍一下，好吗？

9. 饭馆后边有一条胡同，对吗？

2 语法 Grammar

1. 方位词　Nouns of locality

Words like "lǐbian 里边" (inside), "wàibian 外边" (outside), "zuǒbian 左边" (left), "yòubian 右边" (right), "pángbiān 旁边" (beside), "shàngbian 上边" (above), "xiàbian 下边" (below), "qiánbian 前边" (front), "hòubian 后边" (back; behind), "dōngbian 东边" (east), "xībian 西边" (west), "nánbian 南边" (south), "běibian 北边" (north), and "duìmiàn 对面" (opposite) are all nouns of locality. They can be used as a subject, an object, or a modifier. They can also be modified.

Example

Qiánbian yǒu méi yǒu yí ge fànguǎn?
（1）前边　有　没　有　一个　饭馆？ Is there a restaurant in front?

Yínháng zài túshūguǎn dōngbian.
（2）银行　在　图书馆　东边。The bank is east of the library.

Yòubian de lóu shì xīn tóngxué de sùshèlóu.
（3）右边　的楼　是　新　同学　的宿舍楼。
The building on the right is the dormitory for new students.

Notes:

❶ When a noun of locality is used as a modifier, "de 的" must be used between the modifier and the modified. For example, "yòubian de lóu 右边的楼" (the building on the right) and "qiánbian de chāoshì 前边的超市" (the supermarket in front). When a noun of locality is used as the modified word, there is usually no "的" before the modified word. For example, "xuéxiào lǐbian 学校里边" (inside the school) and "shítáng pángbiān 食堂旁边" (beside the cafeteria).

❷ The word "lǐbian 里边" usually cannot be added after the name of a country or a very large place. For example, one may say "zài Zhōngguó 在中国" (in China) and "zài Běijīng 在北京" (in Beijing), but not "* 在中国里边" or "* 在北京里边".

❸ Usually monosyllabic words like "lǐ 里" (in; inside), "wài 外" (out; outside), "qián 前" (front), "hòu 后" (back), "shàng 上" (up), "xià 下" (down), "dōng 东" (east), "xī 西" (west), etc. cannot be used alone, but often can be modified by other nouns, such as "xuéxiào li 学校里" (in school), "xiàomén wài 校门外" (outside the school gate), "lóu shàng 楼上" (upstairs), "lóu xià 楼下" (downstairs), "lù dōng 路东" (east of the street), and so on. These monosyllabic words may modify other nouns, for example, "qián mén 前门" (front gate), "hòu mén 后门" (back door), "nán lóu 南楼" (south building), and "běi lóu 北楼" (north building).

Exercise I　Substitute the underlined parts and complete the dialogues.

（1）A：银行在前边吗？

　　　B：银行不在前边，在对面。

校门	西边	东边
体育馆	左边	右边
超市	楼里边	楼外边

（2）A：左边的食堂是学生食堂吗？

　　　B：左边的食堂不是学生食堂，

　　　　是老师的食堂。

前边的楼　图书馆　　教学楼
东边的门　学校大门　后门

Exercise II　Look at the pictures and the underlined parts, and complete the dialogues.

超市

食堂

北

Example

A：请问学校里边有超市吗？

B：有一个超市。

A：超市在哪儿？

B：超市在食堂旁边。

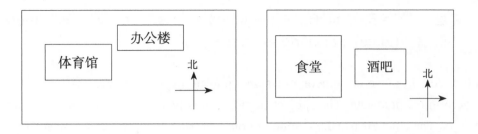

2. 用"在"表方位的句子　A sentence with "zài 在" (to be in/on/at) indicating location

To express the idea that someone or something is located in a certain place, usually "在" (to be in/on/at) is used as the main verb. The subject of this type of sentence usually is a person or thing. The object is the noun that indicates the location.

Subject (person or thing)	Verb 在		Object (noun of locality)
我		在	他右边。
大为的宿舍		在	学校里边吗?
图书馆	不	在	食堂西边。

Exercise I　Substitute the underlined parts and complete the dialogues.

A：请问，图书馆在哪儿?

B：图书馆在教学楼右边。

办公楼　　宿舍楼前边
清真餐厅　学生食堂旁边
体育馆路　前边

Exercise II　Look at the picture and introduce the people and the objects.

（1）A：谁是林强?（马大为　王小云　林娜）

　　B：林强在＿＿＿＿＿＿＿＿＿＿。

（2）A：蛋糕在哪儿?（巧克力　咖啡　寿面）

　　B：＿＿＿＿＿＿＿＿＿＿＿＿＿。

3. 用 "有" "是" 表存在的句子 A sentence with either " yǒu 有" (there is/are; to have) or "shì 是" (to be) indicating existence

To explain a certain place or someone or something in a certain place, "有" or "是" is often used as the main verb in the predicate. The subject (topic) of this type of sentence usually is a noun or noun phrase of locality. The object is usually a noun or noun phrase that expresses the person or the thing.

Subject or Topic (noun or noun phrase of locality)	Verb 有 / 是	Object (person or thing)
学校里边	有	银行。
办公楼对面	没有	超市。
前边	有没有	一个小饭馆？
食堂旁边	是	办公楼。
图书馆东边	不是	教学楼。
你对面	是不是	一个银行？
你前边	是	谁？

Note:

A sentence with "是" and a sentence with "有" differ in the following ways:

The object of a sentence with "有" makes a general reference, whereas the object of a sentence with "是" makes a specific reference. Therefore, we can say "Túshūguǎn qiánbian yǒu yí ge sùshèlóu. 图书馆前边有一个宿舍楼。" (In front of the library there is a dormitory), but we do not say "*Túshūguǎn qiánbian you wǒmen de sùshèlóu. 图书馆前边有我们的宿舍楼。" In order to express what the latter means, we can say "Túshūguǎn qiánbian shì wǒmen de sùshèlóu. 图书馆前边是我们的宿舍楼。" (In front of the library is our dormitory) or "Wǒmen de sùshèlóu zài túshūguǎn qiánbian. 我们的宿舍楼在图书馆前边。" (Our dormitory is in front of the library).

Exercise I   Substitute the underlined parts and complete the dialogues.

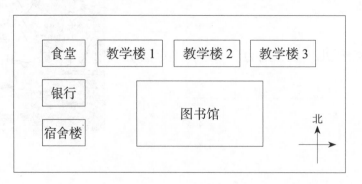

A：宿舍楼北边有什么？

B：宿舍楼北边有一个银行。

银行后边	一个食堂
食堂东边	三个教学楼
教学楼前边	一个图书馆

Exercise II　Look at the picture in Exercise I and complete the sentences below with the words given.

> 是　　不是　　有没有

（1）银行的前边_____图书馆。

（2）教学楼的西边_____食堂。

（3）宿舍楼的后边_____一个银行？

（4）图书馆的前边_____宿舍楼。

4. 介词结构（1）：跟 / 给 + 代词 / 名词　The prepositional construction (1): "gēn 跟" (with) / "gěi 给" (to; for) + Pronoun/Noun

The preposition "跟" is often combined with a noun or a pronoun to form a prepositional phrase. It is placed before the verb, indicating the manner of the action.

跟 + Pronoun/Noun (Person) + Verb (+ Object)

Subject	Predicate		
	跟 + Pronoun/Noun	Verb	Object
你	跟　我	来。	
我	跟	老师　学	中文。
林娜	跟	同学　去	食堂。

The preposition "给", combined with a noun or a noun phrase, forms a prepositional phrase. When placed before the verb, the prepositional phrase indicates the receiver of the action.

给 + Pronoun/Noun (Person) + Verb (+ Object)

Subject	Predicate		
	给 + Pronoun/Noun	Verb	Object
我	给　你	介绍一下。	
马大为	给　大家	唱	美国歌。
林娜	给　哥哥	做	寿面。

Note:

The prepositional phrase using "跟……" or "给……" must be placed before the verb. You can only say "Nǐ gēn wǒ lái. 你跟我来。" (You with me come → Come with me) or "Wǒ gěi nǐ jièshào yíxià. 我给你介绍一下。" (I to you introduce briefly → Let me introduce).

Exercise I Substitute the underlined parts and complete the dialogues.

（1）A：星期天你常常去哪儿？

B：我常常去超市。

A：你常跟谁去超市？

B：我常跟王小云一起去超市。

图书馆	我同学
体育馆	我哥哥
朋友家	我女朋友

（2）A：宋华给林娜介绍什么？

B：宋华给林娜介绍老北京的胡同。

老师	我们	汉字的历史
小云	大为	上海的点心
林娜	大家	英语教学

Exercise II Look at the pictures and complete the sentences.

（1）   （2）

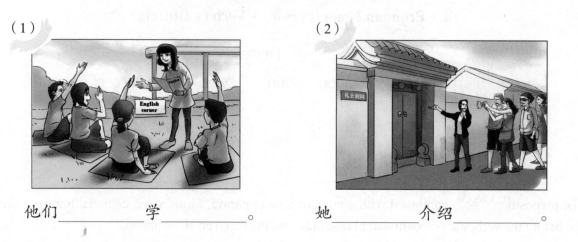

他们＿＿＿＿＿＿学＿＿＿＿＿＿。   她＿＿＿＿＿＿介绍＿＿＿＿＿＿。

5. 用"……，好吗？""……，对吗？"提问 Asking a question with "……, hǎo ma 好吗?" or "……, duì ma 对吗?"

The question "……, hǎo ma 好吗?" is often used to make a suggestion in order to solicit the opinion of other people. The first half of the sentence is a suggestion. The affirmative response may be "hǎo a 好啊" or "hǎo 好", etc. The negative response is often not "*bù hǎo 不好", but rather "zhēn bù hǎoyìsi 真不好意思，……", "duìbuqǐ 对不起……", "kǒngpà bù xíng 恐怕不行", etc.

Example

Wǒmen mǎi yí ge dà dàngāo, hǎo ma?
（1）我们　买一个大 蛋糕，好 吗？
Shall we buy a big cake? (Literally, we buy a big cake, OK?)

Nǐ jiāo wǒ Hànyǔ, hǎo ma?
（2）你 教 我 汉语，好 吗？
Could you teach me Chinese? (Literally, you teach me Chinese, OK?)

The question "……，duì ma 对吗？" is often used to indicate that the speaker is asking with some assurance and confidence. The first part of the sentence could be affirmative or negative. The response could be "duì 对" or "bú shì 不是".

Example

Nǐ shì Zhōngguórén, duì ma?
A：你 是　中国人，　对 吗？
You are Chinese, is that right?

Duì, wǒ shì Zhōngguórén. / Bú shì, wǒ shì Měiguórén.
B：对，我 是　中国人。／ 不 是，我 是 美国人。
Yes, I am Chinese. / No, (I am not Chinese.) I am American.

四、练习与运用 PRACTICE AND APPLICATION

补充词语 Supplementary Words

2-06-06

1.	卫生间	wèishēngjiān	N	washroom; bathroom　去卫生间 卫生间在哪儿
2.	卧室	wòshì	N	bedroom　回卧室 卧室旁边
3.	客厅	kètīng	N	living room　在客厅 客厅后边
4.	阳台	yángtái	N	balcony　在阳台 阳台里
5.	厨房	chúfáng	N	kitchen　厨房里 厨房左边
6.	书房	shūfáng	N	study　在书房写字
7.	咖啡厅	kāfēitīng	N	coffee shop; café　去咖啡厅 咖啡厅里
8.	酒吧	jiǔbā	N	bar　酒吧前面
9.	清真餐厅	qīngzhēn cāntīng		Muslim restaurant; halal restaurant 在清真餐厅吃饭
10.	操场	cāochǎng	N	sports field　操场南边 操场上
11.	那儿	nàr	Pr	there　去那儿
12.	左边	zuǒbian	N	left (side)　左边的办公楼 在食堂左边

13.	上边	shàngbian	N	above; over; on top of	钢琴<u>上边</u>
14.	下边	xiàbian	N	below; under; underneath	楼<u>下边</u>
15.	外边	wàibian	N	outside	去<u>外边</u> 银行<u>外边</u>

1 语音练习 Pronunciation Drills 2-06-07

Listen and read aloud: Add tone marks to the following words and sentences, and then read them aloud.

❶ nar
❷ zher
❸ pangbian
❹ qianbian
❺ zhaoji
❻ chaoshi
❼ tiyuguan
❽ sushelou
❾ Women de sushelou zai zher, dui ma?
❿ Fanguan houbian you yi tiao hutong.

2 会话练习 Conversation Practice

Pair activity: Create dialogues based on the scenes and the requirements below.

1. Asking directions

For the scenes below, choose a question and then in pairs of two start a dialogue.

Scene 1: You cannot find your classroom.

Scene 2: You want to go to a bank to withdraw some money.

Scene 3: You cannot find a washroom on the road.

A. 请问，401 教室在哪儿？

B. 请问，学校里边有银行吗？

C. 请问，哪儿有卫生间？

2. Describing the locations

Based on the picture below, describe the campus to your friends.

我的宿舍楼北边有……，东边是……，
西边是……，……在……。

3. Expressing not hearing clearly or understanding

Pair activity: A makes a statement and B says that he or she has not heard A clearly.

(1) In a very low voice, A says "Nǐ duō dà? 你多大？" (How old are you?)

(2) Speaking very quickly, A says "Qǐng gēn wǒ lái. 请跟我来。" (Please come with me.)

The following words may be helpful to you:

不好意思　等一下　你说什么

4. Asking about words that you don't understand

In response to the scenes below, which questions would you ask? Assume that you do not know the words in parentheses.

Scene 1: The class is almost over. The teacher says, "今天的作业是……"（作业 zuòyè）

Scene 2: A Chinese person asks you, "您贵姓？"（贵姓 guìxìng）

Scene 3: A Chinese friend suggests that you eat "火锅".（火锅 huǒguō）

The following words may be helpful to you:

不好意思　等一下　你说什么　什么意思

 听后复述 Listening and Repeating　 2-06-08

Listen to the following dialogues and repeat what you hear.

（1）A：请问餐厅在哪儿？

　　B：在楼上。

　　A：谢谢！

　　B：不客气。

（2）A：请问这儿有银行吗？

　　B：不好意思，我也不知道。

（3）A：学校东边是什么地方？

　　B：学校东边是超市。

　　A：那个超市大不大？

　　B：不太大。

（4）A：不好意思，您说什么？

　　B：我说明天你有空儿吗？

　　A："有空儿"是什么意思？

　　B：就是"有时间"。

4 阅读理解 Reading Comprehension

Ⅰ

我们学校的食堂在校门右边，那儿的包子和饺子很好吃。校门外还有一个饭馆，我们也常去那儿。学校食堂旁边是办公楼。教学楼在食堂东边，图书馆在食堂北边。图书馆旁边有个很大的操场，东边有一个银行。宿舍楼在银行后边，宿舍楼旁边有一个小超市，我们很喜欢去那儿。

Decide whether the statements are true (T) or false (F).

（1）校门的左边是我们学校的食堂。（　　　）

（2）食堂在图书馆的南边。　　　　　（　　　）

（3）小超市也在银行后边。　　　　　（　　　）

Ⅱ

这是我的新家。我家有两个卧室、一个客厅、一个厨房和一个卫生间。大卧室在客厅的东边，小卧室在客厅的西边。客厅的南边有一个很大的阳台。厨房和卫生间在客厅的对面。厨房不太大，卫生间很大，在厨房的西边。我的新家怎么样？欢迎你来我们家。

Read the paragraph and then sketch a map of the apartment.

5 任务与活动 Task and Activity

1. Making a phone call – Got lost

Pair activity: A invites B to the dormitory to have fun. B gets lost on campus, so B calls A and asks for directions. A must ask B where he or she is located and gives directions to B. Hint: The following sketch map can be used as reference.

A：你现在在哪儿？

B：_____。

A：_____。

（东边、西边、南边、北边、旁边、教学楼、食堂、体育馆、图书馆、超市、银行）

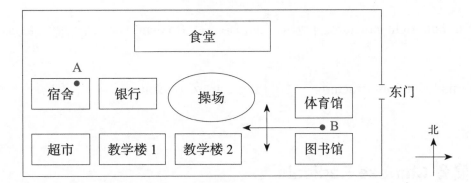

2. Doing research – Our country is here

Group activity: Everyone introduces where his or her country is located on the map of the world, and indicates which continent it belongs to, as well as the neighboring countries or the seas to the north, south, east, and west.

6 写作练习 Writing Exercise

Based on the second exercise under Task and Activity above, write out the words you have used in your campus tour.

The following sentences may be helpful to you:

> 我们国家在……。东边是……，西边是……。
>
> 我们国家南边有……，……在我们国家北边。

五、汉字 *CHINESE CHARACTERS*

1 汉字知识 Knowledge about Chinese Characters

The structure of Chinese characters (V)

A compound character made of two or more components:

(1) Compound left-right structure: e.g., yǔ 语 (language) and dōu 都 (all; both)

(2) Compound top-bottom structure: e.g., nín 您 (you) and sù 宿 (to stay overnight)

(3) Left-middle-right structure: e.g., xiè 谢 (to thank) and zuò 做 (to do)

(4) Top-middle-bottom structure: e.g., yì 意 (meaning)

2 汉字偏旁 Chinese Radicals

Radical	Name	Stroke Order	No. of Strokes	Example	Explanation
⺮	竹字头	ノ ㇒ ㇏ ㇒ ⺮ ⺮	6	等 děng (to wait)	Related to "bamboo"
⻊	足字旁	㇏ 丷 ㅁ ㅁ ㇉ ⻊ ⻊	7	跟 gēn (to follow; with) 路 lù (road) 跳 tiào (to jump)	Related to "foot"
彳	双人旁	ノ ㇒ 彳	3	街 jiē (street) 很 hěn (very)	Related to "walking" or "road"

3 认写基本汉字 Learn and Write the Basic Chinese Characters

（1）足 ㇏ 丷 ㅁ ㅁ 무 무 무 足

zú   foot   7 strokes

（2）书　　ᆨ ᄀ 书 书

shū　　book　　　　　　　　　　　　4 strokes

（3）西　　一 ᆨ 兀 丙 两 西

xī　　west　　　　　　　　　　　　6 strokes

（4）东　　一 ᄂ 东 东 东

dōng　　east　　　　　　　　　　　5 strokes

（5）舌　　ノ 二 千 千 舌 舌

shé　　tongue　　　　　　　　　　6 strokes

（6）方　　丶 亠 方 方

fāng　　square　　　　　　　　　　4 strokes

（7）走　　一 十 土 キ キ 走 走

zǒu　　to walk　　　　　　　　　　7 strokes

（8）矢　　ノ ᆫ 二 午 矢

shǐ　　arrow　　　　　　　　　　　5 strokes

（9）竹　　ノ ᄼ 仁 仃 竹 竹

zhú　　bamboo　　　　　　　　　　6 strokes

4　认写课文中的汉字 Learn and Write the Chinese Characters in the Text

（1）宿舍 sùshè

舍 ⟶ 人 + 舌　　　　　　　　　　　　8 strokes

（2）超市 chāoshì

超 ⟶ 走 + 刀 + 口　　　　　　　　　12 strokes

（3）知道 zhīdào

知 ⟶ 矢 + 口　　　　　　　　　　　　8 strokes

（4）等 děng

等 ⟶ 竹 + 土 + 寸　　　　　　　　　12 strokes

（5）跟 gēn

跟 —→ 𧾷 + 艮

13 strokes

（6）马路 mǎlù

路 —→ 𧾷 + 夂（夂：ノ ク 夂）+ 口

13 strokes

（7）银行 yínháng

行 —→ 彳 + 亍（亍：一 二 亍）

6 strokes

（8）街道 jiēdào

街 —→ 彳 + 土 + 土 + 亍

12 strokes

六、文化知识 *CULTURAL KNOWLEDGE*

The Local-style Dwellings in China

Due to the different natural environments and cultural customs, a variety of different features have appeared in the dwelling structures across China.

The "sìhéyuàn 四合院" is a typical northern courtyard dwelling surrounded by buildlings on all four sides. The entrance of the main residence, where senior family members live, faces south, with the back rooms facing north. The younger generations live in the east and west wings. Between the main residence and the wings, there are corridors for walks and relaxation.

The dwelling with the "tiānjǐng 天井" courtyard is mainly in the area south of the Yangtze River. The four sides are connected by two- or three-storey houses with a small courtyard in the

middle. The diverse special designs, integrating the stone sculpture, wood sculpture, or brick sculpture, make the architecture very elegant.

The "yáodòng 窑洞" cave dwellings are traditional residences in the northwest loess plateau. They were dug into the mountains and have doors and windows in front. "窑洞" is a product of the loess plateau,

symbolizing the characteristics of the people in northern Shaanxi Province.

The "měnggǔbāo 蒙古包", the Mongolian yurt, is the residence for the herdsmen on the steppes in Inner Mongolia. A yurt is easily constructed and moved, suitable for livestock farming and the nomadic way of life. The roof of a

yurt is like a crown, which may be big or small. A yurt is usually set up on a grassy area, having very good ventilation. In the winter a yurt is warm and in the summer it is cool, withstanding wind and rain. It is convenient and comfortable.

七、自我评估　SELF-EVALUATION

I can basically do the following things in Chinese:

☐ I can describe the surroundings of the place where I live.

☐ I can talk about the location of something.

☐ I can ask directions.

☐ When I encounter a language problem, I am able to ask others for help.

趣味汉语　Fun with Chinese

A Funny Story: Three Turtles

Sān zhī wūguī qù hē kāfēi,　tāmen gāng dào kāfēidiàn ménkǒu jiù xià yǔ le.　Dà wūguī duì xiǎo
三只乌龟去喝咖啡，它们 刚 到咖啡店 门口 就 下雨了。大乌龟对小

wūguī shuō:　"Nǐ huí jiā qǔ sǎn ba."　Xiǎo wūguī shuō:　"Nǐmen bù hē wǒ de kāfēi,　wǒ jiù qù."
乌龟 说："你回家取伞吧。" 小 乌龟 说："你们不喝我的咖啡， 我 就去。"

Dà wūguī hé zhōng wūguī huídá:　"Wǒmen bù hē,　nǐ qù ba."
大乌龟和 中 乌龟回答："我们不喝，你去吧。"

Liǎng nián hòu,　dà wūguī duì zhōng wūguī shuō:　"Wǒ xiǎng tā kěndìng bù huílai le,　wǒmen
两 年后，大乌龟对 中 乌龟说："我 想 它肯定不回来了，我们

kěyǐ　hē tā de kāfēi le."　Zhè shí yí ge shēngyīn cóng mén wài chuánlai:　"Nǐmen yào hē wǒ de
可以喝它的咖啡了。" 这时一个 声音 从 门外 传来："你们要喝我的

kāfēi,　wǒ jiù bú qù le."
咖啡，我就不去了。"

Three turtles went to drink coffee. As soon as they arrived at the coffee shop, it began to rain. The oldest turtle said to the little turtle: "You go back home and get an umbrella." The little turtle said: "If you don't drink my coffee, I will go." The oldest turtle and the second turtle said: "We won't drink your coffee. You go back."

Two years later, the oldest turtle said to the second turtle: "I think that he definitely will not be coming back, so we can drink his coffee." At this moment, a voice came from outside the door: "You want to drink my coffee, so I won't go."

7

Píngguǒ   duōshao qián   yì   jīn

苹果多少钱一斤

How much is half a kilo of apples

In this lesson you will learn how to count from 100 to 9,999 and learn about Chinese currency. You will also learn how to use the two words "xiǎng 想" (would like) and "kěyǐ 可以" (can; may) to express what you want, and ask for help when you encounter a language problem. Then you can go shopping in Chinese in a store, or bargain for a lower price on the street.

一、热身 *WARM-UP*

1 思考 **Think**

Think about the following questions:

(1) What currency is used in your country? What are the units of this currency?

(2) In your country, do people bargain when they go shopping? If they do, how do they bargain?

(3) Do you use a credit card or debit card when you go shopping? In general, what kind of card do people use?

2 活动 **Activity**

Of the following coins and banknotes, guess which ones are "rénmínbì 人民币"?

二、课文 *TEXT*

（一）  2-07-01

老板： 您好，您要什么？
Lǎobǎn： Nín hǎo, nín yào shénme?

马大为： 我想买点儿苹果。①
Mǎ Dàwéi： Wǒ xiǎng mǎi diǎnr píngguǒ.

老板： 先生，您的汉语真好。
Lǎobǎn： Xiānsheng, nín de Hànyǔ zhēn hǎo.

> 称赞与回应
> **Praise and response**

马大为： 哪里，我的汉语不太好。② 苹果多少钱一斤？③
Mǎ Dàwéi： Nǎli, wǒ de Hànyǔ bú tài hǎo. Píngguǒ duōshao qián yì jīn?

老板： 五块五一斤。④
Lǎobǎn： Wǔ kuài wǔ yì jīn.

> 问价
> **Asking about the price**

马大为： 这个…… 我问您一个问题：这个汉语怎么说？
Mǎ Dàwéi： Zhège Wǒ wèn nín yí ge wèntí: zhège Hànyǔ zěnme shuō?

老板： 这叫"草莓"。
Lǎobǎn： Zhè jiào "cǎoméi".

> 遇到语言困难求助
> **Encountering a language problem and asking for help**

马大为： 草莓怎么卖？
Mǎ Dàwéi:　Cǎoméi　zěnme mài?

老板： 十六块一斤。
Lǎobǎn:　Shíliù　kuài　yì　jīn.

马大为： 您的草莓真贵。
Mǎ Dàwéi:　Nín de　cǎoméi zhēn guì.

老板： 不贵，我的草莓好吃。您可以尝一下。
Lǎobǎn:　Bú　guì,　wǒ　de cǎoméi hǎochī.　Nín　kěyǐ　cháng yíxià.

马大为： 便宜点儿吧，⑤ 十四块一斤，好吗？
Mǎ Dàwéi:　Piányi　diǎnr　ba,　shísì　kuài　yì　jīn,　hǎo ma?

老板： 三十块两斤。
Lǎobǎn:　Sānshí　kuài liǎng jīn.

砍价
Bargaining

马大为： 好吧。我买两斤草莓和四斤苹果。
Mǎ Dàwéi:　Hǎo ba.　Wǒ mǎi liǎng jīn cǎoméi hé　sì　jīn píngguǒ.

老板： 一共五十二块钱。我送您两个草莓。您还要什么？
Lǎobǎn:　Yígòng　wǔshí'èr kuài qián.　Wǒ sòng nín liǎng ge cǎoméi.　Nín hái yào shénme?

马大为： 不要了，谢谢。⑥ 给您钱。
Mǎ Dàwéi:　Bú　yào　le,　xièxie.　Gěi nín qián.

付钱
Paying for something

老板： 好，您给我六十，我找您八块。
Lǎobǎn:　Hǎo,　nín gěi wǒ　liùshí,　wǒ zhǎo nín　bā kuài.

好吃您再来。⑦
Hǎochī nín zài lái.

生词 New Words　　2-07-02

1. 老板	lǎobǎn	N	shopkeeper; proprietor; boss　王老板　丁老板
2. 想	xiǎng	V/OpV	to think; to think about / to want; would like　想问题 想一下　想来　想参加　想看电影　不想去上海
3. 买	mǎi	V	to buy　买点心　买书　买礼物　不买　买什么

4. （一）点儿	(yì) diǎnr	Nu-M	a little; some　吃点儿饺子　喝点儿什么　看点儿书
5. 苹果	píngguǒ	N	apple　买点儿苹果　好吃的苹果
6. 先生	xiānsheng	N	sir; Mr.　张先生　宋先生
7. 哪里	nǎli	IE	*(an expression of modesty)* not at all　哪里哪里
8. 钱	qián	N	money　多少钱　有钱的人　没有钱
9. 斤	jīn	M	*jin* (500g)　一斤　十斤苹果　多少钱一斤
10. 块（钱）	kuài (qián)	M	*kuai (a colloquial measure word for dollar)*　五块（钱）　五块（钱）一斤
11. 怎么	zěnme	QPr	how　怎么说　怎么做　怎么写　怎么去　怎么学
12. 草莓	cǎoméi	N	strawberry　买点儿草莓　两斤草莓
13. 卖	mài	V	to sell　卖苹果　草莓怎么卖
14. 贵	guì	A	expensive　真贵　不贵
15. 可以	kěyǐ	OpV	may; can　可以参加　可以去　可以看一下　不可以
16. 尝	cháng	V	to taste　尝一下　可以尝一下
17. 便宜	piányi	A	inexpensive; cheap　很便宜　不便宜　便宜点儿
18. 给	gěi	V	to give　给老板钱　给他草莓　给你咖啡
19. 找	zhǎo	V	to give change　找钱　找我两块
20. 再	zài	Adv	again　再吃点儿　再坐一会儿　再等一会儿　再唱一个

注释　Notes

① 我想买点儿苹果。

I'd like to buy some apples.

The word "yìdiǎnr 一点儿" is an indefinite measure word to modify a noun, meaning a small amount or some. For example, "yìdiǎnr chá 一点儿茶" (some tea), "yìdiǎnr diǎnxin 一点儿点心" (some snack), "yìdiǎnr qián 一点儿钱" (some money). When "一点儿" is not at the beginning of a sentence, "yī 一" can be omitted. For example, "chī diǎnr miàntiáo 吃点儿面条" (eat some noodles), "hē diǎnr kāfēi 喝点儿咖啡" (drink some coffee), "sòng diǎnr lǐwù 送点儿礼物" (give some gifts), and "kàn diǎnr shū 看点儿书" (do some reading), etc.

② 哪里，我的汉语不太好。

No, my Chinese is not very good.

"nǎli 哪里" is actually an interrogative pronoun meaning "where", but "哪里" in this context has a negative connotation. It is often used to express modesty when responding to praise. We can also use "Shì ma? 是吗？" (Is that so? Really?) to express doubt. For example, "Shì ma? Wǒ de Hànyǔ bú tài hǎo. 是吗？我的汉语不太好。" (Really? My Chinese is not very good). Whether we use a word expressing negation or doubt, the purpose is to show that a person accepts other people's compliments with modesty. In Chinese culture, this is regarded as an appropriate and expected response.

③ 苹果多少钱一斤？

How much is one *jin* of apples?

"……duōshao qián yì jīn? 多少钱一斤？" (How much is one *jin* of...?) is a common expression used to ask the price of something when shopping. *Jin* is the commonly used unit of weight in China. One *jin* is equivalent to half a kilogram or 1.1023 pounds. The legal measurement stipulated by the Chinese government is "qiānkè 千克" (1,000 grams) or "gōngjīn 公斤" (kilogram), but in daily life, people just use the word *jin*.

④ 五块五一斤。

Five *kuai* (Chinese dollars) 50 cents per *jin*.

The currency in circulation in China now is "rénmínbì 人民币" (literally, the People's Currency). The units of the currency are "yuán 元", "jiǎo 角" (one tenth of a "元"), and "fēn 分" (one percent of a "元"). When speaking Chinese, people often say "kuài 块" and "máo 毛" instead of the written forms "元" and "角". When "毛" and "分" are at the end, they may be omitted. For example,

1.75 yuán   yí kuài qī máo wǔ (fēn qián)
1.75 元 → 一 块 七 毛 五（分 钱）

5.50 yuán   wǔ kuài wǔ (máo qián)
5.50 元 → 五 块 五（毛 钱）

Note:

When an amount of money begins with the number "2", say "liǎng 两". For example,

2.20 yuán   liǎng kuài èr
2.20 元 → 两 块 二

0.22 yuán   liǎng máo èr
0.22 元 → 两 毛 二

⑤ 便宜点儿吧。

Could you make the price a bit lower?

⑥ 不要了，谢谢。

　　No, thanks.

⑦ 好吃您再来。

　　If it tastes good, come back again.

（二）  2-07-03

丁力波：您好，这件衬衫多少钱？①
Dīng Lìbō：Nín hǎo，　zhè jiàn chènshān duōshao qián?

售货员：三百九十九块。
Shòuhuòyuán：Sānbǎi　jiǔshíjiǔ　kuài.

丁力波：我可以试一下吗？
Dīng Lìbō：Wǒ　kěyǐ　shì　yíxià　ma?

请求与允许

Making a request and
giving permission

售货员：当然可以。②
Shòuhuòyuán：Dāngrán　kěyǐ.

丁力波：这件太小，有大号的衬衫吗？③
Dīng Lìbō：Zhè jiàn tài xiǎo，　yǒu dàhào　de chènshān ma?

挑选衣服

Choosing clothes

售货员：有，左边有大号的衬衫。您再试一下这件吧。
Shòuhuòyuán: Yǒu, zuǒbian yǒu dàhào de chènshān. Nín zài shì yíxià zhè jiàn ba.

丁力波：这件很合适。有没有牛仔裤？
Dīng Lìbō: Zhè jiàn hěn héshì. Yǒu méi yǒu niúzǎikù?

售货员：有。这条牛仔裤怎么样？
Shòuhuòyuán: Yǒu. Zhè tiáo niúzǎikù zěnmeyàng?

丁力波：很好，我要这条。我还想买一件羽绒服。
Dīng Lìbō: Hěn hǎo, wǒ yào zhè tiáo. Wǒ hái xiǎng mǎi yí jiàn yǔróngfú.

售货员：您看这件怎么样？
Shòuhuòyuán: Nín kàn zhè jiàn zěnmeyàng?

丁力波：我不喜欢黑色，有绿色的羽绒服吗？
Dīng Lìbō: Wǒ bù xǐhuan hēisè, yǒu lǜsè de yǔróngfú ma?

售货员：有，您可以看一下这件。
Shòuhuòyuán: Yǒu, nín kěyǐ kàn yíxià zhè jiàn.

丁力波：这件不错。这些衣服一共多少钱？
Dīng Lìbō: Zhè jiàn búcuò. Zhèxiē yīfu yígòng duōshao qián?

售货员：衬衫三百九十九块，牛仔裤五百八十七块，
Shòuhuòyuán: Chènshān sānbǎi jiǔshíjiǔ kuài, niúzǎikù wǔbǎi bāshíqī kuài,

羽绒服一千二百零五块，
yǔróngfú yìqiān èrbǎi líng wǔ kuài,

一共两千一百九十一块。
yígòng liǎngqiān yìbǎi jiǔshíyī kuài.

结账
Settling a bill

丁力波：可以打折吗？
Dīng Lìbō: Kěyǐ dǎzhé ma?

售货员：不好意思，现在不打折。
Shòuhuòyuán: Bù hǎoyìsi, xiànzài bù dǎzhé.

丁力波：可以刷卡吗？
Dīng Lìbō: Kěyǐ shuākǎ ma?

售货员：没问题。④
Shòuhuòyuán: Méi wèntí.

生词 New Words　2-07-04

1. 件	jiàn	M	item/article (of clothing)　两件　这件	
2. 衬衫	chènshān	N	shirt; blouse　一件衬衫　买衬衫　新衬衫	
3. 售货员	shòuhuòyuán	N	salesperson　女售货员　一个售货员	
员	yuán	Suf	(a suffix attached to persons in certain fields) person	
4. 百	bǎi	Nu	hundred　一百　三百九十九　五百八十七	
5. 试	shì	V	to try; to try on　试一下　可以试一下	
6. 当然	dāngrán	Adv	of course　当然可以　当然想去　当然喜欢　当然参加	
7. 左边	zuǒbian	N	left (side)　左边的同学　在校门左边	
左	zuǒ	N	left	
8. 合适	héshì	A	suitable; fitting　很合适　真合适　不合适	
9. 牛仔裤	niúzǎikù	N	jeans　一条牛仔裤　买牛仔裤	
10. 羽绒服	yǔróngfú	N	down coat; down jacket　一件羽绒服　买羽绒服	
11. 黑色	hēisè	N	black　喜欢黑色　黑色的衬衫	
黑	hēi	A	black　黑牛仔裤　黑衬衫	
12. 绿色	lǜsè	N	green　喜欢绿色　绿色的羽绒服	
绿	lǜ	A	green　绿衬衫	
13. 不错	búcuò	A	pretty good　很不错　真不错	
错	cuò	A	wrong	
14. 些	xiē	M	some; a few　一些学生　这些苹果	
15. 衣服	yīfu	N	clothing　这些衣服　一件衣服　买衣服	
16. 千	qiān	Nu	thousand　一千　一千二百六十五　两千二百五十一	
17. 零	líng	Nu	zero　一千二百零五块　三块零五分钱	
18. 打折	dǎzhé	VO	to offer a discount　可以打折　打六折　不打折	
19. 刷卡	shuākǎ	VO	to pay with a credit/debit card　可以刷卡	
卡	kǎ	N	card　银行卡	
20. 没问题	méi wèntí	IE	no problem	
问题	wèntí	N	question; problem; issue　有问题　没有问题	

注释 Notes

① 这件衬衫多少钱？

How much does this shirt cost?

The question "Zhè jiàn chènshān duōshao qián? 这件衬衫多少钱？" and the response "(Zhè jiàn chènshān 这件衬衫) 399 kuài 块。" are both sentences with a nominal predicate. The predicate can be a question pronoun, a numeral-measure-word compound, or a noun phrase. In addition to age, hours and dates that we have learned before, a sentence with a nominal predicate can also express a price, an amount of money, and so on.

② 当然可以。

Of course you can.

It is used to express permission.

③ 有大号的衬衫吗？

Do you have a large size shirt?

For outer garments, shirts, T-shirts, etc. sold in Chinese stores, the size could be S for small, M for medium, L for large, and XL or XXL for extra large.

④ 没问题。

No problem.

The meaning of "Méi wèntí 没问题。" is "I am fine (literally, have no problem)." In spoken Chinese, it often reflects a positive and confident manner of speaking. For example,

    Míngtiān nǐ bā diǎn lái, hǎo ma?
A: 明天 你八点来，好 吗？ Come at eight o'clock tomorrow, OK?

    Méi wèntí, wǒ bā diǎn lái.
B: 没 问题，我八点来。No problem. I will come at eight o'clock.

三、语言点 LANGUAGE POINTS

1 核心句 Key Sentences   2-07-05

1. 我想买点儿苹果。
2. 苹果多少钱一斤？
3. 草莓怎么卖？
4. 这个汉语怎么说？

5. 这件衬衫多少钱？

6. 便宜点儿吧，十四块一斤，好吗？

7. 您给我六十，我找您八块。

8. 一共两千一百九十一块。

9. 可以刷卡吗？

10. 您再试一下这件吧。

2 语法 Grammar

1. 百、千的称数法　Numbers from 100 to 9,999

	1……9 一……九	10……99 十……九十九
100 一百	101……109 一百零一……一百零九	110、111……199 一百一十、一百一十一……一百九十九
200 二百	201……209 二百零一……二百零九	210、211……299 二百一十、二百一十一……二百九十九
⋮	⋮	⋮
900 九百	901……909 九百零一……九百零九	910、911……999 九百一十、九百一十一……九百九十九
1000 一千		
1001 一千零一	1010 一千零一十	1052 一千零五十二
1100 一千一百	2109 两千一百零九	2543 两千五百四十三
4222 四千二百 二十二	8990 八千九百九十	9999 九千九百九十九

Note:

When "2" appears before "qiān 千", it is read out as "liǎng 两".

Exercise I　Read the red numbers in the table above aloud.

Exercise II　Read the following numbers aloud.

| 110 | 246 | 658 | 703 | 962 | 1050 | 2287 |

2. 能愿动词谓语句（1）：想、可以　A sentence with an optative verb (1): "xiǎng 想" (would like) or "kěyǐ 可以" (may; can)

Optative verbs such as "想", "可以", "yào 要" (will; to want), "néng 能" (can), and "yīnggāi 应该" (should) are often placed before a verb, expressing intention, possibility or capability. The word "想" expresses one's subjective intention or hope. Its negative form is "bù xiǎng 不想".

Subject	Predicate		
	Optative Verb	Verb	Object
丁力波	想	买	一件绿色的羽绒服。
林娜	想不想	看	北京的胡同？
我	不想	去	上海。

The word "可以" often expresses objective conditions that permit or forbid someone to do something. The negative form is "bù néng 不能" (cannot) or "bù kěyǐ 不可以" (cannot).

Subject	Predicate		
	Optative Verb	Verb	Object
您	可以	给我介绍一下吗？	
我	可以不可以	试一下	这件衣服？
现在	不能／不可以	过	马路。

Notes:

❶ In a sentence with an optative verb, the verb/adjective-not-verb/adjective question is applied to the optative verb rather than the action verb. For example,

Nǐ xiǎng bu xiǎng kàn diànyǐng?
（1）你 想 不 想 看 电影？ Would you like to watch a movie?

Lín Nà xiǎng bu xiǎng liànxí kǒuyǔ?
（2）林娜 想 不 想 练习 口语？ Does Lin Na want to practice speaking (Chinese)?

❷ To give a simple answer to a question, the answer can be just an optative verb. For example,

Kěyǐ shuākǎ ma?
A: 可以 刷卡 吗？ Can I pay with a credit/debit card?

Kěyǐ.
B: 可以。 Yes, you can.

194

❸ Some optative verbs are simply verbs, such as "想" (to think about) as in "xiǎng wèntí 想问题" (to think about a question/issue) and "xiǎng yǔfǎ 想语法" (to think about grammar).

Exercise I   Make dialogues based on the pictures and prompts.

Example

A：您要什么？

B：我想买点儿苹果。

Exercise II   Substitute the underlined parts and complete the dialogues.

（1）A：你想不想<u>买中文书</u>？

　　B：我不想<u>买中文书</u>，我想<u>买中文地图</u>。

去图书馆	去超市
买草莓	买苹果
试这件衬衫	试那条牛仔裤
学中文歌	看中国电影

（2）A：现在可以<u>问问题</u>吗？

　　B：不好意思，现在不能／不可以<u>问问题</u>。

| 刷卡 |
| 说英语 |
| 看书 |
| 进体育馆 |

3. 双宾语动词谓语句（2）：给、问、找   A sentence with a two-object verbal predicate (2): "gěi 给" (to give), "wèn 问" (to ask), and "zhǎo 找" (to give change)

The verbs "给"，"问" and "找" can be followed by two objects, with the first object indicating the recipient and the second one indicating the thing given.

给、问、找 + Pronoun/Noun (Person) + Noun (Phrase) (Thing)

Subject	Predicate		
	Verb 给、问、找	Object₁	Object₂
您	给	我	六十（块）。
老板	给	大为	两个草莓。
妈妈	给	儿子	一盒巧克力。
马大为	问	老板	一个问题。
他	问	她	明天的课。
医生	问	你	什么？
我	找	您	八块。

Exercise I   Complete the sentences with the words and phrases given.

Example   我 → 老板（给）   <u>我给老板二十块钱。</u>（￥20）

（1）我 → 售货员（给）　＿＿＿＿＿＿＿＿＿＿。（￥1000）

（2）同学 → 我（给）　＿＿＿＿＿＿＿＿＿＿。（一张照片）

（3）林娜 → 哥哥（送）　＿＿＿＿＿＿＿＿＿＿。（一件衬衫）

（4）我 → 老师（问）　＿＿＿＿＿＿＿＿＿＿。（这个汉字）

（5）宋华 → 林娜（问）　＿＿＿＿＿＿＿＿＿＿。（英语的问题）

Exercise II   Following the example, put the words and phrases in order to form sentences.

Example   大为　老板　送　两个草莓 → <u>老板送大为两个草莓。</u>

（1）售货员　八块　找　我 → ＿＿＿＿＿＿＿＿＿＿＿＿＿＿＿＿＿＿。

（2）老师　名字　问　她的　我 → ＿＿＿＿＿＿＿＿＿＿＿＿＿＿＿＿＿。

（3）妈妈　两斤　小云　苹果　给 → ＿＿＿＿＿＿＿＿＿＿＿＿＿＿＿＿。

（4）大为　唱　大家　教　美国歌 → ＿＿＿＿＿＿＿＿＿＿＿＿＿＿＿＿。

（5）她哥哥　给　一条　小云　牛仔裤　黑色的 → ＿＿＿＿＿＿＿＿＿＿＿＿。

（6）林娜　一盒　宋华　送　英国茶 → ＿＿＿＿＿＿＿＿＿＿＿＿＿＿＿＿。

4. 用疑问代词的问句（3）：怎么　An interrogative sentence with a question pronoun (3): "zěnme 怎么" (how)

The question pronoun "怎么" placed before a verb forms an interrogative sentence. The pattern "怎么 + verb" is often used to ask about a certain action or about how to do something, such as "zěnme shuō 怎么说" (how do you say), "zěnme zuò 怎么做" (how do you make), "zěnme qù 怎么去" (how do you go), "zěnme xiě 怎么写" (how do you write), and so on.

Subject	Predicate
草莓	怎么卖?
寿面	怎么做?
这个汉字	怎么写?
"discount"	汉语怎么说?
这个	汉语怎么说?

Note:

In this type of sentence, the subject is often the recipient of the action, but is also the topic of the comment.

Exercise I　Complete the sentences based on the prompts.

Example　苹果　卖 → <u>苹果怎么卖</u>?

（1）这件衬衫　卖 → _____?

（2）包子　做 → _____?

（3）这个汉字　写 → _____?

（4）这个歌　唱 → _____?

Exercise II　Complete the dialogues using "zěnme 怎么".

（1）A：_____?

　　B：这叫"草莓"。

（2）A：_____?

　　B：苹果五块一斤。

（3）A：请问 _____ ?

B：对不起，我也不知道蛋糕怎么做。

（4）A：请问 _____ ?

B：真不好意思，我也不知道这个汉字怎么写。

四、练习与运用 *PRACTICE AND APPLICATION*

补充词语 Supplementary Words　2-07-06

1.	元	yuán	M	*yuan (the official measure word for dollar)* 一百二十九元
2.	角	jiǎo	M	*jiao (the official measure word for 10 cents)* 八十元六角
3.	毛	máo	M	*mao (a colloquial measure word for 10 cents)* 五毛钱
4.	分	fēn	M	*fen (a measure word for one cent)* 三元五角五分
5.	橙子	chéngzi	N	orange 一个橙子 买橙子
6.	葡萄	pútao	N	grape 两个葡萄
7.	香蕉	xiāngjiāo	N	banana
8.	樱桃	yīngtao	N	cherry
9.	水果	shuǐguǒ	N	fruit
10.	裙子	qúnzi	N	skirt 一条裙子
11.	T恤	T xù	N	T-shirt 一件 T 恤
12.	白色	báisè	N	white
13.	红色	hóngsè	N	red
14.	穿	chuān	V	to wear; to put on 穿衣服 穿衬衫 穿牛仔裤 穿裙子
15.	拍照	pāizhào	VO	to take a picture 喜欢拍照 不可以拍照
16.	吸烟	xī yān	V O	to smoke 不可以吸烟 想吸烟
17.	称呼	chēnghu	V	to call; to address 怎么称呼

1 语音练习 Pronunciation Drills

 2-07-07

Listen and read aloud: Add tone marks to the following words and sentences, and then read them aloud.

❶ heise

❷ heshi

❸ zenme

❹ chenshan

❺ niuzaiku

❻ yurongfu

❼ chang yixia

❽ pianyi dianr

❾ Wo mai san jin caomei he liang jin pingguo.

❿ Nin gei wo yibai, wo zhao nin qi kuai.

2 会话练习 Conversation Practice

Pair activity: Create dialogues based on the scenes and the requirements below.

1. To go shopping

Based on the information in the pictures and the hints, ask and answer questions.

（1）

15.8 元 / 斤

6 元 / 斤

4.5 元 / 斤

（……多少钱？ / 我买……。/ 一共多少钱？ / 我给你……）

（2）

1150 元

388 元

99 元

（可以试……？ / 这儿有大号……？ / 打折 / 刷卡）

2. Language difficulties

Complete the dialogues below based on the scenes expressed in the pictures.

（1）

A：您好，这个＿＿＿＿＿＿＿＿＿？

B：这叫＿＿＿＿＿＿＿＿＿。

（京剧脸谱 jīngjù liǎnpǔ）

A：多少钱一个？

B：＿＿＿＿＿＿＿＿＿。

A：太贵了，＿＿＿＿＿＿＿＿＿，

300块一个，好吗？

B：340吧。

A：好吧。我要＿＿＿＿＿＿＿＿＿。

－－－－－－－－－－－－－－－－－－－－－－

（2）

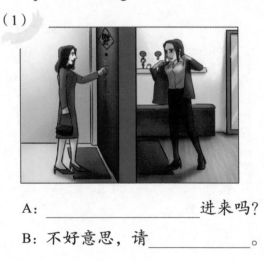

A：您好，＿＿＿＿＿＿＿＿＿？

B：这叫＿＿＿＿＿＿＿。（旗袍 qípáo）

A：这件旗袍＿＿＿＿＿＿＿＿＿？

B：880元。

A：您的旗袍真贵，＿＿＿＿＿＿＿＿＿，

800元，好吗？

B：您买两件，一共给1600元。

A：好吧。我可以给我妹妹一件。

3. Requests and permission

Complete the dialogues below based on the scenes expressed in the pictures.

（1）

（2）

A：＿＿＿＿＿＿＿＿＿进来吗？

B：不好意思，请＿＿＿＿＿。

A：＿＿＿＿＿＿＿＿＿问题吗？

B：当然＿＿＿＿＿＿。

（3）

A: 我可以＿＿＿＿＿＿＿＿？

B: 没问题，＿＿＿＿＿＿＿＿。

（4）

A: ＿＿＿＿＿＿参加你们的活动吗？

B: ＿＿＿＿＿＿＿＿，欢迎！

3 听后复述 Listening and Repeating 2-07-08

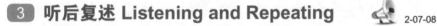

Listen to the following dialogues and repeat what you hear.

（1）A: 您要什么？

B: 饺子多少钱一斤？

A: 20 块一斤。

B: 包子呢？

A: 包子两块钱一个。

B: 我要半斤饺子，四个包子。

A: 一共 18 块钱。

B: 不好意思，这是一百块。

A: 我找您 82 块。

（2）A: 您的汉语真好。

B: 哪里，我刚学汉语，我的口语不太好。

A: 你常常说汉语吗？

B: 是啊。我的中国朋友常常跟我说汉语。我也常常问他们问题。

（3）A: 里面可以看一下吗？

B: 可以，请进。

A: 这儿可以拍照吗？

B: 不好意思，这儿不可以拍照。

（4）A: 你是我们学校的学生吗？

B: 我是。

A: 你好，你贵姓？

B: 我姓丁，叫丁力波。你怎么称呼？

A: 我叫牛小英（Niú Xiǎoyīng），是王小云的同学。

B: 牛小姐，认识你很高兴。

A: 你可以叫我小英。

4 阅读理解 Reading Comprehension

马大为想买点儿苹果，苹果五块五一斤。他还想买点儿草莓，草莓很贵，一斤十六块，两斤三十。他想买两斤草莓和四斤苹果，一共五十二块钱。他给老板六十块，老板找他八块，还送他两个草莓。

Answer the following questions:

(1) 马大为想买什么？

(2) 一共多少钱？

林娜想买一件羽绒服，她想买大号衣服，大号的羽绒服很合适。她喜欢绿色，这件绿色的羽绒服七百八十块钱，售货员说可以打八五折，是六百六十三块钱。她还想买一条牛仔裤，她想买中号的牛仔裤，这条大号的牛仔裤不合适，太大。她喜欢黑色，那条黑色的牛仔裤四百九十块钱，售货员说可以打七折，是三百四十三块钱，很便宜。羽绒服和牛仔裤一共一千零六块钱。售货员说可以刷卡，刷卡还可以打九五折，一共是九百五十五块钱。林娜没有卡，她给售货员一千零一十块钱，售货员找她四块钱。

Answer the following questions:

(1) 林娜想买什么？

(2) 她想买小号的羽绒服吗？

(3) 她喜欢黑色吗？

(4) 那件绿色的羽绒服可以打几折？

(5) 那条黑色的牛仔裤贵不贵？多少钱？

(6) 可以刷卡吗？刷卡可以打折吗？

(7) 林娜给售货员多少钱？售货员找她多少钱？

5 任务与活动 Task and Activity

1. Role-play

In groups of two, create a dialogue based on the following sentence patterns. One will play the salesperson, and the other the customer.

119 元　　　　968 元　　　　99 元

398 元　　　388 元（9 折）　　　1150 元（5 折）

（……多少钱？ / 我可以试一下吗？ / 真贵 / 再试一下…… / 可以打折吗？ / 可以刷卡吗？）

2. Marketing research

Go to a fruit market in your city and investigate the prices of the fruits below. Based on the hints below, report your findings to the class. You may also add other sentence patterns.

大家好！我来介绍一下这个水果超市。这个超市叫……，在我们家的……（东边 / 南边 / 西边 / 北边）。超市非常大 / 不太大，水果很多 / 不太多，很贵 / 不太贵。橙子……一斤，苹果……一斤，葡萄……一斤，草莓……一斤，樱桃……一斤，香蕉……一斤。你可以尝一下这些水果。我妈妈喜欢吃……，我爸爸喜欢吃……，我喜欢吃……。

6 学习活动 Learning Activity

In your group, summarize the measure words learned so far and the nouns that they go with. Make a list and report back to the class.

7 写作练习 Writing Exercise

Write about one of your experiences of buying fruits or clothes.

Requirements: (1) State the time and place;

(2) Specify the different varieties, (designs) and prices of the fruits or clothes;

(3) Explain why you decided to buy a certain kind of fruit or piece of clothing.

The following words may be helpful to you:

> 买　贵　想　给　找　送　喜欢

五、汉字 *CHINESE CHARACTERS*

1 汉字知识 Knowledge about Chinese Characters

Locating Chinese characters in a dictionary based on the radical

Chinese "zìdiǎn 字典" (character dictionaries) and "cídiǎn 词典" (word dictionaries) are arranged according to the shapes of the characters. In general, a component on the top, bottom, left or right, etc. is used as a radical. For example, in the Chinese characters "hǎo 好" (good), "tā 她" (she; her), "mā 妈" (mom), "jiě 姐" (elder sister), "mèi 妹" (younger sister), "nà 娜" (a female name) and so on, the component "nǚ 女" (female) on the left is the radical. In the Chinese characters "yì 意" (meaning), "sī 思" (thinking), "xiǎng 想" (to think about), "nín 您" (you), "yuàn 愿" (willing) and so on, the component "xīn 心" (heart) at the bottom is the radical. Of the characters with the same radical, those with fewer strokes are put before those with more strokes. When using the radical to consult a character in a dictionary, first you must know the radical of the character, then you count the number of strokes left over. In the example of the character "zuò 做" (to do), in addition to the radical "亻" itself, there are nine strokes. You can find "做" under the "亻" radical, and it is listed under nine strokes.

2　汉字偏旁 Chinese Radicals

Radical	Name	Stroke Order	No. of Strokes	Example	Explanation
扌	提手旁	一 十 扌	3	打 dǎ (to hit) 折 zhé (to break)	Related to "hand"
衤	衣字旁	丶 亠 才 衤 衤	5	衬 chèn (lining) 衫 shān (shirt; blouse) 裤 kù (pants)	Related to "colthes"
钅	金字旁	丿 卜 𠂉 钅 钅	5	钱 qián (money) 银 yín (silver)	Related to "metal"

3　认写基本汉字 Learn and Write the Basic Chinese Characters

(1) 果　丶 冂 冂 日 旦 甲 甲 果
guǒ　fruit　8 strokes

(2) 草　一 十 艹 艹 芍 苩 苩 茸 草
cǎo　grass　9 strokes

(3) 且　丨 冂 冃 月 且
qiě　and　5 strokes

(4) 衣　丶 亠 亠 才 衣 衣
yī　clothes　6 strokes

(5) 手　一 二 三 手
shǒu　hand　4 strokes

4　认写课文中的汉字 Learn and Write the Chinese Characters in the Text

(1) 便宜 piányi

宜 —→ 宀 + 且　8 strokes

（2）钱 qián

钱 —→ 钅 + 戋 （戋：一 二 チ 夫 戋） | 10 strokes

（3）衬衫 chènshān

衬 —→ 衤 + 寸 | 8 strokes

衫 —→ 衤 + 彡 （彡：ノ 彡 彡） | 8 strokes

（4）牛仔裤 niúzǎikù

裤 —→ 衤 + 库 （库：丶 一 广 广 庐 庐 库） | 12 strokes

（5）打折 dǎzhé

打 —→ 扌 + 丁 （丁：一 丁） | 5 strokes

折 —→ 扌 + 斤 （斤：ノ ノ 斤 斤） | 7 strokes

六、文化知识 *CULTURAL KNOWLEDGE*

The Currency of China Today: Rénmínbì

The official currency in use in China today is "rénmínbì 人民币" (literally, the People's Currency). It was first issued on December 1, 1948 when the People's Bank of China was established. As of October 1, 1999, five sets of "人民币" were issued. The abbreviation for the name of the currency is CNY for Chinese Yuan, but the more common name is RMB. In general, adding the sign of "¥" indicates the face value of the "人民币".

There are two types of "人民币" in daily use: the paper notes and the coins. The primary currency unit for "人民币" is "yuán 元 (kuài 块)"; the secondary units are "jiǎo 角 (máo 毛)" (10 cents) and "fēn 分" (cent).

There are altogether 13 denominations for "人民币":

Paper notes:

(1) Primary currency:

One Hundred Yuan (100 元), Fifty Yuan (50 元), Twenty Yuan (20 元), Ten Yuan (10 元), Five Yuan (5 元), Two yuan (2 元), and One Yuan (1 元)

(2) Secondary currency:

Fifty Cents (5 角), Twenty Cents (2 角), and Ten Cents (1 角)

Coins:

One Yuan (1 元), Fifty Cents (5 角), Ten Cents (1 角), Five Cents (5 分), Two Cents (2 分), and One Cent (1 分)

七、自我评估　SELF-EVALUATION

I can basically do the following things in Chinese:

☐ I can say large numbers in the thousands.

☐ I can ask about the price of something that I would like to buy.

☐ I can choose the fruit and clothing that I would like to buy.

☐ I can bargain and pay for the things that I buy.

☐ I can ask someone for permission to do something.

趣味汉语　Fun with Chinese

Brain Teasers

Zhōngguó yí ge rén yǒu yí ge、quán guó zhǐ yǒu shí'èr ge de dōngxi shì shénme?
1. 中国　一个人有一个、全国只有十二个的东西是什么?

Xiǎomíng jīnnián 12 suì，wèi shénme zhǐ guòle sān cì shēngrì?
2. 小明　今年12岁，为什么只过了三次生日?

Mǎi yì shuāng xié yào 360 yuán，yì zhī xié ne?
3. 买一双鞋要360元，一只鞋呢?

Shéi yì nián zhǐ zài 12 yuè gōngzuò yì tiān?
4. 谁一年只在12月工作一天?

Dàxióngmāo yìshēng zuì dà de yíhàn shì shénme?
5. 大熊猫　一生最大的遗憾是什么?

(1) Every Chinese has one and there are only 12 of them across the country. What is it?

(2) Xiaoming is 12 years old this year, but why has he celebrated his birthday only three times?

(3) It costs 360 *yuan* to buy a pair of shoes. How much does it cost to buy only one shoe?

(4) Who works only one day in December in a year?

(5) What is the greatest regret of a giant panda?

8

Wǒ quánshēn dōu bù shūfu

我全身都不舒服

I am not feeling well at all

Ma Dawei is sick. You go with him to a Chinese hospital to see a doctor. You will learn how to talk about your health conditions in Chinese and learn how to talk with your doctor. At the same time, you will develop a command of a new way of asking questions and a new sentence pattern in Chinese.

一、热身 *WARM-UP*

1 思考 Think

Think about the following questions:

(1) In your country, if you have a headache or a sore throat, what will you do?

(2) To stay healthy, do you often exercise? What do you have to pay attention to in your daily life?

(3) Do you know about traditional Chinese medicine? Have you ever taken any traditional Chinese medicine? If you have, what kind of medicine have you taken?

2 活动 Activity

Below are some of the methods used by doctors of traditional Chinese medicine. Which ones have you seen? Tell us what you think about them.

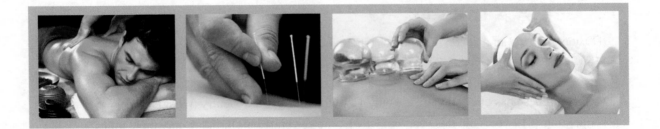

二、课文 *TEXT*

（一）　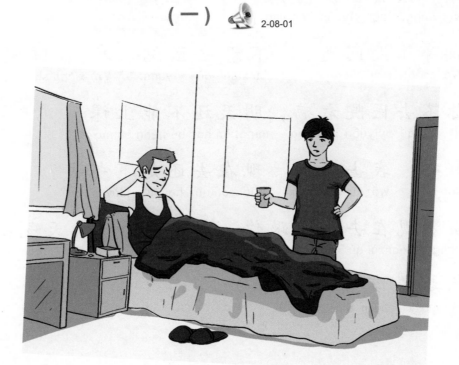 2-08-01

(In the dormitory of Ma Dawei and Ding Libo)

丁力波：大为，　快起床！① 你每天早上都六点去运动，②
Dīng Lìbō：Dàwéi,　　kuài qǐchuáng!　Nǐ měi tiān zǎoshang dōu liù diǎn qù yùndòng,

今天为什么九点还不起床？③
jīntiān　wèi shénme jiǔ diǎn hái bù qǐchuáng?

> 催促
> Urging someone to do something

马大为：我想起床，可是我头很疼。
Mǎ Dàwéi：Wǒ xiǎng qǐchuáng,　kěshì wǒ tóu hěn téng.

丁力波：对不起，我不知道你不舒服。④
Dīng Lìbō：Duìbuqǐ,　wǒ bù zhīdào nǐ bù shūfu.

> 道歉
> Apologizing

马大为：没关系。
Mǎ Dàwéi：Méi guānxi.

丁力波：你嗓子疼不疼？
Dīng Lìbō：Nǐ sǎngzi téng bu téng?

> 询问身体状况
> Asking about someone's health

马大为：我嗓子也有点儿疼。⑤
Mǎ Dàwéi: Wǒ sǎngzi yě yǒudiǎnr téng.

丁力波：你应该去医院看病。
Dīng Lìbō: Nǐ yīnggāi qù yīyuàn kànbìng.

> 表示必要
> Expressing a need

马大为：我身体没问题，⑥不想去医院。我想睡觉。
Mǎ Dàwéi: Wǒ shēntǐ méi wèntí, bù xiǎng qù yīyuàn. Wǒ xiǎng shuìjiào.

丁力波：你不去医院看病，明天还不能上课。
Dīng Lìbō: Nǐ bú qù yīyuàn kànbìng, míngtiān hái bù néng shàngkè.

> 表示可能
> Expressing a possibility

马大为：好吧，我去看病。现在去还是下午去？
Mǎ Dàwéi: Hǎo ba, wǒ qù kànbìng. Xiànzài qù háishi xiàwǔ qù?

丁力波：当然现在去，我跟你一起去。⑦今天天气很冷，
Dīng Lìbō: Dāngrán xiànzài qù, wǒ gēn nǐ yìqǐ qù. Jīntiān tiānqì hěn lěng,

你要多穿点儿衣服。
nǐ yào duō chuān diǎnr yīfu.

生词 New Words 2-08-02

1. 快	kuài	Adv/A	quickly / quick 快来 快说 很快 快点儿
2. 起床	qǐchuáng	VO	to get up 快起床 六点起床
床	chuáng	N	bed 一张床
3. 每	měi	Pr	each; every 每天 每年 每个人
4. 运动	yùndòng	V	to do sports; to take exercise 去运动
5. 为什么	wèi shénme	QPr	why 为什么还不起床 为什么不去
6. 可是	kěshì	Conj	but
7. 头	tóu	N	head
8. 疼	téng	A	painful 头疼 哪儿疼
9. 对不起	duìbuqǐ	V	(to be) sorry
10. 舒服	shūfu	A	comfortable 很舒服 不舒服
11. 没关系	méi guānxi	IE	it doesn't matter; never mind

12.	嗓子	sǎngzi	N	throat　嗓子疼　嗓子不好
13.	有（一）点儿	yǒu (yì) diǎnr	Adv	somewhat; a little　有点儿累　有点儿疼　有点儿忙 有点儿小　有点儿着急
14.	应该	yīnggāi	OpV	should; ought to　应该做　应该知道　应该学习 应该试一下　不应该去
	该	gāi	OpV	should　该做　该去　不该去
15.	医院	yīyuàn	N	hospital　去医院　大医院
16.	看病	kànbìng	VO	to see a doctor　去看病　去医院看病
	病	bìng	N/V	illness / to be sick　有病　没有病
17.	身体	shēntǐ	N	body; health　身体很好　身体没问题　身体不太好
18.	睡觉	shuìjiào	VO	to sleep; to go to bed　想睡觉　快去睡觉
	睡	shuì	V	to sleep　想睡一会儿
19.	能	néng	OpV	can; to be able to　能八点起床　能参加　恐怕不能来
20.	上课	shàngkè	VO	to go to class　不能上课　几点上课
21.	还是	háishi	Conj	(used in a choice-type question) or　睡觉还是起床 现在去还是下午去
22.	天气	tiānqì	N	weather　天气很好　好天气
23.	冷	lěng	A	cold　天气很冷　有点儿冷
24.	穿	chuān	V	to wear (clothing); to put on　穿衣服　多穿点儿衣服 穿衬衫　穿牛仔裤

注释　Notes

① 快起床！

Get up soon!

"kuài 快 + verb (phrase)" expresses urging someone to do something, such as "kuài lái 快来" (come quickly) and "kuài shuō 快说" (hurry up and tell me/us).

② 你每天早上都六点去运动。

You go exercise at six o'clock every morning.

When "měi 每" modifies a noun, it usually requires a measure word such as "měi ge xuésheng 每个学生" (every student) and "měi jīn píngguǒ 每斤苹果" (every *jin* of apples).

However, when "每" modifies "tiān 天" (day) or "nián 年" (year), it cannot take a measure word, for example, "měi tiān 每天" (every day) and "měi nián 每年" (every year).

In addition, when "每" modifies "yuè 月" (month) or "xīngqī 星期" (week), it may or may not take a measure word, such as "měi ge yuè 每个月" or "měi yuè 每月" (every month), or "měi ge xīngqī 每个星期" or "měi xīngqī 每星期" (every week).

The word "每" is often used with "dōu 都" (both; all). For example,

Tā měi tiān dōu qù túshūguǎn.
（1）他 每 天 都 去 图书馆。 He goes to the library every day.

Tā měi ge yuè dōu huí jiā.
（2）她 每 个 月 都 回家。 She goes home every month.

③ 今天为什么九点还不起床？

It's already nine o'clock; why haven't you gotten up yet today?

The adverb "hái 还" (still), other than the meaning "in addition", is often put before an adjective or a verb expressing an ongoing state of being. For example,

Wǎnshang shí'èr diǎn tā bú shuìjiào, yī diǎn tā hái bú shuìjiào.
（1）晚上 十二 点 她不 睡觉，一点 她还 不 睡觉。
She was not sleeping at 12 midnight and at one o'clock she was still not asleep.

Tā bàba hěn máng, Xīngqītiān hái gōngzuò.
（2）他爸爸很 忙， 星期天 还 工作。 His father is very busy and is still working on Sunday.

Wǒ gēge xiànzài hái méi yǒu háizi.
（3）我 哥哥 现在 还 没 有 孩子。 By now, my elder brother still does not have a child yet.

Zuótiān hěn lěng, jīntiān hái hěn lěng.
（4）昨天 很 冷，今天 还 很 冷。 Yesterday was cold, and today it is still cold.

Note:

The negative adverb "bù 不" or verb "yǒu 有 / méi yǒu 没有" must be placed after "还" as we see in examples (1) and (3) above.

An interrogative sentence with the question pronoun "wèi shénme 为什么" is often used to ask the reason for something. For example,

Mǎ Dàwéi wèi shénme bù lái shàngkè?
（1）马 大为 为 什么 不来 上课？
Why hasn't Ma Dawei come to class?

–Tā tóu téng.
——他头 疼。
– He has a headache.

Lín Nà wèi shénme bú qù kàn diànyǐng?
（2）林 娜 为 什么 不去 看 电影？
Why didn't Lin Na go to watch the movie?

–Tā tèbié máng.
——她特别 忙。
– She was particularly busy.

④ 对不起，我不知道你不舒服。

Sorry, I didn't know that you were not feeling well.

"nǐ bù shūfu 你不舒服" is a subject-predicate phrase used as the object of the verb "zhīdào 知道" in the sentence.

⑤ 我嗓子也有点儿疼。

My throat is a bit sore, too.

When "yǒu (yì) diǎnr 有（一）点儿" ("一" is often omitted) is placed before an adjective or verb as an adverbial, it expresses a certain degree. When it is before an adjective, it often carries the meaning of "unsatisfactory" or being negative. For example, "yǒudiǎnr bù gāoxìng 有点儿不高兴" (to be a little unhappy), and "yǒudiǎnr lèi 有点儿累" (to be a little tired).

Note:

The usages of "yǒu yìdiǎnr 有一点儿" and "yìdiǎnr 一点儿" are different. "有一点儿" is used as an adverbial modifying an adjective or a verb. "一点儿" is used as a modifier of a noun. For example, "yìdiǎnr cǎoméi 一点儿草莓" (some strawberries), "yìdiǎnr qián 一点儿钱" (some money), and "yìdiǎnr yào 一点儿药" (some medicine). "一点儿 + noun" is often placed after a verb and acts as the object. For example, "Wǒ qù mǎi yìdiǎnr dōngxi. 我去买一点儿东西。" (I am going to buy something). "一点儿" cannot replace "有一点儿". For example,

Tā yǒudiǎnr bù gāoxìng.
（1）他 有点儿 不 高兴。（We can't say "＊他一点儿不高兴。"）
　　　He is a little unhappy.

Wǒ yǒudiǎnr tóu téng.
（2）我 有点儿 头 疼。（We can't say "＊我一点儿头疼。"）
　　　I have a slight headache.

⑥ 我身体没问题。

I am fine.

The word "shēntǐ 身体" refers to the human body and also one's health. "Nǐ shēntǐ zěnmeyàng? 你身体怎么样？" (How are you?) is also a greeting among friends.

⑦ 我跟你一起去。

I will go with you.

When the prepositional construction "gēn 跟 + pronoun / noun phrase" is placed before a verb as an adverbial, it is often used with "yìqǐ 一起" (together). "跟 + pronoun / noun phrase + 一起 + verb phrase" expresses to do something with someone. For example,

Lìbō gēn Dàwéi yìqǐ qù yīyuàn.
（1）力波跟 大为一起去 医院。Libo went to the hospital with Dawei.

Lín Nà gēn Sòng Huá yìqǐ liànxí kǒuyǔ.
（2）林 娜 跟 宋 华一起练习 口语。Lin Na practiced spoken Chinese with Song Hua.

（二） 2-08-03

(In the hospital)

丁力波： 你 在 这儿 等 一下， 我 去 给 你 挂号。
Dīng Lìbō: Nǐ zài zhèr děng yíxià, wǒ qù gěi nǐ guàhào.

马大为： 好。
Mǎ Dàwéi: Hǎo.

丁力波： 请问， 头疼、 嗓子疼 应该 挂 什么 科？
Dīng Lìbō: Qǐngwèn, tóu téng、 sǎngzi téng yīnggāi guà shénme kē?

护士： 挂 内科。
Hùshi: Guà nèikē.

丁力波： 内科 在 一 层 还是 二 层？
Dīng Lìbō: Nèikē zài yī céng háishi èr céng?

护士： 在 二 层。
Hùshi: Zài èr céng.

> 挂号
> Registering in a hospital

＊＊＊＊＊＊＊＊＊＊＊＊＊＊＊＊＊＊＊＊＊

医生： 你 哪儿 不 舒服？①
Yīshēng: Nǐ nǎr bù shūfu?

马大为： 我头疼，嗓子疼，全身都不舒服。
Mǎ Dàwéi: Wǒ tóu téng, sǎngzi téng, quánshēn dōu bù shūfu.

陈述病情
Talking about one's health

医生： 先 量一下体温吧。
Yīshēng: Xiān liáng yíxià tǐwēn ba.

马大为： 大夫， 多少度？
Mǎ Dàwéi: Dàifu, duōshao dù?

医生： 38 度 4。我看一下嗓子。你嗓子有点儿发炎，②
Yīshēng: 38 dù 4. Wǒ kàn yíxià sǎngzi. Nǐ sǎngzi yǒudiǎnr fāyán,

去验一下血吧。
qù yàn yíxià xiě ba.

(The doctor reads the result of a blood test.)

马大为： 要不要打针？
Mǎ Dàwéi: Yào bu yào dǎzhēn?

医生： 不用打针。你要多喝水，多休息。
Yīshēng: Búyòng dǎzhēn. Nǐ yào duō hē shuǐ, duō xiūxi.

看病
Treating an illness

你可以吃中药吗？
Nǐ   kěyǐ chī zhōngyào ma?

马大为： 可以， 听说中药不错。
Mǎ Dàwéi: Kěyǐ, tīngshuō zhōngyào búcuò.

医生： 好， 你先吃一点儿中药， 下星期一再来。
Yīshēng: Hǎo, nǐ xiān chī yìdiǎnr zhōngyào, xià Xīngqīyī zài lái.

马大为： 谢谢大夫。
Mǎ Dàwéi: Xièxie   dàifu.

医生： 不用谢。
Yīshēng: Búyòng xiè.

生词 New Words 🔊 2-08-04

| 1. | 在 | zài | Prep | at, in, on 在这儿等我 在宿舍学习 |
| 2. | 挂号 | guàhào | VO | to register (in a hospital) 给你挂号 |

	挂	guà	V	to register (in a hospital)　挂什么号　挂一个号
3.	科	kē	N	department　什么科　挂什么科
4.	内科	nèikē	N	department of internal medicine　挂内科　看内科 内科医生
	内	nèi	N	internal; inside　办公楼内　医院内
5.	层	céng	M	floor　一层　二层　十层
6.	全身	quánshēn	N	the whole body; all over　全身不舒服　全身疼
	全	quán	A	whole; complete; total　全校　全班　全家
7.	量	liáng	V	to measure　量衣服
8.	体温	tǐwēn	N	body temperature　量体温
9.	大夫	dàifu	N	doctor　王大夫　女大夫　内科大夫
10.	度	dù	M	degree　37度　38度4　多少度
11.	发炎	fāyán	VO	to be inflamed　嗓子发炎　有点儿发炎
12.	验血	yànxiě	VO	to have a blood test　验一下血
	血	xiě	N	blood
13.	打针	dǎzhēn	VO	to give an injection; to get a shot　不想打针 要不要打针
	针	zhēn	N	injection　打一针　打几针
14.	不用	búyòng	Adv	no need　不用打针　不用验血
15.	水	shuǐ	N	water　喝水　多喝水
16.	休息	xiūxi	V	to rest; to take a break　多休息　休息一下　休息一会儿 不用休息
17.	中药	zhōngyào	N	traditional Chinese medicine　吃中药　买中药
	药	yào	N	medicine　吃药　吃点儿药　买药

注释 Notes

① 你哪儿不舒服？

Where do you feel sick? (What's wrong with you?)
This is a common question that a doctor asks a patient.

② 你嗓子有点儿发炎。

Your throat is a bit inflamed.

三、语言点 LANGUAGE POINTS

1 核心句 Key Sentences

2-08-05

1. 今天（你）为什么九点还不起床？
2. 你应该去医院看病。
3. 现在去还是下午去？
4. 今天天气很冷，你要多穿点儿衣服。
5. 你在这儿等一下。
6. 我头疼，嗓子疼，全身都不舒服。
7. 你嗓子有点儿发炎。
8. 不用打针。
9. （你）明天还不能上课。

2 语法 Grammar

1. 主谓谓语句 A sentence with a subject-predicate phrase as the predicate

This type of sentence, at the first level, is composed of a subject (subject$_1$) and a predicate (predicate$_1$). The predicate itself, at the second level, is also composed of a subject (subject$_2$) and a predicate (predicate$_2$). Subject$_2$ under predicate$_1$ is often one part or one aspect of the subject (subject$_1$) of the whole sentence.

In the negative form, the adverb "bù 不" is placed at the second level. The question with verb/adjective-not-verb/adjective also occurs at the second level.

Subject$_1$ (Topic)	Predicate$_1$ (Comment)	
	Subject$_2$	Predicate$_2$
马大为	头	疼。
他	全身	都不舒服。
你	身体	好吗？
宋华	学习	怎么样？
今天	天气	冷不冷？
这个	汉语	怎么说？

Exercise I   Following the example, put the words and phrases in order to form sentences.

Example　马大为　疼　头 → 马大为头疼。

（1）陈老师　很好　身体 → _____。

（2）林娜　很不错　汉语 → _____。

（3）昨天　有点儿冷　天气 → _____。

（4）很忙　我爸爸　工作 → _____。

Exercise II   Following the example, change the form of the sentences.

Example　他头疼。→ 他头不疼。→ 他头疼不疼？

（1）马大为嗓子疼。→ _____。 → _____？

（2）今天天气很冷。→ _____。 → _____？

（3）他学习很好。→ _____。 → _____？

（4）我妈妈工作很忙。→ _____。 → _____？

2. 选择疑问句　An interrogative sentence with a choice-type question

An interrogative sentence with a choice-type question uses "háishi 还是" (or) to connect choice A and choice B. The responder needs to choose A or B.

Question			Response (choice A or B)
Choice A	还是	Choice B	
现在去	还是	下午去？	现在去。（choice A）
内科在一层	还是	二层？	在二层。（choice B）
你是老师	还是	学生？	我是学生。（choice B）
她学习汉语	还是	学习英语？	她学习汉语。（choice A）

Exercise I   Complete the sentences following the example.

Example　我们现在去还是明天去？（现在去 / 明天去）

（1）我们_____？（下午去 / 晚上去）

（2）银行在_____？（二层 / 三层）

（3）大为要_____？（买苹果 / 买巧克力）

（4）林娜晚上_____？（练习口语 / 看电影）

Exercise II　Match the phrases on the left with the phrases on the right.

他是老师		宿舍楼？
你买牛仔裤		看外科（wàikē, surgical department）？
宋华上午有课	还是	学生？
马大为看内科		下午有课？
这是教学楼		买羽绒服？

3. 连动句（1）：表示目的　A sentence with serial verbs (1): Expressing a purpose

In a sentence with serial verbs (1), the subject has two serial verbs or verb phrases as the predicate. The sequence of the two verbs is set. Verb$_2$ explains the purpose of verb$_1$. The negative adverb "bù 不" is usually placed before verb$_1$.

$$\text{Subject} + \text{Verb}_1 \text{ (Object}_1) + \text{Verb}_2 \text{ (Object}_2)$$

Subject	Predicate		
	Adverbial	Verb$_1$ (Object$_1$)	Verb$_2$ (Object$_2$)
马大为		去医院	看病。
他	下午　不	回学校	运动。
你们	明天	去不去超市	买苹果？

Note:

When there is an optative verb in a sentence, the negative adverb "不" should be placed before the optative verb. For example,

　　Nǐ bù yīnggāi qù fànguǎn chī fàn.
（1）你 不 应该 去 饭馆 吃 饭。You should not eat in a restaurant.

　　Nǐ bù néng zài zhèr xī yān.
（2）你 不 能 在这儿吸 烟。You cannot smoke here.

Exercise I　Substitute the underlined parts and complete the dialogues.

A：你现在去哪儿？

B：我现在回学校。

A：你回学校做什么？

B：我回学校上课。

去超市　　买咖啡
去朋友家　参加生日聚会
回家　　　看妈妈

Exercise II　Following the example, put the words and phrases in order to form sentences.

Example　马大为　看病　去医院 → 马大为去医院看病。

（1）挂号　我们　去二层 → _____。

（2）我　学习　去图书馆 → _____。

（3）去饭馆　丁力波　吃饭 → _____。

（4）回家　我　睡觉 → _____。

4. 能愿动词谓语句（2）：应该、要、能　A sentence with an optative verb (2): "yīnggāi 应该" (should), "yào 要" (need; to want), and "néng 能" (can; to be able to)

The optative verb "应该" expresses "it is necessary to do something".

Subject	Predicate	
	Optative Verb	Verb-Object
马大为	应该	去医院看病。
你	不应该	买那件很贵的衬衫。

Exercise I　Based on the hints, complete the sentences using "yīnggāi 应该" or "bù yīnggāi 不应该".

（1）你嗓子有点儿发炎，_____。（医院　打针）

（2）今天天气很冷，你_____。（穿　衣服）

（3）你明天有很多课，今天晚上_____。（去　看电影）

（4）现在是早上九点，_____。（睡觉）

Exercise II Following the example, put the words and phrases in order to form sentences.

> Example 应该 你 休息 多 → <u>你应该多休息</u>。

（1）吃 应该 马大为 中药 一点儿 → _____。

（2）大家 练习 应该 口语 → _____。

（3）咖啡 多喝 你们 应该 不 → _____。

（4）祝 应该 生日 我们 林娜 快乐 → _____。

The optative verb "要" often expresses "need to do something". The negative form is "búyòng 不用" (no need). For example,

Subject	Predicate	
	Optative Verb	Verb-Object
马大为	要不要	验血？
马大为	不用	验血。
我	要	给他女儿买礼物吗？
你	要	给她买点儿巧克力。

Exercise I Following the example, change the form of the sentences.

> Example 他要打针。→ <u>他不用打针。</u> → <u>他要不要打针？</u>

（1）这孩子要验血。→ _____。→ _____？

（2）我朋友要量体温。→ _____。→ _____？

（3）那个同学要吃中药。→ _____。→ _____？

（4）我们要参加聚会。→ _____。→ _____？

Exercise II Complete the dialogues based on the context.

（1）A：_____？

　　B：要去医院。

（2）A：_____？

　　B：要验血。

（3）A：要不要去医院看病？

　　B：_____，我跟你一起去。

（4）A：要不要打针？

　　B：_____，先吃点儿药吧。

The optative verb "能" often expresses the meaning of "can; to be able to". The negative form is "bù néng 不能" (cannot; to be unable to).

Subject	Predicate		
	Adverbial	Optative Verb	Verb-Object
大为	明天	能	上课吗？
我	晚上	不能	来学校。
小云	星期六	能	参加聚会吗？

Exercise I　Substitute the underlined parts and complete the dialogues.

（1）A：明天你有没有时间？

　　B：什么事儿？

　　A：明天你能不能来学校？

　　B：我能来学校。

参加生日聚会
教我汉字
去陆雨平家喝茶

（2）A：星期天你能不能去我家？

　　B：不好意思，星期天我特别忙。

　　　我不能去你家。

去唱歌
去看电影
跟我一起去超市

Exercise II　Complete the dialogues based on the context.

（1）A：_____？

　　B：星期天我能去参加聚会。

（2）A：你今天能来上课吗？

　　B：对不起，_____。

（3）A：你现在能不能来一下？

　　　B：_____。

（4）A：_____？

　　　B：星期六我能跟你们去跳舞。

5. 介词结构（2）：在 + 代词 / 名词　The prepositional construction (2): "zài 在" (in/on/ at) + Pronoun/Noun

The word "在" is a verb as well as a preposition. The preposition "在" followed by a noun or a phrase, which is usually a place word, forms a prepositional construction. It is placed before the verbal predicate, indicating the place where the action happens.

Subject	Predicate		Verb / Verb Phrase
	Preposition 在 + Pronoun/Noun		
你	在	这儿	等一下。
她爸爸	在	哪儿	工作？
她爸爸	在	医院	工作。
张老师	不　在	我们班	上课。

Exercise I　Substitute the underlined parts and complete the dialogues.

A：你在哪儿工作？

B：我在北京工作。

学习汉语　　北京大学
休息　　　　咖啡厅
吃饭　　　　食堂
买衬衫　　　超市

Exercise II　Following the example, put the words and phrases in order to form sentences.

Example　中国　汉语　我　学习　在 → 我在中国学习汉语。

（1）医院　我　在　工作　妈妈 → _____。

（2）林娜　汉字　宿舍　在　写 → _____。

（3）常常　我　苹果　在　这儿　买 → _____。

（4）等　在　你　哪儿　马大为 → _____？

四、练习与运用 *PRACTICE AND APPLICATION*

补充词语 Supplementary Words　2-08-06

1.	眼睛	yǎnjing	N	eye　大眼睛　眼睛小
2.	牙	yá	N	tooth　牙疼
3.	胃	wèi	N	stomach　胃不舒服
4.	脖子	bózi	N	neck
5.	胳膊	gēbo	N	arm
6.	腰	yāo	N	lower back; waist
7.	腿	tuǐ	N	leg
8.	发烧	fāshāo	VO	to have a fever　有点儿发烧　不发烧
9.	拉肚子	lā dùzi	V O	to have loose bowels; to have diarrhea　不拉肚子
10.	感冒	gǎnmào	V	to have a cold　有点儿感冒
11.	急诊	jízhěn	N	emergency　挂急诊
12.	外科	wàikē	N	surgical department
13.	西药	xīyào	N	Western medicine　吃西药
14.	透视	tòushì	V	to have an X-ray exam　要不要透视
15.	针灸	zhēnjiǔ	N	acupuncture and moxibustion　要针灸　不用针灸
16.	大便	dàbiàn	N	feces, stool　化验大便
17.	小便	xiǎobiàn	N	urine　化验小便

1 语音练习 Pronunciation Drills　2-08-07

Listen and read aloud: Add tone marks to the following words and sentences, and then read them aloud.

❶ tou teng　　　❷ sangzi　　　❸ qichuang

❹ shuijiao　　　❺ quanshen　　　❻ shufu

❼ yanxie　　　❽ daifu

❾ Wo tou teng, sangzi teng, quanshen dou bu shufu.

❿ Ni sangzi youdianr fayan, yan yixia xie ba.

2 会话练习 Conversation Practice

Pair activity: Create dialogues based on the scenes and the requirements below.

1. Asking about one's health

Based on the information in the pictures, ask and answer questions.

Example

A：你哪儿不舒服？

B：我牙疼。

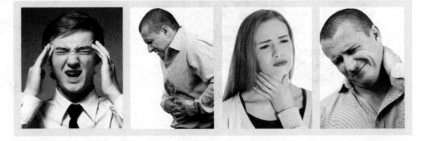

2. Expressing a need

Based on the context and the prompts, complete the dialogues.

（1）马大为：力波，你每天晚上都十点半睡觉，今天为什么十一点半还不睡觉？

　　丁力波：我肚子有点儿疼。

　　马大为：_____？（要不要……）

　　丁力波：我不想去医院。

　　马大为：你不去医院看病，明天可能不能上课。

　　丁力波：好吧。你跟我一起去，好吗？

　　马大为：好的。晚上很冷，你_____。（应该……）

（2）王小云：妈妈，我嗓子有点儿疼。

　　妈妈：你_____？（要不要……）

　　王小云：不用。我不喜欢吃药。

　　妈妈：你_____。（应该……）

　　王小云：好吧。水在哪儿？我去喝水。

3. Visiting a doctor

Based on the scenes in the pictures and the context, complete the dialogues.

（1）

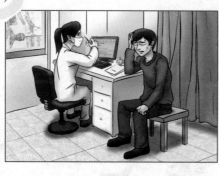

大夫：_____？

宋华：我头疼。

大夫：先量一下体温吧。

宋华：_____？

大夫：37度9，有点儿发烧。

- -

（2）

大夫：_____？

老人：我嗓子有点儿疼。

大夫：_____？

老人：不发烧。

大夫：我看一下嗓子。嗓子有点儿发

　　　炎。_____？

老人：我可以吃中药。

大夫：好的。你先吃点儿中药，下周

　　　三再来。

- -

（3）

　大夫：你哪儿不舒服？

陆雨平：她_____。

　大夫：_____？

陆雨平：拉肚子。

　大夫：先验一下大便，再验一下血吧。

(The doctor reads the result of a stool test.)

陆雨平：大夫，_____？

　大夫：要打针，还要吃一点儿药。

4. Urging someone to do something

Based on the scene in the picture, complete the dialogue.

A: _____

B: _____

5. Apologizing

Based on the scenes in the pictures, complete the dialogue.

A: _____

B: _____

3 听后复述 Listening and Repeating 🔊 2-08-08

Listen to the following dialogues and repeat what you hear.

（1）A：你每天晚上几点回家？

B：七点半回家。

A：你在学校食堂吃晚饭还是回家吃晚饭？

B：我回家吃晚饭。

（2）A：明天我们有个聚会，你能参加吗？

B：我很想参加，可是今天晚上我去上海。真对不起。

A：没关系。

（3）A：你认识她吗？

　　B：认识。她是我同学。

　　A：她怎么样？

　　B：她学习很好，汉语不错，眼睛很大，人也很漂亮。

　　A：谢谢你的介绍。

4 阅读理解 Reading Comprehension

I

　　马大为每天都六点起床去运动，今天九点还没起床。他想起床，可是头很疼，嗓子也有点儿疼。丁力波跟他一起去医院看病。头疼应该挂内科，内科在二层。医生给他量体温，他的体温是38度4，嗓子也有点儿发炎。医生说不用打针，要多喝水，还要吃点儿中药。下星期一大为再去医院。

Answer the following questions:

（1）马大为身体怎么样？

（2）他的体温是多少度？

（3）他要不要打针？

II

　　王小云每天早上七点起床去上课，可是今天早上她不能去上课。她头疼，嗓子也疼，全身都不舒服。她妈妈跟她一起去友谊医院（Yǒuyì Yīyuàn）看病，她妈妈的朋友张大夫在那儿工作。友谊医院就在她们家旁边。张大夫说小云的体温是37度8，嗓子也有点儿发炎。她说小云不用打针，可是要吃点儿西药和中药，还要多喝水，多休息。她还说天气冷，小云应该多运动。

Answer the following questions:

（1）小云每天几点起床去上课？她今　　（4）谁在友谊医院工作？
　　　天能去上课吗？

　　　　　　　　　　　　　　　　　　（5）友谊医院在哪儿？
（2）她今天哪儿不舒服？

　　　　　　　　　　　　　　　　　　（6）小云要不要打针？要不要吃药？
（3）谁跟小云一起去医院看病？

　　　　　　　　　　　　　　　　　　（7）张大夫说天气冷，小云应该做什么？

5 任务与活动 Task and Activity

1. Role-play

Lin Qiang, Lin Na's elder brother, had a stiff neck. Lin Na took him to the hospital. Dr. Chen at the hospital knew Lin Na and suggested that Lin Qiang try acupuncture and moxibustion. Lin Qiang was afraid and did not want to try it. Lin Na told him not to be afraid. When she had a stiff neck before, Dr. Chen applied acupuncture and moxibustion and they were very beneficial. Lin Qiang agreed. After the acupuncture and moxibustion therapy, his neck no longer hurt.

In groups of three, one person will play Lin Qiang, one person Lin Na, and the other person Dr. Chen. Create a dialogue based on the sentence patterns below. You may also use some other patterns that you have previously learned.

> 我……疼。/ 你应该……。/ 跟……一起去。/ 我去给你挂号。/ 给你介绍一下，
> 这是……。/ 这是我哥哥，他叫……。/ 你哪儿不舒服？ / 要不要……？ / 给
> 他做针灸。/ 不想……。/ ……，还……。

2. Interview

Refer to the following questions and interview one of your Chinese friends.

（1）你身体怎么样？ 你每天都运动吗？

（2）你学习什么专业？ 你学习怎么样？

（3）你家里有几口人？ 你爸爸 / 妈妈做什么工作？ 他 / 她工作忙不忙？

6 写作练习 Writing Exercise

Based on the requirements and prompts below, write a short passage about an experience of taking your family member or friend to see a doctor in a hospital.

Your writing should cover:
(1) Persuading the family member or friend to go to a hospital;
(2) Procedures of registering in a hospital;
(3) Conversation with the doctor.

Prompts:

> （1）我……疼。/ 你应该……。/ 跟……一起去。
>
> （2）……疼挂什么科？ / ……科在几层？
>
> （3）你哪儿不舒服？ / 量体温 / 验血 / 吃药 / 打针……

五、汉字 *CHINESE CHARACTERS*

1 汉字知识 Knowledge about Chinese Characters

Locating Chinese characters in a dictionary based on pīnyīn

In many Chinese dictionaries, the entries are arranged alphabetically according to "Hànyǔ pīnyīn 汉语拼音". The "Xīnhuá Zìdiǎn《新华字典》" (*Xinhua Dictionary*) and the "Xiàndài Hànyǔ Cídiǎn《现代汉语词典》" (*Modern Chinese Dictionary*), the two most commonly used dictionaries, are arranged in this way. When the standard Chinese pronunciation of a character is known, it is easy to locate a character by using "pīnyīn 拼音".

2 汉字偏旁 Chinese Radicals

Radical	Name	Stroke Order	No. of Strokes	Example	Explanation
疒	病字头	丶 一 广 广 疒	5	病 bìng (illness) 疼 téng (painful)	Related to "illness"
月	肉月旁	丿 刀 月 月	4	脖 bó (neck) 肚 dù (belly) 腰 yāo (lower back; waist)	Related to "flesh"
目	目字旁	丨 冂 冃 目 目	5	睡 shuì (to sleep) 看 kàn (to look)	Related to "eye"
广	广字头	丶 一 广	3	床 chuáng (bed) 度 dù (degree) 应 yīng (should)	Related to "shelter"

3 认写基本汉字 Learn and Write the Basic Chinese Characters

（1）头　　丶 丶 二 头 头
tóu　　head　　　　　　　　　　5 strokes

（2）身　　丿 亻 冂 乃 冎 身 身
shēn　　body　　　　　　　　　　7 strokes

（3）牙 一 二 于 牙
yá tooth 4 strokes

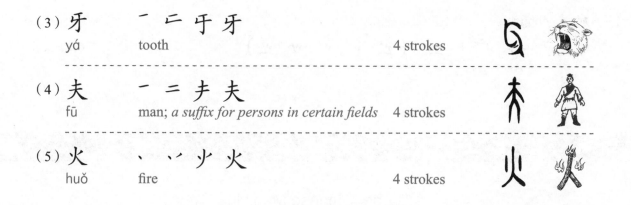

（4）夫 一 二 弌 夫
fū man; *a suffix for persons in certain fields* 4 strokes

（5）火 丶 丷 少 火
huǒ fire 4 strokes

4 认写课文中的汉字 Learn and Write the Chinese Characters in the Text

（1）疼 téng

疼 —— 疒 + 冬（冬:丿 ㄅ 夂 冬 冬） 10 strokes

（2）看病 kànbìng

病 —— 疒 + 丙（丙:一 厂 冂 丙 丙） 10 strokes

（3）肚子 dùzi

肚 —— 月 + 土 7 strokes

（4）睡觉 shuìjiào

睡 —— 目 + 垂（垂:丿 一 千 壬 乑 乑 垂 垂） 13 strokes

（5）穿 chuān

穿 —— 穴 + 牙 9 strokes

（6）发炎 fāyán

炎 —— 火 + 火 8 strokes

（7）起床 qǐchuáng

床 —— 广 + 木 7 strokes

（8）度 dù

度 —— 广 + 廿（廿:一 十 廿 廿）+ 又 9 strokes

（9）应该 yīnggāi

应 → 广 + 㡌 （㡌：丶 丷 丷 㡌）   7 strokes

六、文化知识 *CULTURAL KNOWLEDGE*

Traditional Chinese Medicine

Chinese medicine refers to traditional Chinese medicine (TCM). It is a medical science based on Chinese philosophy. The major diagnostic methods are: "wàng 望" (observing), "wén 闻" (listening and smelling), "wèn 问" (inquiring), and "qiè 切" (pulse feeling and palpation). The most common methods for treating illnesses are traditional Chinese medicine, herbs, acupuncture, moxibustion, *tuina* massage (a form of Chinese manipulative therapy), cupping, scraping, etc. There were many distinguished doctors in Chinese

history, such as "Biǎn Què 扁鹊" (c. 407 – 310 BCE), "Zhāng Zhòngjǐng 张仲景" (c. 150 – c. 219), "Lǐ Shízhēn 李时珍" (1518 – 1593), and so on. "李时珍" was a famous doctor in the Ming Dynasty (1368 – 1644).《Běncǎo Gāngmù (本草纲目)》(*The Compendium of Materia Medica*) written by him is a comprehensive work of pharmacognosy in ancient China.

TCM has been used by Chinese doctors for thousands of years. TCM and Western medicine differ in that the former does not use artificially created chemicals but uses essences from natural substances. Traditional Chinese remedies can be divided into three categories according to their sources: medicines from plants, animals, and minerals. TCM is effective in preventing and curing many diseases. With the advancement of the modernization of TCM, more and more people in the world are benefiting from it.

七、自我评估 *SELF-EVALUATION*

I can basically do the following things in Chinese:

☐ I can urge someone to do something.

☐ I can express something that I have to do.

☐ I can express something that I may do.

☐ I can ask about a person's health.

☐ I can register in a hospital.

☐ I can describe my illness to a doctor.

趣味汉语 Fun with Chinese

Chinese Proverbs about Health

Fàn hòu bǎi bù zǒu, huódào jiǔshíjiǔ.

1. 饭 后 百 步 走，活 到 九 十 九。

Jīnrì bù yǎngshēng, míngrì bì yǎng bìng.

2. 今日不 养生， 明日必 养 病。

Xiào yi xiào, shí nián shào; chóu yi chóu, báile tóu.

3. 笑 一 笑， 十 年 少；愁 一 愁， 白 了 头。

(1) Walk hundreds of steps after meals, and you will live as long as 99.

(2) Neglect your health today, and you'll treat your illness tomorrow.

(3) Smiles make one young, and worries make one old.

Tiānqì liángkuai le

天气凉快了

It's getting cool

Having studied this lesson, you can talk with your friends about the seasons, changes in the weather, family activities at different times of the year, and travel arrangements. You will see how people in Beijing use public transportation.

一、热身 WARM-UP

1 思考 Think

Think about the following questions:

(1) In your country, how many seasons are there in a year? How is the weather in every season?

(2) Which is your favorite season? In this season, what do you like to do?

(3) If you go on a short trip within your city, what means of transportation is your first choice? Can you tell us why?

2 活动 Activity

Based on the situation in your country, list the ways you get around your city from the most to the least popular.

bicycle

bus

taxi

private car

motorcycle

subway

skateboard

Popularity:

_____ > _____ > _____ > _____ > _____ > _____ > _____

二、课文 TEXT

（一）  2-09-01

(Ma Dawei and Wang Xiaoyun are talking in the park.)

马大为：今天天气真好啊！①
Mǎ Dàwéi:　Jīntiān　tiānqì　zhēn hǎo　a!

王小云：是啊，现在是秋天了，天气凉快了。
Wáng Xiǎoyún:　Shì　a,　xiànzài　shì　qiūtiān　le,　tiānqì　liángkuai le.

马大为：今天空气也特别好。
Mǎ Dàwéi:　Jīntiān　kōngqì　yě　tèbié　hǎo.

王小云：秋天是北京最好的季节。②
Wáng Xiǎoyún:　Qiūtiān　shì　Běijīng　zuì　hǎo　de　jìjié.

> 谈论季节和天气
>
> Talking about the seasons and the weather

天气不冷，也不热，很舒服。
Tiānqì　bù lěng,　yě bú rè,　hěn shūfu.

马大为：北京的春天怎么样？
Mǎ Dàwéi:　Běijīng　de chūntiān zěnmeyàng?

王小云： 春天很暖和，可是常常刮风。在你们家乡，你
Wáng Xiǎoyún: Chūntiān hěn nuǎnhuo, kěshì chángcháng guā fēng. Zài nǐmen jiāxiāng, nǐ

最喜欢什么季节？
zuì xǐhuan shénme jìjié?

马大为： 我最喜欢春天。春天树都绿了，很漂亮。
Mǎ Dàwéi: Wǒ zuì xǐhuan chūntiān. Chūntiān shù dōu lù le, hěn piàoliang.

王小云： 夏天和冬天怎么样？
Wáng Xiǎoyún: Xiàtiān hé dōngtiān zěnmeyàng?

马大为： 夏天天气很热，常常下雨。冬天很冷，常常
Mǎ Dàwéi: Xiàtiān tiānqì hěn rè, chángcháng xià yǔ. Dōngtiān hěn lěng, chángcháng

下雪。
xià xuě.

王小云： 夏天你可以游泳，冬天你可以滑雪。多好啊！
Wáng Xiǎoyún: Xiàtiān nǐ kěyǐ yóuyǒng, dōngtiān nǐ kěyǐ huáxuě. Duō hǎo a!

马大为： 对。我特别喜欢游泳和滑雪。小云，你会滑
Mǎ Dàwéi: Duì. Wǒ tèbié xǐhuan yóuyǒng hé huáxuě. Xiǎoyún, nǐ huì huá-

雪吗？
xuě ma?

王小云： 以前我不会，现在刚学。我只会一点儿。
Wáng Xiǎoyún: Yǐqián wǒ bú huì, xiànzài gāng xué. Wǒ zhǐ huì yìdiǎnr.

马大为： 欢迎你来我的家乡，③ 我可以教你游泳和滑雪。
Mǎ Dàwéi: Huānyíng nǐ lái wǒ de jiāxiāng, wǒ kěyǐ jiāo nǐ yóuyǒng hé huáxuě.

王小云： 谢谢。今年冬天你回国吗？
Wáng Xiǎoyún: Xièxie. Jīnnián dōngtiān nǐ huí guó ma?

> 谈打算
> Talking about one's plans

马大为： 我想回国，可是（飞）机票太贵了。④
Mǎ Dàwéi: Wǒ xiǎng huí guó, kěshì (fēi)jīpiào tài guì le.

王小云： 没关系。你可以不坐飞机。
Wáng Xiǎoyún: Méi guānxi. Nǐ kěyǐ bú zuò fēijī.

马大为： 不坐飞机？我怎么回国？
Mǎ Dàwéi: Bú zuò fēijī? Wǒ zěnme huí guó?

王小云： 你会游泳，可以游泳啊！
Wáng Xiǎoyún: Nǐ huì yóuyǒng, kěyǐ yóuyǒng a!

生词 New Words 🔊 2-09-02

1.	秋天	qiūtiān	N	autumn; fall 北京的秋天
2.	了	le	Pt	*an aspect particle indicating something that has happened or a change* 大了 小了 秋天了
3.	凉快	liángkuai	A	cool 凉快的天气 很凉快
4.	空气	kōngqì	N	air 空气很好 空气不好
5.	最	zuì	Adv	most; to the highest degree 最好 最贵 最漂亮 最喜欢
6.	季节	jìjié	N	season 四个季节 哪个季节
7.	热	rè	A	hot 天气很热 有点儿热 我很热
8.	春天	chūntiān	N	spring 喜欢春天 春天了
9.	暖和	nuǎnhuo	A	warm 暖和的天气 很暖和
10.	刮风	guā fēng	V O	to be windy
	风	fēng	N	wind 大风
11.	家乡	jiāxiāng	N	hometown 我的家乡
12.	树	shù	N	tree 绿树 大树 树绿了
13.	夏天	xiàtiān	N	summer 很热的夏天 喜欢夏天
14.	冬天	dōngtiān	N	winter 很冷的冬天 喜欢冬天
15.	下雨	xià yǔ	V O	to rain
	雨	yǔ	N	rain 大雨 小雨
16.	下雪	xià xuě	V O	to snow
	雪	xuě	N	snow 下雪 下大雪
17.	游泳	yóuyǒng	VO	to swim 喜欢游泳 去游泳
18.	滑雪	huáxuě	VO	to ski 去滑雪 喜欢滑雪
19.	会	huì	OpV/V	can; to be able to / to have knowledge of 会滑雪 会说汉语 会一点儿
20.	以前	yǐqián	N	before; previously 以前不会 以前学英语
21.	(飞)机票	(fēi)jīpiào	N	airplane ticket 买飞机票
	飞机	fēijī	N	airplane
	票	piào	N	ticket 买票 电影票 一张票
22.	坐	zuò	V	to sit; to go/travel somewhere by means of 坐飞机 坐公共汽车

注释 Notes

① 今天天气真好啊！

It's really nice today!

We have learned "a 啊" at the end of a declarative sentence expressing affirmation, such as "Shì a. 是啊。" in Lesson 3. It is also used to urge someone to do something, such as "Nǐ yào duō chuān diǎnr yīfu a! 你要多穿点儿衣服啊！" (You need to put on more clothing!) In addition, when used at the end of a statement, "啊" can also express an exclamation, e.g., "Jīntiān tiānqì zhēn liángkuai a! 今天天气真凉快啊！" (It's really cool today!), "Tā de Hànzì zhēn piàoliang a! 她的汉字真漂亮啊！" (How nice her Chinese characters look!) The punctuation mark is usually an exclamation point (!).

② 秋天是北京最好的季节。

Autumn is the best season in Beijing.

The "zuì 最 + adjective" expresses the idea that someone or something exceeds everyone or everything else in the same category. For example, "Zuótiān zuì rè. 昨天最热。" (Yesterday was the hottest (hotter than any other days)), "Tā shì wǒ zuì xiǎo de dìdi. 他是我最小的弟弟。" (He is my youngest brother (younger than any other brothers)). "最" can also be put before some verbs about ideas expressing the superlative meaning. For example,

　　　　Mǎ Dàwéi zuì xǐhuan yóuyǒng.
（1）马 大为 最喜欢　游泳。Ma Dawei likes swimming the most.

　　　　Nǐ zuì bù xǐhuan shénme jìjié?
（2）你 最 不 喜欢　什么 季节？　Which season do you like the least?

　　　　Lín Nà zuì xiǎng kàn Běijīng de hútòng.
（3）林 娜 最 想　看 北京 的 胡同。Lin Na would like to see the *hútòng* in Beijing the most.

③ 欢迎你来我的家乡。

Welcome to my hometown.

④ 可是（飞）机票太贵了。

But the airplane ticket is too expensive.

The "tài 太 + adjective + le 了" expresses the meaning that the degree of the adjective is very high, exceeding the ordinary. If the nature of the adjective is negative, such as "tài guì le 太贵了" or "tài rè le 太热了", it expresses a mood of excessiveness and dissatisfaction. If the nature of the adjective is positive, such as "tài hǎo le 太好了" or "tài piàoliang le 太漂亮了", it expresses satisfaction and exclamation.

（二） 2-09-03

(On the weekend, Song Hua makes a date with Lin Na to see an art gallery.)

宋华:　听说博物馆有个很好的展览，咱们今天去看，
Sòng Huá:　Tīngshuō bówùguǎn yǒu ge hěn hǎo de zhǎnlǎn,　zánmen jīntiān qù kàn,

怎么样？
zěnmeyàng?

| 提活动建议 |
| Suggesting an activity |

林娜:　好啊。今天我也有时间了，① 咱们一起去看。
Lín Nà:　Hǎo a.　Jīntiān wǒ yě yǒu shíjiān le,　zánmen yìqǐ qù kàn.

现在几点了？
Xiànzài jǐ diǎn le?

| 问时间（2） |
| Asking about time (2) |

宋华:　快十点了。②
Sòng Huá:　Kuài shí diǎn le.

林娜:　咱们什么时候去？
Lín Nà:　Zánmen shénme shíhou qù?

宋华:　现在去，好吗？
Sòng Huá:　Xiànzài qù,　hǎo ma?

林娜： 现在？ 好吧。 博物馆在天安门， 咱们怎么去？ 我
Lín Nà: Xiànzài? Hǎo ba. Bówùguǎn zài Tiān'ān Mén, zánmen zěnme qù? Wǒ

朋友有车， 咱们能开车去吗？
péngyou yǒu chē, zánmen néng kāichē qù ma?

宋华： 我不会开车。 你呢？
Sòng Huá: Wǒ bú huì kāichē. Nǐ ne?

林娜： 我会开车。 可是我没有中国驾照， 在这儿不能
Lín Nà: Wǒ huì kāichē. Kěshì wǒ méi yǒu Zhōngguó jiàzhào, zài zhèr bù néng

开。 咱们打车去吧。
kāi. Zánmen dǎchē qù ba.

宋华： 现在路上可能堵车。 打车去可能很慢， 也不便宜。③
Sòng Huá: Xiànzài lùshang kěnéng dǔchē. Dǎchē qù kěnéng hěn màn, yě bù piányi.

咱们坐地铁和公共汽车， 怎么样？
Zánmen zuò dìtiě hé gōnggòng qìchē, zěnmeyàng?

> 讨论出行交通
> Talking about transportation

林娜： 好啊。 先坐地铁还是先坐公共汽车？
Lín Nà: Hǎo a. Xiān zuò dìtiě háishi xiān zuò gōnggòng qìchē?

宋华： 先坐961路公共汽车到苹果园。 在苹果园换地铁
Sòng Huá: Xiān zuò 961 lù gōnggòng qìchē dào Píngguǒyuán. Zài Píngguǒyuán huàn dìtiě

1号线到天安门。
1 hào xiàn dào Tiān'ān Mén.

林娜： 咱们几点能到？
Lín Nà: Zánmen jǐ diǎn néng dào?

宋华： 12点能到。 别着急。
Sòng Huá: 12 diǎn néng dào. Bié zháojí.

林娜： 我不着急， 可是我的肚子有点儿着急。
Lín Nà: Wǒ bù zháojí, kěshì wǒ de dùzi yǒudiǎnr zháojí.

宋华： 对， 我也饿了。 咱们可以先吃点儿点心。
Sòng Huá: Duì, wǒ yě è le. Zánmen kěyǐ xiān chī diǎnr diǎnxin.

生词 New Words  2-09-04

1.	博物馆	bówùguǎn	N	museum 去博物馆
2.	展览	zhǎnlǎn	V	to exhibit 在博物馆展览 看展览
3.	时候	shíhou	N	time; moment 什么时候 这时候
4.	车	chē	N	vehicle 坐车 有车 买车 卖车
5.	开车	kāichē	VO	to drive a car (or any type of vehicle) 会开车
	开	kāi	V	to drive
6.	驾照	jiàzhào	N	license 有驾照 我的驾照
7.	打车	dǎchē	VO	to take a taxi; (to go somewhere) by taxi
8.	路上	lùshang	N	on the way 路上车多 路上人少
9.	可能	kěnéng	OpV	may; maybe; (to be) possible 可能堵车 可能下雨
10.	堵车	dǔchē	VO	to be congested with traffic; to be in a traffic jam 路上堵车 堵车了
	堵	dǔ	V	to block 太堵了
11.	慢	màn	A	slow 很慢 有点儿慢
12.	地铁	dìtiě	N	subway 坐地铁
13.	公共汽车	gōnggòng qìchē	N	bus 坐公共汽车
	公共	gōnggòng	A	public
	汽车	qìchē	N	vehicle; car 坐汽车 开汽车
14.	路	lù	N	route; road 111 路公共汽车
15.	换	huàn	V	to transfer; to change 换地铁 换 56 路公共汽车
16.	线	xiàn	N	line; route 地铁线 1 号线
17.	饿	è	A	hungry 肚子饿 有点儿饿 很饿 饿了
18.	天安门	Tiān'ān Mén	PN	Tian'anmen
19.	苹果园	Píngguǒyuán	PN	Pingguoyuan (Apple Orchard, name of a subway station in Beijing)

注释 Notes

① 好啊。今天我也有时间了。

Good. I also have time today.

In a conversation, if the listener agrees with the speaker, the answer can be "hǎo 好", "hǎo de 好的", "hǎo a 好啊", or "hǎo ba 好吧". Generally speaking, "好" and "好的" only express agreement; "好啊" implies a pleasant agreement, whereas "好吧" may imply a brief hesitation because of the "ba 吧" ending that softens the adjective or suggests reservation.

Lin Na said "Jīntiān wǒ yě yǒu shíjiān le. 今天我也有时间了。" because last time when Song Hua made a date with her to see a movie, she did not have time.

② 快十点了。

It's almost 10 o'clock now.

③ 打车去可能很慢，也不便宜。

To go by taxi can be very slow, and not cheap, either.
The verb phrase "dǎchē qù 打车去" is the subject as well as the topic of this sentence. In Chinese, not only nouns or pronouns but also verbs, other parts of speech, or phrases can function as a subject.

三、语言点 LANGUAGE POINTS

1 核心句 Key Sentences 🔊 2-09-05

1. 现在是秋天了。
2. 天气凉快了。
3. 今天我也有时间了。
4. 现在几点了？
5. 今天天气真好啊！
6. 你最喜欢什么季节？
7. 咱们打车去吧。
8. 打车去可能很慢。
9. 咱们坐地铁和公共汽车，怎么样？
10. 飞机票太贵了。
11. 我会开车。可是我没有中国驾照，在这儿不能开。

2 语法 Grammar

1. 助词 "了" 在句尾（1）：表示情况的变化　The particle "le 了" at the end of a sentence (1): Expressing change of status

The particle "了" at the end of a sentence expresses a change in status or a new situation. This usage often appears in a sentence with an adjective or a noun as the predicate, as well as in a sentence using the verb "shì 是" (to be) or "yǒu 有" (to have; there is/are), etc.

Declarative Sentence	Question Ending with "ma 吗" (Whether status has changed)	Negative Sentence (No change in status)
天气凉快了。 (It was hot before.)	天气凉快了吗？	天气没有凉快。
树都绿了。 (It was not green before.)	树都绿了吗？	树没有绿。
现在是秋天了。 (It was summer before.)	现在是秋天了吗？	现在不是秋天。
今天我（也）有时间了。 (I did not have any time before.)	今天你有时间了吗？	今天我没有时间。

For whether or not a status has changed, we often use the question ending with "吗". If the status has not changed, we often use "méi yǒu 没有" (see the first, second, and fourth sentences above). If a sentence contains "是", the negative is "bú shì 不是" (see the third sentence above).

Exercise I　Substitute the underlined parts and complete the dialogues.

（1）A：你累不累？

　　B：我累了，我想休息。

饿	吃点心
渴	喝茶
困	睡觉

（2）A：现在是秋天了。

　　B：是啊，天气凉快了。

春天	暖和
夏天	热
十二月	冷

（3）A：现在几点了？

B：七点了，你快起床吧。

A：好吧。

8:00	去上课
12:00	去吃饭
23:00	睡觉

（4）A：你弟弟现在怎么样？

B：他 / 她很好。他 / 她现在有女朋友了。

你朋友	工作
王小云	驾照
陈老师	女儿

Exercise II　Look at the pictures and describe what you see.

（1）

以前他不忙，现在他＿＿＿＿＿＿＿＿＿＿＿＿＿＿＿。

（2）

七月天气很热，现在十月了，＿＿＿＿＿＿＿＿＿＿＿＿。

（3）

2010 年她学习汉语，现在她＿＿＿＿＿＿＿＿＿＿＿＿＿＿。

（4）

乔丹（Qiáodān）以前是运动员（yùndòngyuán, athlete），现在他_____。

2. 连动句（2）：表示方式　A sentence with serial verbs (2): Expressing means or manner

In Lesson 8, we have learned "a sentence with serial verbs (1): expressing a purpose". In this lesson, the first verb of a sentence with a serial verb phrase usually expresses the means or manner of the second verb. For example,

Tā měi tiān zuò gōnggòng qìchē huí jiā.
（1）他每天坐 公共 汽车回家。He returns home by bus every day.

Wǒmen kāichē qù Wángfǔjǐng.
（2）我们 开车 去 王府井。We drove to Wangfujing.

Dàwéi kěyǐ yóu(yǒng) huí guó ma?
（3）大为 可以 游（泳）回国 吗？ Can Dawei swim back to his country?

Exercise I　Following the example, choose the means of transportation that you often use and tell the class.

Example　我常常坐飞机 去上海。

坐地铁　　去学校

坐飞机　　去朋友家

打车　　　回国

开车　　　去上海

坐公共汽车　回家

Exercise II　Complete the sentences using the words given.

（1）A：你每天怎么去学校？

B：我每天_____。（公共汽车）

（2）A：你今天怎么回家？

B：我今天 _____。（公共汽车）

（3）A：你们老板坐飞机去上海吗？

B：不，他 _____。（开车）

（4）A：咱们怎么去王府井？

B：咱们 _____ 吧。（地铁）

3. 能愿动词谓语句（3）：会、可能　A sentence with an optative verb (3): "huì 会" (can; to be able to) and "kěnéng 可能" (possible)

The optative verb "会" is often used before a verb to express ability, and this kind of ability can be learned through study or practice. For example, "huì kāichē 会开车" (can drive), "huì yóuyǒng 会游泳" (can swim), and "huì shuō Hànyǔ 会说汉语" (can speak Chinese).

Subject	Predicate	
	Optative Verb	Verb-Object
你	会不会	说汉语？
宋华	不会	开车。
丁力波	会	写这个汉字。
谁	会	滑雪？

The optative verb "可能" expresses "possibility" and is often an estimate with uncertainty.

Subject	Predicate		
	Time Word	Optative Verb	Verb-Object / Adjective
陆雨平	八月	可能	去上海。
马大为	现在	不可能	睡觉。
王小云	明天	可能	来学校吗？
打车去		可能	很慢。

Exercise I　Substitute the underlined parts and complete the dialogues.

A：你会不会<u>跳舞</u>？

B：我会一点儿。

A：你今天能去<u>跳舞</u>吗？

B：不好意思，我今天<u>很忙</u>，不能去。

游泳	很累
滑雪	不舒服
唱中文歌	嗓子疼

Exercise II　Substitute the underlined parts and complete the dialogues.

A：咱们<u>开车</u>去吧。

B：<u>开车</u>去可能<u>堵车</u>。

打车	很贵
坐公共汽车	很慢
走路（zǒulù, to walk）	很累

4. 用疑问代词的问句（4）：怎么样　An interrogative sentence with a question pronoun (4): "zěnmeyàng 怎么样" (How is/are...? / How about...?)

The use of "……，怎么样？" is similar to the use of "……，hǎo ma 好吗？" at the end of a sentence. It is often used to make a suggestion or to seek the opinion of others. The first half of the sentence is a statement, expressing a suggestion. For example,

Wǒmen mǎi yí ge dà dàngāo, zěnmeyàng?
（1）我们　买一个大 蛋糕，怎么样？　How about buying a big cake?

Xiànzài qù, zěnmeyàng?
（2）现在　去，怎么样？　How about going now?

An affirmative response is often "hǎo a 好啊", "hǎo 好", "hǎo de 好的", "hǎo ba 好吧", or "tài hǎo le 太好了", etc.; the negative response could be "bù xíng 不行" (no) or "zhēn bù hǎoyìsi 真不好意思，……" (I'm really sorry), or "duìbuqǐ 对不起，……" (sorry), etc., with an explanation of the reason for this response.

Exercise I　Substitute the underlined parts and complete the dialogues.

（1）A：咱们去<u>吃饭</u>，怎么样？

　　B：好啊。/ 对不起，我现在不想去。

游泳
看电影
唱歌

（2）A：我们一起<u>去上海</u>，怎么样？

　　B：好啊。/ 对不起，最近我没有时间。

去北京
去王府井
回英国

Exercise II Decide whether the following sentences are right (√) or wrong (×).

（1）这件羽绒服怎么样卖？　　　　　　　　　（　　　）

（2）我们一起去跳舞，怎么？　　　　　　　　（　　　）

（3）我们坐地铁去，怎么样？　　　　　　　　（　　　）

（4）咱们几点去，怎么样？　　　　　　　　　（　　　）

四、练习与运用 PRACTICE AND APPLICATION

补充词语 Supplementary Words　　2-09-06

1. 火车	huǒchē	N	train　坐火车
2. 火车站	huǒchēzhàn	N	railway station　去火车站
3. 船	chuán	N	ship; boat　坐船
4. 机场	jīchǎng	N	airport　去机场
5. 骑	qí	V	to ride (a bicycle or horse)
6. 自行车	zìxíngchē	N	bicycle　骑自行车
7. 走路	zǒulù	VO	to walk　走路去
8. 滑冰	huábīng	VO	to go ice-skating; to skate
9. 篮球	lánqiú	N	basketball　打篮球
10. 排球	páiqiú	N	volleyball　打排球
11. 踢	tī	V	to kick; to play (soccer, etc.)
12. 足球	zúqiú	N	soccer　踢足球
13. 城里	chénglǐ	N	city; town　去城里
14. 美术馆	měishùguǎn	N	art gallery　去美术馆
15. 参观	cānguān	V	to visit (a place)　参观画展　参观博物馆
16. 公园	gōngyuán	N	park　去公园
17. 售票员	shòupiàoyuán	N	ticket seller; (of a bus) conductor; box-office clerk
18. 师傅	shīfu	N	*(a respectful form of address for workers, e.g., drivers, etc.)* master

1 语音练习 Pronunciation Drills   2-09-07

Listen and read aloud: Add tone marks to the following words and sentences, and then read them aloud.

❶ chuntian ❷ qiutian ❸ dongtian

❹ dache ❺ duche ❻ jiaxiang

❼ liangkuai ❽ gonggong qiche ❾ Jintian tianqi zhen hao a!

❿ Bu zuo feiji? Wo zenme hui guo?

2 会话练习 Conversation Practice

Pair/Group activity: Create dialogues based on the scenes or the requirements below.

1. Talking about the seasons and the weather

(1) Act out the dialogues below.

A：今天天气真好。

B：是啊，很暖和。

A：明天天气怎么样？

B：可能也不错。

A：什么季节去北京最好？

B：秋天吧，不冷也不热。

(2) Choose a place you are familiar with and complete the dialogue.

A：你是哪儿人？

B：我是＿＿＿＿＿＿＿＿人。

A：你们家乡现在天气怎么样？

B：＿＿＿＿＿＿＿＿＿＿＿＿＿。

2. Talking about the change of status

In groups of four, talk about why the characters in the pictures are angry or look embarrassed. Then give your suggestions about what the characters should say.

3. Talking about plans

Look at the dialogue and the pictures, and then talk about your plans for the weekend.

Example

A：星期日你想做什么？

B：我想看电影。

4. Giving suggestions for activities

(1) You are studying in Beijing. Your friend is visiting you from your country. You would like to accompany him/her to go sightseeing around Beijing. Based on the picture below, you give him/her some suggestions. (Use "……，zěnmeyàng 怎么样？" or "……，hǎo ma 好吗？")

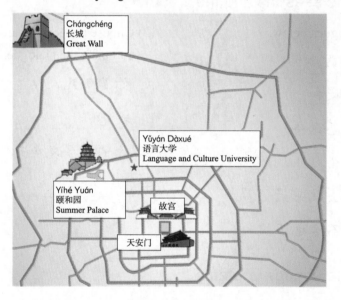

Chángchéng
长城
Great Wall

Yǔyán Dàxué
语言大学
Language and Culture University

Yíhé Yuán
颐和园
Summer Palace

故宫

天安门

(2) Your Chinese friend is going to your country. What suggestions do you have for him/her about travelling in your city?

5. Talking about means of transportation

You will take a friend with you on a day trip in your city. Plan to visit two to four scenic spots, talk about the means of transportation you will take, draw a map of your trip, and then report back to the class. Use the questions below:

❶ 我们怎么去……？

❷ 我们坐地铁去还是坐公共汽车去？

❸ 我们骑自行车去……，怎么样？

3 **听后复述 Listening and Repeating** 　2-09-08

Listen to the following dialogues and repeat what you hear.

（1）A：请上车吧。你去哪儿？

　　B：我去王府井（Wángfǔjǐng）大街。师傅，七点半能到吗？

　　A：不堵车，能到。

（2）A：售票员，买票。

　　B：您去哪儿？

　　A：请问，111 路到美术馆吗？

　　B：到。

　　A：多少钱一张票？

　　B：两块。

　　A：买两张。

（3）A：请问首都机场（Shǒudū Jīchǎng, Capital International Airport）怎么走？

　　B：可以坐地铁去。先坐地铁 13 号线到西直门（Xīzhí Mén），在西直门换 2 号线到东直门（Dōngzhí Mén），在东直门换机场线到首都机场。

4 **阅读理解 Reading Comprehension**

Ⅰ

　　马大为的家乡一年有四个季节，春天、夏天、秋天和冬天。春天天气暖和了，树都绿了，很漂亮；夏天天气很热，马大为常常去游泳；秋天天气凉快了，不冷也不热。马大为最喜欢秋天，因为水果都熟（shú, ripe）了，他可以吃很多水果。冬天天气很冷，马大为常常去滑雪。

Answer the following questions:

（1）马大为的家乡有几个季节？都是什么季节？

（2）马大为最喜欢哪个季节？为什么？

Ⅱ

　　到 2014 年 12 月，北京地铁有 17 条线了。坐 1 号线，你可以到有名的西单（Xīdān）、天安门、王府井，你可以在西单买东西，在王府井吃北京小吃。坐 2 号线，你可以到雍和宫（Yōnghé Gōng），还可以到火车站。在西直门地铁站，你可以换 4 号线、13 号线。坐 4 号线，北边可以到颐和园（Yíhé

Yuán）、圆明园（Yuánmíng Yuán）、北京大学和中关村（Zhōngguān Cūn）。如果你想去机场，可以坐2号线，在东直门换机场线。地铁2号线上有很多"门"，比如"西直门"。你数数（shǔshu, to count），一共有多少个"门"？

Answer the following questions:

（1）到2014年12月，北京地铁有多少条线了？

（2）如果你想去王府井，最好坐几号线？

（3）从西直门去机场，怎么换车？

（4）看北京地铁线路图（Beijing Subway Map），数数2号线上有多少个"门"。

（5）看北京地铁线路图，数数2号线上有多少个换乘站（huànchéngzhàn, transfer station），分别是什么站。

Beijing Subway Map (Part)

5 任务与活动 Task and Activity

1. Interview

In groups of two, ask about the seasons and weather conditions in each other's hometowns or the cities where you live. Complete the chart below and then report your findings back to the class.

季节	天气	常做什么

Sample questions:

❶ 你的家乡 / 城市有几个季节？都是什么季节？

❷ 春天 / 夏天 / 秋天 / 冬天天气怎么样？

❸ 你最喜欢什么季节？为什么？

❹ 春天 / 夏天 / 秋天 / 冬天你常做什么？

2. Role-play

In groups of two, suppose you are at Beijing Language and Culture University. Based on the table below, select a weekend activity, the means of transportation, and the routes, and then perform.

目的地 Destination	目的 Purpose	距离 Distance	交通方式 Means of Transportation	用时 Cost of Time	费用 Cost of Money
北京大学	买书	3km	307 路公共汽车	16 分钟	2 元
			打车	10 分钟	13 元
			骑自行车	22 分钟	
			走路	45 分钟	
国家博物馆	看画展	15km	375 路→13 号线→4 号线→1 号线	57 分钟	7 元
			13 号线→4 号线→1 号线	1 小时 9 分	5 元
			打车	40 分钟	41 元
			骑自行车	1 小时 40 分	
王府井	看电影	16km	375 路→13 号线→4 号线→1 号线	59 分钟	7 元
			13 号线→4 号线→1 号线	1 小时 19 分	5 元
			打车	41 分钟	43 元
			骑自行车	1 小时 46 分	

A：听说……有个……，你想去吗？

B：好啊。什么时候去？

A：……，怎么样？

B：好。咱们怎么去？

……

6　写作练习 Writing Exercise

Write a paragraph introducing the seasons and weather in your hometown.

Example　我的家乡一年有……个季节，……。我最喜欢……，天气……了，树……了。我会……，常常跟……一起，坐……去……。

五、汉字 *CHINESE CHARACTERS*

1 汉字知识 Knowledge about Chinese Characters

Pictophonetic characters

Many Chinese characters are composed of two parts, one of which denotes an approximate sound, called "shēngpáng 声旁" (phonetic component), and the other denotes an approximate meaning, called "xíngpáng 形旁" (pictographic/semantic component). This type of character is called "xíngshēngzì 形声字" (pictophonetic character). For example,

(1) mā 妈 (mom):
pictographic/semantic component: nǚ 女 (woman); phonetic component: mǎ 马

(2) bà 爸 (dad):
pictographic/semantic component: fù 父 (father); phonetic component: bā 巴

(3) qī 期 (period of time):
pictographic/semantic component: yuè 月 (moon; month); phonetic component: qí 其

2 汉字偏旁 Chinese Radicals

Radical	Name	Stroke Order	No. of Strokes	Example	Explanation
氵	三点水	丶丶氵	3	滑 huá (to slip) 汽 qì (vapor; steam) 泳 yǒng (to swim) 游 yóu (to swim; to travel)	Related to "water"
冫	两点水	丶冫	2	凉 liáng (cool) 冷 lěng (cold)	Related to "ice"
纟	绞丝旁	乚纟纟	3	线 xiàn (line; thread) 绒 róng (fine hair; down) 绿 lǜ (green)	Related to "silk"
灬	四点底	丶丶丶灬	4	热 rè (hot) 照 zhào (to shine)	Related to "fire"
穴	穴字头	丶丶八宀穴	5	空 kōng (empty) 窄 zhǎi (narrow)	Related to "cave"

3 认写基本汉字 Learn and Write the Basic Chinese Characters

(1)　禾　　一 二 千 千 禾
　　hé　　standing grain　　　　　　5 strokes

(2)　穴　　、 丶 宀 宀 穴
　　xué　　cave; hole　　　　　　　5 strokes

(3)　冬　　ノ ク 久 冬 冬
　　dōng　　winter　　　　　　　　5 strokes

(4)　水　　丿 才 水 水
　　shuǐ　　water　　　　　　　　　4 strokes

(5)　雨　　一 厂 币 币 雨 雨 雨 雨
　　yǔ　　rain　　　　　　　　　　8 strokes

(6)　开　　一 二 于 开
　　kāi　　to open; to begin; to drive　　4 strokes

(7)　车　　一 七 乞 车
　　chē　　vehicle　　　　　　　　4 strokes

4 认写课文中的汉字 Learn and Write the Chinese Characters in the Text

(1) 秋天 qiūtiān

　　秋 —→ 禾 + 火　　　　　　　　9 strokes

(2) 空气 kōngqì

　　空 —→ 穴 + 工　　　　　　　　8 strokes

(3) 凉快 liángkuai

　　凉 —→ 冫 + 京（京：、 一 亠 亠 方 亨 京 京）　　10 strokes

(4) 热 rè

　　热 —→ 扌 + 丸（丸：丿 九 丸）+ 灬　　10 strokes

（5）游泳 yóuyǒng

游 —→ 氵 + 方 + 𠂉 + 子   12 strokes

泳 —→ 氵 + 永   8 strokes

（6）滑雪 huáxuě

滑 —→ 氵 + 骨（骨：丶 冂 冎 冎 骨 骨 骨 骨）   12 strokes

雪 —→ 雨 + 彐（彐：𠃌 彐 彐）   11 strokes

（7）汽车 qìchē

汽 —→ 氵 + 气   7 strokes

（8）线 xiàn

线 —→ 纟 + 戋   8 strokes

六、文化知识 *CULTURAL KNOWLEDGE*

The Climate of China

China is situated in East Asia and on the west side of the Pacific Ocean. It has a land area of over 9,600,000 square kilometers. It is connected with 14 countries and has eight maritime countries as neighbors. Most parts of China are located in the North Temperate Zone, with a mild climate and four distinct seasons, and are suitable for habitation. The characteristics of the climate are cold with some

snow in the winter and hot with high temperatures and plenty of rain in the summer, which provide favorable conditions for agriculture.

Because of such a vast territory, China's climate varies within these climate types: Mòhé 漠河 in the most northern part of China is at latitude 53 North and has a boreal climate; Nánshā Qúndǎo 南沙群岛 (The Nansha Islands, known in the West as the Spratlys), located at latitude 3 North, has an equatorial climate; the Qinghai-Tibet Plateau, with an altitude of

over 4,500 meters, has winter throughout the year; the South China Sea Islands are in summer throughout the year; the central part of Yunnan Province has spring-like weather all through the year.

七、自我评估　*SELF-EVALUATION*

I can basically do the following things in Chinese:

☐ I can talk about the seasons and weather of a certain place.

☐ I can talk about my plans.

☐ I can suggest an activity.

☐ I can discuss the means of transportation to go from one place to another.

趣味汉语　**Fun with Chinese**

Guess Which Chinese Character It Is

yí ge rén
1. 一个人

yī jiā yī
2. 一加一

Dà yǔ luò zài héng　　　　shān shang.
3. 大雨落在横（horizontal）山上。

Yì biān lǜ,　yì biān hóng,　lǜ de xǐhuan yǔ,　hóng de xǐhuan fēng.
4. 一边绿，一边红，绿的喜欢雨，红的喜欢风。

(1) One person ("one" plus "person")

(2) One plus (+) one

(3) Rain above a horizontal mountain.

(4) One part is green and the other is red; the green likes rain and the red likes wind.

10

Zhù nǐ Shèngdàn kuàilè
祝你圣诞快乐
Merry Christmas

Christmas is coming. Ding Libo wants to prepare gifts for his family and phone his mother in Canada. In this lesson, you will learn how to give your holiday wishes and send your regards to someone through someone else. You will also learn how to talk about things that have happened. You are now studying the last lesson of Book 1 in the *New Practical Chinese Reader* series. This lesson will summarize the main grammatical points covered in the entire book. You will see that you have already learned how to speak Chinese in a variety of sentence patterns.

一、热身 *WARM-UP*

1 思考 Think

Think about the following questions:

(1) In your country, which is the most important holiday? What do you do on this holiday?

(2) On a holiday, what gifts will you give your family members and friends? What kind of wishes will you give others?

(3) Do you know the most important holiday in China? Do you know the customs of this holiday?

2 活动 Activity

From the pictures below, select suitable small gifts for your family or friends as Christmas or New Year gifts, and then choose a few of these gifts and present them to your classmates.

| toy | traditional Chinese knot | paper-cut | facial mask in traditional Chinese operas | choth shoes | red packet |

二、课文 *TEXT*

（一） 2-10-01

(Ding Libo meets Lu Yuping in the subway.)

丁力波： 陆雨平， 你好！ 好久不见了， 你去哪儿？①
Dīng Lìbō: Lù　Yǔpíng,　　nǐ hǎo!　　Hǎojiǔ　bú jiàn le,　　nǐ qù　nǎr?

陆雨平： 是你啊， 力波。② 我去电影学院， 他们请我做
Lù Yǔpíng: Shì　nǐ　a,　　　Lìbō.　　Wǒ qù diànyǐng xuéyuàn,　tāmen qǐng wǒ zuò

报告。 你去哪儿了？
bàogào.　 Nǐ qù　nǎr　le?

丁力波： 我去王府井了。
Dīng Lìbō: Wǒ qù Wángfǔjǐng le.

> 谈已经发生的事情
> Talking about something
> that has happened

我去给爸爸妈妈买圣诞节礼物了。
Wǒ qù gěi bàba māma mǎi Shèngdàn Jié lǐwù le.

陆雨平： 你爸爸妈妈都好吗？
Lù Yǔpíng: Nǐ bàba māma dōu hǎo ma?

丁力波： 他们 都 很 好， 谢谢。
Dīng Lìbō： Tāmen dōu hěn hǎo, xièxie.

陆雨平： 听说 你 爸爸 妈妈 的 专业 也 是 中文？
Lù Yǔpíng： Tīngshuō nǐ bàba māma de zhuānyè yě shì Zhōngwén?

丁力波： 我 爸爸 是 加拿大人， 中文 名字 叫 古波。 他 以前 也
Dīng Lìbō： Wǒ bàba shì Jiānádàrén, Zhōngwén míngzi jiào Gǔ Bō. Tā yǐqián yě

在 语言 学院 学 汉语， 现在 是 中国
zài Yǔyán Xuéyuàn xué Hànyǔ, xiànzài shì Zhōngguó

> 谈某人的变化
> Talking about someone who has changed

文学 教授 了。 我 妈妈 叫 丁云， 是 中国人。 她 的
wénxué jiàoshòu le. Wǒ māma jiào Dīng Yún, shì Zhōngguórén. Tā de

专业 是 美国 文学， 现在 在 加拿大 教 汉语。 我们 一
zhuānyè shì Měiguó wénxué, xiànzài zài Jiānádà jiāo Hànyǔ. Wǒmen yì

家 人 都 喜欢 中文， 都 说 中文。
jiā rén dōu xǐhuan Zhōngwén, dōu shuō Zhōngwén.

陆雨平： 今年 你 在 北京 过 圣诞节， 是 不 是？
Lù Yǔpíng： Jīnnián nǐ zài Běijīng guò Shèngdàn Jié, shì bu shì?

丁力波： 是 啊。 北京 也 是 我 的 家。 我 哥哥 和 弟弟 都 在 北京。
Dīng Lìbō： Shì a. Běijīng yě shì wǒ de jiā. Wǒ gēge hé dìdi dōu zài Běijīng.

弟弟 跟 我 外婆 一起 住。
Dìdi gēn wǒ wàipó yìqǐ zhù.

陆雨平： 现在 他们 回 加拿大 过节 了 吗？
Lù Yǔpíng： Xiànzài tāmen huí Jiānádà guòjié le ma?

丁力波： 没有。 弟弟 没有 回 加拿大， 他 去 旅行 了。 哥哥 可
Dīng Lìbō： Méiyǒu. Dìdi méiyǒu huí Jiānádà, tā qù lǚxíng le. Gēge kě-

能 回国 看 爸爸 妈妈， 他 还 没有 决定。 雨平， 中国
néng huí guó kàn bàba māma, tā hái méiyǒu juédìng. Yǔpíng, Zhōngguó-

人 是 不 是 也 过 圣诞节？
rén shì bu shì yě guò Shèngdàn Jié?

陆雨平: 中国 最重要的节日是春节。
Lù Yǔpíng: Zhōngguó zuì zhòngyào de jiérì shì Chūnjié.

现在很多年轻人也喜欢过西方的节日。对了，我
Xiànzài hěn duō niánqīng rén yě xǐhuan guò Xīfāng de jiérì. Duìle, wǒ-

们有个美国朋友，我爱人让我给他儿子买一件
men yǒu ge Měiguó péngyou, wǒ àiren ràng wǒ gěi tā érzi mǎi yí jiàn

圣诞礼物。你说，该买什么？③
Shèngdàn lǐwù. Nǐ shuō, gāi mǎi shénme?

> 谈论节日
> Talking about a holiday

丁力波: 他儿子几岁了？
Dīng Lìbō: Tā érzi jǐ suì le?

> 问年龄（3）
> Asking about one's age (3)

陆雨平: 六岁了。
Lù Yǔpíng: Liù suì le.

丁力波: 你给他买一个小汽车吧，男孩子都喜欢汽车。
Dīng Lìbō: Nǐ gěi tā mǎi yí ge xiǎo qìchē ba, nán háizi dōu xǐhuan qìchē.

陆雨平: 好。谢谢你！我到了。④ 祝你圣诞快乐！⑤ 再见！
Lù Yǔpíng: Hǎo. Xièxie nǐ! Wǒ dào le. Zhù nǐ Shèngdàn kuàilè! Zàijiàn!

丁力波: 再见！ 也祝你圣诞快乐！
Dīng Lìbō: Zàijiàn! Yě zhù nǐ Shèngdàn kuàilè!

> 节日祝愿
> Holiday greetings

生词 New Words　2-10-02

1.	好久不见	hǎojiǔ bú jiàn	IE	long time no see	
	好久	hǎojiǔ	A	very long; for a long time	等好久了
2.	学院	xuéyuàn	N	institute; college	电影学院 在汉语学院学习

3.	报告	bàogào	N	speech; lecture; report　做报告　听报告
4.	语言	yǔyán	N	language　语言专业　在语言学院学习
5.	文学	wénxué	N	literature　中国文学　英国文学　文学专业
6.	教授	jiàoshòu	N	professor　中文教授　丁教授
7.	过节	guòjié	OV	to spend a holiday; to celebrate a festival
	过	guò	V	to spend (time)　过生日
	节	jié	N	holiday; festival　过节
8.	外婆	wàipó	N	(maternal) grandmother　我外婆
9.	住	zhù	V	to live　住学生宿舍　跟我外婆一起住
10.	旅行	lǚxíng	V	to travel　去旅行　喜欢旅行　常常旅行
11.	看	kàn	V	to see; to visit (someone)　看外婆　看妈妈　看朋友
12.	决定	juédìng	V	to decide　决定去　决定参加　还没有决定
13.	重要	zhòngyào	A	important　重要的决定　重要的活动　重要的报告　重要的事　很重要的问题
14.	节日	jiérì	N	festival; holiday　重要的节日　节日快乐
15.	年轻	niánqīng	A	young　很年轻　年轻人　年轻的医生
16.	西方	Xīfāng	N	the West　西方国家　西方人　西方文学
17.	爱人	àiren	N	husband or wife　我爱人　我朋友的爱人
	爱	ài	V	to love　爱妈妈　爱家乡　爱国　我爱你
18.	儿子	érzi	N	son　他儿子　老师的儿子　小儿子
19.	王府井	Wángfǔjǐng	PN	Wangfujing, a famous shopping area in Beijing
20.	圣诞节	Shèngdàn Jié	PN	Christmas; Christmas Day　圣诞节礼物
21.	加拿大	Jiānádà	PN	Canada
22.	古波	Gǔ Bō	PN	Gu Bo, Chinese name of Ding Libo's father
23.	丁云	Dīng Yún	PN	Ding Yun, Chinese name of Ding Libo's mother
24.	春节	Chūnjié	PN	Spring Festival; Chinese New Year　过春节　春节快乐

注释 Notes

① 你去哪儿?

Where are you going?

Both "Nǐ qù nǎr? 你去哪儿?" and "Nǐ qù nǎr le? 你去哪儿了?" (Where did you go? / Where have you been?) are common expressions used among friends. You may respond vaguely. These are merely common greetings, which are used as a social interaction.

② 是你啊,力波。

It's you, Libo.

"shì nǐ a 是你啊" is often used when you meet a friend on the street or when you recognize someone on the phone, expressing a surprise.

③ 你说,该买什么?

Tell me, what should I buy?

Here "nǐ shuō 你说" (tell me) (or "nǐ kàn 你看" (in your opinion)) is to ask for the other person's opinion.

④ 我到了。

Here I am.

Sometimes one may say "(a place) dào le 到了" (I/We have arrived at (a place)), such as "Diànyǐng Xuéyuàn dào le. 电影学院到了。" (I/We have arrived at the Film Academy).

⑤ 祝你圣诞快乐!

Merry Christmas!

"zhù 祝 + someone + congratulatory phrase" expresses one's good wishes. It is used for a holiday or birthday. For example,

Zhù nǐ Chūnjié kuàilè!
(1)祝 你 春节 快乐! Happy Chinese New Year (to you)!

Zhù nǐ shēngrì kuàilè!
(2)祝 你 生日 快乐! Happy Birthday (to you)!

Zhù nǐ zhōumò kuàilè!
(3)祝 你 周末 快乐! Have a nice weekend!

You may also just say "春节快乐!", "生日快乐!", "周末快乐!", and so on.

（二）  2-10-03

马大为： **力波，刚才你不在，你的手机响了。**
Mǎ Dàwéi: Lìbō, gāngcái nǐ bú zài, nǐ de shǒujī xiǎng le.

丁力波： **我去学校商店了。**
Dīng Lìbō: Wǒ qù xuéxiào shāngdiàn le.

(Looking at his cell phone)

是我哥哥的短信。他让我给妈妈打电话。
Shì wǒ gēge de duǎnxìn. Tā ràng wǒ gěi māma dǎ diànhuà.

(Making a phone call)

丁力波： **喂，是我。**① **妈妈，您好！**
Dīng Lìbō: Wèi, shì wǒ. Māma, nín hǎo!

> 打电话
> Making a phone call

丁云： **是力波啊，你好吗？**
Dīng Yún: Shì Lìbō a, nǐ hǎo ma?

丁力波： **我很好。您和爸爸最近怎么样？**
Dīng Lìbō: Wǒ hěn hǎo. Nín hé bàba zuìjìn zěnmeyàng?

丁云：　　我们都很好。你外婆身体怎么样？
Dīng Yún:　Wǒmen dōu hěn hǎo.　Nǐ wàipó shēntǐ zěnmeyàng?

丁力波：　外婆身体不错。她让我问你们好。②
Dīng Lìbō:　Wàipó shēntǐ búcuò.　Tā ràng wǒ wèn nǐmen hǎo.

转达问候

Passing on someone's regards

丁云：　　我们也问她好。你要常回家看外婆，多帮她做
Dīng Yún:　Wǒmen yě wèn tā hǎo.　Nǐ yào cháng huí jiā kàn wàipó,　duō bāng tā zuò

点儿事儿。
diǎnr shìr.

丁力波：　我和哥哥都常去看她。我们都很想你们。
Dīng Lìbō:　Wǒ hé gēge dōu cháng qù kàn tā.　Wǒmen dōu hěn xiǎng nǐmen.

丁云：　　我们也很想你们。你现在学习怎么样？
Dīng Yún:　Wǒmen yě hěn xiǎng nǐmen.　Nǐ xiànzài xuéxí zěnmeyàng?

丁力波：　我现在有很多中国朋友了，他们常常帮我复习
Dīng Lìbō:　Wǒ xiànzài yǒu hěn duō Zhōngguó péngyou le,　tāmen chángcháng bāng wǒ fùxí

课文、练习口语。我还常常问他们语法问题。对
kèwén、 liànxí kǒuyǔ.　Wǒ hái chángcháng wèn tāmen yǔfǎ wèntí.　Duì-

了，我现在会用汉语词典了，
le,　wǒ xiànzài huì yòng Hànyǔ cídiǎn le,

谈学习（2）

Talking about studying (2)

也会上中文网了。③
yě huì shàng Zhōngwén wǎng le.

丁云：　　这很好。力波，今年你在中国过圣诞节，我和
Dīng Yún:　Zhè hěn hǎo.　Lìbō,　jīnnián nǐ zài Zhōngguó guò Shèngdàn Jié,　wǒ hé

你爸爸要给你寄一件圣诞礼物。
nǐ bàba yào gěi nǐ jì yí jiàn Shèngdàn lǐwù.

丁力波：　谢谢爸爸妈妈。你们来北京，是我们最想要的
Dīng Lìbō:　Xièxie bàba māma.　Nǐmen lái Běijīng,　shì wǒmen zuì xiǎng yào de

礼物。妈妈，我爱你！
lǐwù.　Māma,　wǒ ài nǐ!

丁云：　　我也爱你，力波。再见！
Dīng Yún:　Wǒ yě ài nǐ,　Lìbō.　Zàijiàn!

生词 New Words 2-10-04

1.	刚才	gāngcái	N	just now 刚才你不在 刚才我有事儿
2.	手机	shǒujī	N	cell phone 手机号 买手机
	手	shǒu	N	hand
3.	响	xiǎng	V	to ring 手机响了
4.	商店	shāngdiàn	N	shop; store 去商店
	店	diàn	N	shop; store 药店 饭店 面包店
5.	短信	duǎnxìn	N	text message 手机短信 一条短信
	短	duǎn	A	short 很短 有点儿短
6.	让	ràng	V	to let; to allow 妈妈让我早点儿去
7.	打电话	dǎ diànhuà	VO	to call someone 给妈妈打电话
	电话	diànhuà	N	telephone 一个电话 电话响了
8.	喂	wèi	Int	*(usually on the phone)* hello 喂，是我 喂，是大为吗
9.	问好	wènhǎo	VO	to send one's regards (to someone); to say hello (to someone) 向您问好 问你好 问他好
10.	帮	bāng	V	to help 请帮我一下
11.	想	xiǎng	V	to miss 想家 想妈妈 很想你
12.	复习	fùxí	V	to review 复习语法 复习汉字
13.	课文	kèwén	N	text 复习课文 学习课文 这课课文
14.	用	yòng	V	to use 用手机 用一下电话
15.	词典	cídiǎn	N	dictionary 汉语词典 会用汉语词典 用一下词典 买汉语词典
16.	上网	shàngwǎng	VO	to go online; to go on the Internet 会上网 能上网 上网学习
	网	wǎng	N	net; Internet 中文网
17.	寄	jì	V	to post; to mail 寄礼物 寄书 寄词典 寄衣服 寄钱

注释 Notes

① 喂，是我。

Hello, it's me.

"wèi 喂" is often used on the phone, expressing a greeting or a response. For example,

Wèi, shì Dīng Lìbō ma?

（1）喂，是 丁 力波 吗？　Hello, is that Ding Libo?

Wèi, wǒ shì Mǎ Dàwéi.

（2）喂，我 是 马 大为。Hello, this is Ma Dawei.

Wèi, nǐ hǎo! Qǐngwèn Wáng Xiǎoyún zài ma?

（3）喂，你 好！请问 王 小云 在 吗？　Hello, may I ask if Wang Xiaoyun is there?

② 她让我问你们好。

She asked me to send her regards to you.

"……wèn 问……hǎo 好" is a way to pass on one's regards. For example,

Tā wèn nǐ hǎo.

（1）他 问 你 好。He asked me to send you his regards.

Qǐng nǐ wèn tā hǎo.

（2）请 你 问 他 好。I would like to ask you to send him my regards.

③ 我现在会用汉语词典了，也会上中文网了。

Now I can use a Chinese dictionary as well as a Chinese website.

Sentences with an optative verb (e.g., huì 会, néng 能, kěyǐ 可以, xiǎng 想, etc.) or a word describing psychological activities (e.g., xǐhuan 喜欢, ài 爱, etc.), with the particle "le 了" at the end, also tend to indicate the change of status. For example,

Tā huì yòng Hànyǔ cídiǎn.

（1）他 会 用 汉语 词典。(It only indicates that he has the ability.)
He can use a Chinese dictionary.

Tā huì yòng Hànyǔ cídiǎn le.

他 会 用 汉语 词典 了。(This implies that he was unable to do so before.)
Now he can use a Chinese dictionary.

Dàwéi míngtiān néng lái shàngkè.

（2）大为 明天 能 来 上课。(It only indicates that he can come to class tomorrow.)
Dawei can come to class tomorrow.

Dàwéi míngtiān néng lái shàngkè le.

大为 明天 能 来 上课 了。(This implies that he was unable to do so before.)
Now Dawei can come to class tomorrow.

Tā xiǎng mǎi chē le.

（3）他 想 买 车 了。(This implies that he did not want to buy a car before.)
Now he wants to buy a car.

Tā xǐhuan tiàowǔ le.

（4）他 喜欢 跳舞 了。(This implies that he did not like to dance before.)
Now he likes to dance.

三、语言点 *LANGUAGE POINTS*

1 核心句 Key Sentences   2-10-05

1. 你去哪儿了？
2. 我去学校商店了。
3. 弟弟没有回加拿大，他去旅行了。
4. 他们请我做报告。
5. 中国人是不是也过圣诞节？

6. 他儿子几岁了？
7. 祝你圣诞快乐！
8. 她让我问你们好。
9. 我现在会用汉语词典了。

2 语法 Grammar

1. 助词 "了" 在句尾（2）：肯定事情的发生或实现   The particle "le 了" at the end of a sentence (2): To confirm that something (has) happened

In a sentence with a verbal predicate that denotes an action or behavior, the particle "了" is often used to confirm that something (has) happened or has been completed. Compare the questions and answers in A (without "了") and B (with "了") below:

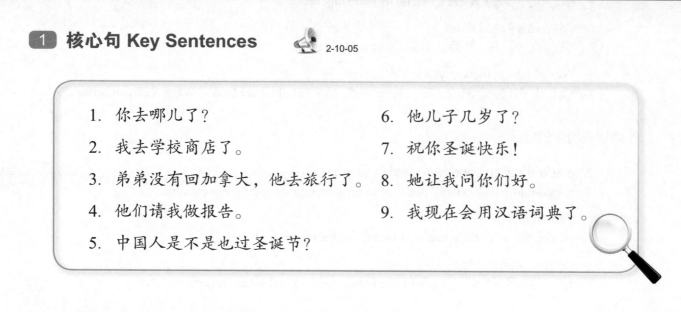

A （without "了"）	B （with "了"）
Nǐ qù nǎr? Q₁: 你 去 哪儿？ Where are you going?	Nǐ qù nǎr le? Q₁: 你 去 哪儿 了？ Where did you go? / Where have you been?
Wǒ qù Wángfǔjǐng. A₁: 我 去 王府井。 I am going to Wangfujing.	Wǒ qù Wángfǔjǐng le. A₁: 我 去 王府井 了。 I went to Wangfujing. / I have been to Wangfujing.
Nǐ qù mǎi shénme? Q₂: 你 去 买 什么？ What would you like to buy?	Nǐ qù mǎi shénme le? Q₂: 你 去 买 什么 了？ What did you buy? / What have you bought?
Wǒ qù mǎi Shèngdàn Jié lǐwù. A₂: 我 去 买 圣诞 节礼物。 I'm going to buy a Christmas gift.	Wǒ qù mǎi Shèngdàn Jié lǐwù le. A₂: 我 去 买 圣诞 节礼物了。 I bought a Christmas gift. / I have bought a Christmas gift.

In dialogue A, the two events "去王府井" and "买圣诞节礼物" did not happen or have not happened; in dialogue B, the two events (have) happened.

For a sentence with the particle "了", the negative form is to add the adverb "méi (yǒu) 没（有）" (but not "bù 不") before the verb, and "了" must be removed. See example 3 in the table below.

To ask a question, put "……吗" or "……没有" at the end of a sentence as we see in examples 4 and 5 in the table below. A "verb - 没 - verb" form may also be used to ask this type of question, and "了" is removed from the end, such as the last example in the table below.

Verb + Object + 了

Subject	Predicate			
	Adverbial	Verb	Object	Particle
你的手机		响		了。
丁力波		去	学校商店	了。
他	没有	去	上海。	
弟弟		回	加拿大	了吗？
你	给妈妈	打电话		了没有？
林娜和宋华		看没看	展览？	

Note:

The particle "了" always denotes that an action or something (has) happened in the past. However, something that (has) happened in the past does not necessarily require "了". It is not necessary to use "了" if it is a general statement that does not stress the confirmation of the thing that has happened, particularly in a series of things or a description of something that happened at a certain time. For example,

Shàng Xīngqīliù tā shàngwǔ qù kàn diànyǐng, xiàwǔ qù cānjiā yí ge jùhuì.
（1）上　星期六他 上午 去看　电影，下午去参加一个聚会。
Last Saturday, he went to (watch) a movie in the morning and went to (attend) a party in the afternoon.

Tā yǐqián yě zài Yǔyán Xuéyuàn xué Hànyǔ.
（2）他以前也在 语言　学院　学 汉语。
Previously he also studied Chinese at the language institute.

Exercise I Substitute the underlined parts and complete the dialogues.

（1）A: 昨天你<u>看电影</u>了吗？

B: 我没有<u>看电影</u>。

A: 你去哪儿了？

B: 我去<u>图书馆</u>了。

上课	医院
去博物馆	银行
参加聚会	我朋友家
去宋华家	超市

（2）A: 上午你做什么了？

B: 我<u>去银行</u>了。

A: 你<u>换没换钱</u>？

B: 我没<u>换钱</u>。

去买水果	买苹果
去图书馆	上网
去看病	验血
回家	复习中文

Exercise II In groups of two, ask and answer the questions and write your answers on the lines.

（1）A: 你吃饭了吗？

B: _____。

（2）A: 昨天你去商店了吗？

B: _____。

（3）A: 昨天晚上 10:00，你睡觉了吗？

B: _____。

（4）A: 2014 年，你去没去中国？

B: _____。

（5）A: 你准备圣诞节礼物了没有？

B: _____。

2. 兼语句 A pivotal sentence

A pivotal sentence is also a sentence with a verbal predicate. Its predicate is composed of two verbal phrases. The object of the first verb is also the subject of the second verb. The first verb in a pivotal sentence is often a verb with the meaning of asking or ordering someone to do something, such as "qǐng 请" (to ask/invite) or "ràng 让" (to allow/let/tell/ask/make).

Both "请" and "让" could mean "to ask someone to do something", but "请" is a politer way to make a request.

Subject$_1$	Predicate			
	Verb$_1$	Object$_1$ (Subject$_2$)	Verb$_2$	Object$_2$
他们	请	陆雨平	做	报告。
你哥哥	昨天让	你	给妈妈打	电话。
他爱人	让	他	买	圣诞礼物了吗？
他们	请	她	唱	中国歌了没有？
妈妈	让不让	小女儿	喝	咖啡？
妈妈	不让	她	喝	咖啡。
她	没有请	他	到	家里。

Both verbs in the predicate of a pivotal sentence can have an adverbial. The negative sentence is usually formed by adding "bù 不" or "méi (yǒu) 没（有）" to the first verb. In an interrogative sentence, add "……ma 吗？", "……le ma 了吗？", or "……le méiyǒu 了没有？" at the end, or use the "verb-not-verb" form for the first verb.

Exercise I　Substitute the underlined parts and complete the dialogues.

（1）A：你给大为打个电话，好吗？

B：什么事儿？

A：让他去 学校。

B：没问题。

来	办公楼
去	博物馆
等	他朋友
去看	张教授

（2）A：你请他做什么？

B：我请他看画展。

A：他能来吗？

B：他能来。

（明天）来我家	来
教我滑雪	去
帮我挂号	去
给大家介绍中国文学	来

（3）A：她可以去旅行吗？

B：不可以，医生不让她去旅行。

说英语	老师	说英语
很晚回家	她爱人	很晚回家
喝咖啡	她外婆	喝咖啡
开车	她爸爸	开车

Exercise II   Look at the pictures and complete the sentences with the words given.

（1）

（让）

大夫＿＿＿＿＿＿＿＿＿＿＿＿＿＿＿。

（3）

（请）

他＿＿＿＿＿＿＿＿＿＿＿＿＿＿＿。

（2）

（让）

他＿＿＿＿＿＿＿＿＿＿＿＿＿＿＿。

（4）

（请）

大家＿＿＿＿＿＿＿＿＿＿＿＿＿＿＿。

3. 用"……，是不是？"提问   Asking a question using "……，shì bu shì 是不是？"

When asking someone a question using "……是不是？" (Is it true that…?) or "……shì ma 是吗？" (…, don't/doesn't you/they/he/she...?), it often expresses an assumption. In response, if you agree, say "shì a 是啊" (Yes); if you disagree, use "bù 不" or "bú shì 不是" (No). For example,

        Nǐ xǐhuan Zhōngguó diànyǐng, shì bu shì?
（1）A：你喜欢　中国　电影，是不是？ You do like Chinese movies, don't you?

        Shì a.
    B：是啊。Yes, I do.

        Nǐ chángcháng shàngwǎng, shì ma?
（2）A：你　常常　　上网，是吗？ You often go on the Internet, don't you?

        Bù, wǒ bú huì shàngwǎng.
    B：不，我不会　上网。No, I don't know how to go on the Internet.

"是不是" may also be placed before a verb or verb phrase. For example,

Zhōngguórén shì bu shì yě guò Shèngdàn Jié? / Zhōngguórén yě guò Shèngdàn Jié, shì bu shì?

中国人　是不是也过　圣诞　节？/ 中国人　也过　圣诞　节，是不是？

Do the Chinese also celebrate Christmas? / The Chinese also celebrate Christmas, don't they?

Exercise I　Substitute the underlined parts and complete the dialogues.

（1）A：你想<u>吃草莓蛋糕</u>，是不是？

　　　B：不是，我想<u>吃巧克力蛋糕</u>。

送他儿子小汽车	送他儿子书
住学生宿舍	住学校外边（wàibian）
复习课文	练习汉字

（2）A：他是不是<u>不喜欢她</u>？

　　　B：不是，<u>他有点儿不好意思</u>。

去商店了	他今天在家休息
秋天去工作	他还没有决定
没有女朋友	他女朋友在上海

Exercise II　In groups of two, make dialogues following the example.

Example

你会游泳吗？

A：你会游泳，是不是？

B：是啊，我会游泳。你是不是也会游泳？

A：不是，我不会游泳。

（1）圣诞节你去旅行吗？

（2）今天晚上 9:00 你在宿舍吗？

（3）你吃早饭了吗？

（4）你给家人买新年礼物了吗？

4. 语法小结（2）：四种汉语句子和常用的六种提问方法　Summary of grammar (2):
Four types of Chinese sentences and six types of questions

(1) 四种汉语句子　Four types of Chinese sentences

Simple Chinese sentences can be divided into four types depending on the main elements in the predicate.

❶ 动词谓语句　A sentence with a verbal predicate

Most Chinese sentences have a verbal predicate and are relatively complex. We have already learned several types and will learn more verbal predicates in the future. For example,

王小云的爸爸是医生。

林娜有两个姐姐。

我也学习汉语。

咱们打车去吧。

我送他一个生日蛋糕。

他想买点儿苹果。

我们请他做报告。

(For more examples, review Grammar 5 of Lesson 4, and related exercises.)

❷ 形容词谓语句　A sentence with an adjectival predicate

In a sentence with an adjectival predicate, "是" is not needed. For example,

我很好。

他最近太忙。

大为今天不舒服。

(For more examples, review Grammar 2 of Lesson 1, and related exercises.)

❸ 名词谓语句　A sentence with a nominal predicate

In a sentence with a nominal predicate, instead of using "是", a noun, noun phrase, or numeral-measure-word compound functions as the main element of the predicate. This type of sentence is mainly used to describe age, price, and so on. In spoken Chinese, a nominal predicate also expresses time, birthplace, and so on. For example,

林强二十七岁。

她今年几岁（了）？

这件衬衫三百九十九块。

现在几点（了）？

现在八点半。

今天星期四。

宋华北京人。

(For more examples, review Grammar 2 of Lesson 5, and related exercises.)

❹ 主谓谓语句　A sentence with a subject-predicate phrase as the predicate

What the subject in the subject-predicate phrase denotes is often a part of what the subject of the whole sentence denotes. The subject-predicate phrase describes and explains the subject of the whole sentence.

In other words, this type of sentence, at the first level, is composed of a subject (subject ₁) and a predicate (predicate ₁). The predicate itself, at the second level, is composed of a subject (subject ₂) and a predicate (predicate ₂). For the table that clearly illustrates the two levels, refer to the table in Grammar 1 of Lesson 8.

你身体怎么样?

我头疼。

他学习很好。

春天树都绿了。

(For more examples, review Grammar 1 of Lesson 8, and related exercises.)

(2) 六种提问方法　Six types of questions

❶ 用 "吗" 提问　Asking a question ending with "ma 吗"

This is the most commonly used type of question. The person who asks this kind of question has some idea about the response. For example,

您是陈老师吗?

你现在忙吗?

明天你不来学院吗?

(For more examples, review Grammar 1 of Lesson 1, and related exercises.)

❷ 正反疑问句　A/An verb/adjective-not-verb/adjective question

This type of question is often used as well. The person who asks this kind of question has no idea about the response. For example,

她是不是英国人?

你有没有弟弟?

他去没去那个饭馆?

你朋友认识不认识他?

图书馆大不大?

(For more examples, review Grammar 4 of Lesson 4, and related exercises)

❸ 用疑问代词的问句　An interrogative sentence with a question pronoun

This type of question specifically asks "shéi 谁" (who), "shénme 什么" (what), "nǎ 哪" (which), "nǎr 哪儿" (where), "zěnme 怎么" (how), "zěnmeyàng 怎么样" (how about), "duōshao 多少" (how many; how much), or "jǐ 几" (how many (for a small number under 10)), "wèi shénme 为什么" (why), etc. For example,

今天几号?

你叫什么名字？

他是哪国人？

你家在哪儿？

谁是贝贝？

你们班一共有多少人？

你现在学习怎么样？

草莓怎么卖？

你为什么九点还不起床？

(For more examples, review Grammar 2 of Lesson 2, Grammar 4 of Lesson 3, Grammar 4 of Lesson 7, Grammar 4 of Lesson 9, and related exercises.)

❹ 用"还是"的选择问句　Asking a choice-type question with "háishi 还是" (or)

The person who asks this type of question assumes that there are two or more possibilities, providing the options for the listener. For example,

他是英国人还是美国人？

我们现在去还是下午去？

内科在一层还是二层？

你喜欢草莓还是喜欢苹果？

(For more examples, review Grammar 2 of Lesson 8, and related exercises.)

❺ 用"好吗？""怎么样？""对吗？""是不是？""是吗？"的问句　Asking a question using "hǎo ma 好吗？", "zěnmeyàng 怎么样？", "duì ma 对吗？", "shì bu shì 是不是？", or "shì ma 是吗？"

A question using "好吗？" or "怎么样？" at the end of a sentence is usually used to ask someone's opinion. A question using "是不是？", "是．吗？" or "对吗？" is usually used to confirm the statement in the main sentence. For example,

我给你介绍一下，好吗？

咱们坐地铁去，怎么样？

饭馆后边有一条胡同，对吗？

今年你在北京过圣诞节，是不是？

你是不是很忙？

丁力波的爸爸以前也在语言学院学汉语，是吗？

(For more examples, review Grammar 5 of Lesson 6, Grammar 3 of Lesson 10, and related exercises.)

❻ 用"呢"的省略式问句 Asking an elliptical question with the particle "ne 呢"

The meaning of this type of question is usually clear from the previous sentence. For example,

我很好。你呢?

他上午没有课。你呢?

(For more examples, review Grammar 6 of Lesson 4, and related exercises.)

Exercise I Ask questions based on the underlined words and the requirements.

（1）我们学校很大。(Use "吗")

（2）我有一个姐姐。(Use "吗")

（3）他是中国人。(Use an interrogative pronoun)

（4）我的宿舍非常好。(Use an interrogative pronoun)

（5）他家有五口人。(Use an interrogative pronoun)

（6）这件衬衫280块。(Use an interrogative pronoun)

（7）我们坐地铁去王府井吧。(Use an interrogative pronoun)

（8）我不喜欢喝咖啡，我喜欢喝茶。(Use "还是")

（9）丁力波是加拿大人。(Use the verb/adjective-not-verb/adjective form)

（10）Taobao 是中国的。(Use an interrogative pronoun)

Exercise II Ask questions based on the following sentences. See who among you asks more questions.

（1）我和朋友坐公共汽车去天安门。

（2）今年我在我爱人的家乡过春节。

（3）他哥哥昨天让他给奶奶打电话。

四、练习与运用 PRACTICE AND APPLICATION

补充词语 Supplementary Words
2-10-06

| 1. 新年 | xīnnián | N | New Year 过新年 |

2.	国庆节	Guóqìng Jié	PN	National Day
3.	清明节	Qīngmíng Jié	PN	Qingming Festival; Tomb Sweeping Day
4.	劳动节	Láodòng Jié	PN	Labor Day
5.	端午节	Duānwǔ Jié	PN	Dragon Boat Festival
6.	儿童节	Értóng Jié	PN	Children's Day
7.	情人节	Qíngrén Jié	PN	Valentine's Day
8.	中秋节	Zhōngqiū Jié	PN	Mid-Autumn Festival; Moon Festival
9.	复活节	Fùhuó Jié	PN	Easter
10.	电脑	diànnǎo	N	computer　用电脑 买电脑
11.	发	fā	V	to send　发短信
12.	电子邮件	diànzǐ yóujiàn		e-mail　发电子邮件
13.	作业	zuòyè	N	homework　做作业
14.	录音	lùyīn	N	recording　听录音
15.	祝贺	zhùhè	V	to congratulate　祝贺你
16.	轻松	qīngsōng	A	relaxed　很轻松 太轻松了
17.	日记	rìjì	N	diary　写日记
18.	晴	qíng	A	sunny　天气晴
19.	第一次	dì-yī cì		the first time
20.	惊喜	jīngxǐ	N	surprise　一个惊喜
21.	通	tōng	V	to connect　通电话
22.	京剧	jīngjù	N	Peking opera　喜欢京剧 唱京剧
23.	火锅	huǒguō	N	hot pot　吃火锅

1 语音练习 Pronunciation Drills　🔊 2-10-07

Listen and read aloud: Add tone marks to the following words and sentences, and then read them aloud.

1 lüxing　　　**2** xueyuan　　　**3** jueding

4 Ding Yun　　　**5** jieri　　　**6** shiqing

7 erzi　　　**8** nü'er　　　**9** Ni qu nar le?

10 Ni mama shi bu shi xing Ding?

2 会话练习 Conversation Practice

Pair activity: Create dialogues based on the scenes and the requirements below.

1. Talking about something that has happened

Do the substitution drills and complete the dialogues.

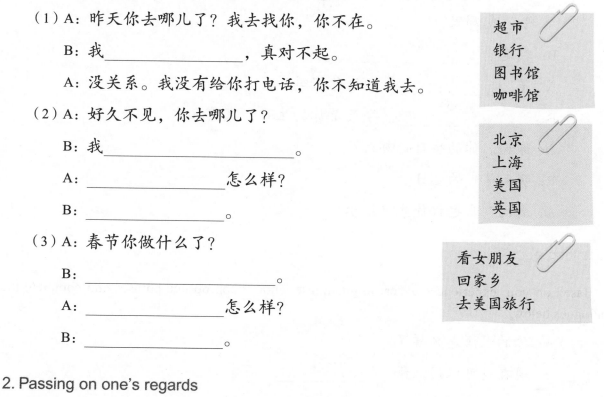

（1）A：昨天你去哪儿了？我去找你，你不在。

　　B：我_____，真对不起。

　　A：没关系。我没有给你打电话，你不知道我去。

（2）A：好久不见，你去哪儿了？

　　B：我_____。

　　A：_____怎么样？

　　B：_____。

（3）A：春节你做什么了？

　　B：_____。

　　A：_____怎么样？

　　B：_____。

超市
银行
图书馆
咖啡馆

北京
上海
美国
英国

看女朋友
回家乡
去美国旅行

2. Passing on one's regards

Complete the dialogues and perform them.

（1）A：好久不见，你好吗？

　　B：我_____。你爸爸妈妈身体怎么样？

　　A：他们_____。

　　B：请你问他们好。

　　A：谢谢。他们也问你好。

（2）A：是你啊！怎么样，工作忙不忙？

　　B：我_____。你呢？

　　A：我现在在学习法语（Fǎyǔ, French），也很忙。

　　B：你女朋友好吗？

　　A：她很好。她让我问你好。

　　B：谢谢。请你也_____。

3. Holiday wishes

Complete the dialogues and perform them.

（1）A：春节好！祝你_____！

B：我也_____！

（2）A：喂，您哪里？

B：我是_____。

A：是_____啊！你好吗？

B：_____。今天是你的生日，我要祝你_____！

A：谢谢。你的生日是哪天？

B：明天是我的生日。

A：真的？我也祝你生日快乐！

4. Talking about studying

Based on your experiences of learning Chinese, choose appropriate phrases and complete the dialogues below.

（1）A：你的汉语怎么样了？

B：现在我可以用汉语_____了。

（打车、买东西、问路、写电子邮件、问好）

（2）A：在汉语课上，你学习什么？

B：我学习_____。（生词、课文、语法、口语、汉字、文化）

（3）A：你觉得学习汉语怎么样？

B：_____。（有意思、容易、轻松、累、难）

3 听后复述 Listening and Repeating 🔊 2-10-08

Listen to the following dialogues and repeat what you hear.

（1）A：好久不见了，你怎么样？

B：我还好。听说你是语言学院的教授了，祝贺你！

A：谢谢。你爱人好吗？

B：她很好，最近去美国学习了。

（2）A：喂，您哪里？

　　B：我是宋华。

　　A：是你啊！你怎么样？有什
　　　么事儿？

　　B：明天你有时间吗？咱们踢
　　　足球好吗？

（3）A：喂，你好！请问您找谁？

　　B：我找林娜。

　　A：好，请等一下。

　　C：喂，我是林娜。

　　B：你好，林娜，我是陆雨平。

（4）A：喂，是 403 号宿舍吗？

　　B：是啊。您找谁？

　　A：丁力波在吗？

　　B：他不在。

　　A：请您告诉他，明天上午 10
　　　点去一下办公楼 301，可以
　　　吗？

　　B：没问题。

4　阅读理解 Reading Comprehension

丁力波的日记

12 月 18 日　星期五　天气晴

　　下星期五是圣诞节。这是我第一次在中国过圣诞节。我要跟小云一起去上海旅行。现在中国人也很喜欢过圣诞节。很多商场都有圣诞老人（Shèngdàn Lǎorén, Santa Claus）。商场东西（dōngxi, things）很多，买东西的人也很多。

　　上午十点，我去王府井给爸爸妈妈买圣诞礼物了。爸爸很喜欢京剧，妈妈也喜欢，我想给他们一个惊喜。我很想家，也想加拿大。

　　上午十点半，哥哥发短信给我，让我给妈妈打电话。

　　中午跟妈妈通电话，我真高兴。爸爸妈妈身体都很好，他们工作都很长。妈妈让我问外婆好。我告诉她外婆身体很好，哥哥和弟弟也都很好。哥哥可能回国，弟弟去旅行了。我现在有很多中国朋友，我会用汉语词典了，还会上中文网了。爸爸妈妈要给我寄一件圣诞礼物，我还不知道那是什么礼物。

Answer the following questions:

（1）圣诞节的时候，力波想去哪儿旅行？

（2）中国人怎么过圣诞节？

（3）力波可能给爸爸妈妈准备什么圣诞礼物？

（4）现在，力波的汉语怎么样？

春节是中国最重要的节日，在北京过春节很有意思。北京人在春节的时候常常去看京剧，或者跟朋友聚会。聚会时，他们常常准备很多礼物。在北京过节时天气很冷，常常下雪。北京人很喜欢在春节的时候吃饺子、吃火锅。我在朋友家第一次吃火锅。饺子和火锅都很好吃，吃的时候也很有意思。

Answer the following questions:

（1）中国最重要的节日是什么？

（2）过春节时，北京的天气怎么样？

（3）北京人过春节的时候常常吃什么？为什么？

5 任务与活动 Task and Activity

1. Role-play

On the street you meet a classmate who you have not seen for a long time. You make arrangements to go to a coffee shop to talk about what each other has been doing lately. Then ask each other to pass on regards to each other's families.

The following sentences may be helpful to you:

> 是你啊！／好久不见了！／你好吗？
>
> ……了吗？／……，是不是？／请问……好。

2. Role-play

In small groups, you and a few friends greet each other on Christmas Eve. One of you inadvertently mentions that today is also his or her birthday. Then everyone together wishes the person a happy birthday.

The following sentences may be helpful to you:

明天是……。/ 祝你……快乐！/……是我的生日。/ 谢谢。

6 写作练习 Writing Exercise

Using the format of the second passage for Reading Comprehension, write a paragraph introducing one of the holidays in your country and explain how you celebrate this holiday.

Your writing should cover:
(1) When is the holiday;
(2) What you eat, do, etc. to celebrate the holiday.

五、汉字 CHINESE CHARACTERS

1 汉字偏旁 Chinese Radicals

Radical	Name	Stroke Order	No. of Strokes	Example	Explanation
攵	反文旁	ノ 亠 ケ 攵	4	教 jiāo (to teach)	Related to "rapping or tapping"
夂	折文旁	ノ ク 夂	3	复 fù (to repeat) 夏 xià (summer)	Related to "walking slowly"
阝	左耳旁	⻖ 阝	2	院 yuàn (courtyard) 陈 Chén (a surname)	Related to "earth" or "stone"
阝	右耳旁	⻖ 阝	2	帮 bāng (to help) 都 dōu/dū (all/capital) 那 nà (that)	Related to "city/state"

2 认写基本汉字 Learn and Write the Basic Chinese Characters

（1）巾　　｜ 冂 巾

jīn　　piece of cloth　　　　　　　　　3 strokes

（2）可　　一　丁　丁　口　可
kě　　　but　　　　　　　　　　　　　　5 strokes

（3）戈　　一　七　戈　戈
gē　　　a type of ancient Chinese weapon　　4 strokes

（4）古　　一　十　十　古　古
gǔ　　　ancient　　　　　　　　　　　5 strokes

3 认写课文中的汉字 Learn and Write the Chinese Characters in the Text

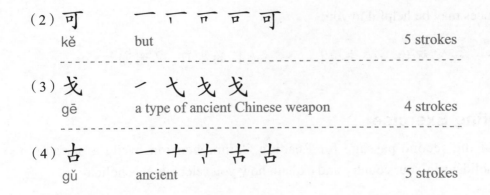

（1）事儿 shìr

事 → 一　丁　丐　写　写　写　事　　　8 strokes

（2）教学 jiàoxué

教 → 耂（耂：一　十　土　耂）+ 子 + 攵　　11 strokes

（3）复习 fùxí

复 → 𠂉 + 日 + 夂　　9 strokes

（4）夏天 xiàtiān

夏 → 一 + 自（自：丿　亻　冂　𦣞　自）+ 夂　　10 strokes

（5）帮 bāng

帮 → 邦 + 巾　　9 strokes

（6）寄 jì

寄 → 宀 + 大 + 可　　11 strokes

（7）找 zhǎo

找 → 扌 + 戈　　7 strokes

六、文化知识　*CULTURAL KNOWLEDGE*

Traditional Chinese Festivals

"Chūnjié 春节", the Spring Festival or Chinese New Year, falls on the first day of the first month on the Chinese lunar calendar. It is the most important and grandest traditional Chinese festival. On Chinese New Year's Eve, people will eat "niányèfàn 年夜饭" (family reunion dinner). Most northerners will eat "jiǎozi 饺子" (dumplings) because "jiǎozi" and "jiāozǐ 交子" (zǐshí 子时) (midnight) are homonyms, symbolizing "out with the old and in with the new". Most southerners will eat "niángāo 年糕" (Chinese New Year cake, made of glutinous rice) because "niángāo" and "niánnián gāo 年年高" (get promoted year after year) are homonyms, symbolizing that life gets better. All Chinese, regardless of southerners or northerners, will eat "yú 鱼" (fish) to represent "niánnián yǒu yú 年年有余" (having abundance every year) because the Chinese word "鱼" for fish is a homonym of "yú 余", the word for abundance. These customs all express a wish for happiness in the coming year. Visiting relatives and friends during the Chinese New Year are common activities. Due to the wide use of computers, cell phones, e-mails, and text messages, there are now new ways to wish others a Happy Chinese New Year. In addition, during this time, there are many forms of entertainment such as setting off fireworks, dragon dances, lion dances, going to temple fairs, and so on.

"Duānwǔ Jié 端午节", the Dragon Boat Festival, is celebrated on the fifth day of the fifth lunar month. Traditionally, the Chinese will eat "zòngzi 粽子" and hold dragon boat races at this time every year. "粽子" are made of glutinous rice wrapped in reed leaves and steamed. According to legend, this festival commemorates the patriotic poet "Qū Yuán 屈原" (c. 340 – 278 BCE), who lived during the Warring  States Period (475 – 221 BCE). Dragon boat racing is the most magnificent activity during "端午节". It has spread to East Asia, Southeast Asia, and all continents. It is becoming more and more popular in Canada and the United States.

"Zhōngqiū Jié 中秋节", the Mid-Autumn Festival (also called the Moon Festival in English), falls on the 15th day of the eighth lunar month. It is a time when the whole family enjoys getting together to look at a full moon and eat various kinds of moon cakes. During this festival,  moon cakes are essential treats and are given as gifts. The round shape of a moon cake symbolizes a family reunion. Appreciating the moon during this time of the year embodies Chinese people's special feelings toward the moon. According to Chinese mythology, the story of "Cháng'é 嫦娥" flying to the moon, combined with the local customs, adds to the poetic and romantic sentiments of the festival.

七、自我评估 *SELF-EVALUATION*

I can basically do the following things in Chinese:

- ☐ I can talk about something that has happened.
- ☐ I can talk about someone who has changed.
- ☐ I can talk about a holiday.
- ☐ I can express some holiday wishes.
- ☐ I can make a phone call in Chinese.
- ☐ I can pass on my regards to someone else.

趣味汉语　Fun with Chinese

Sending Holiday Wishes through Text Messages

Chūnjié: Zhù nǐ zài xīn de yì nián li:　yìfān-fēngshùn、shuāngxǐ-línmén、sānyáng-kāitài、

春节：祝 你 在 新 的 一 年 里：一 帆 风 顺、双 喜 临 门、三 阳 开 泰、

sìjì-fācái、　wǔfú-línmén、　liùliù-dàshùn、　qīxīng-gāozhào、　bāmiàn-línfēng、jiǔjiǔ-guīzhēn、

四 季 发 财、五 福 临 门、六 六 大 顺、七 星 高 照、　八 面 临 风、九 九 归 真、

shíquán-shíměi。　Qíshí jiù shì yí jù huà:　wànshì-rúyì!

十 全 十 美。 其 实 就 是 一 句 话：万 事 如 意！

一帆风顺 May you have a safe journey

双喜临门 May double happiness enter your home

三阳开泰 May the spring bring luck to you three times

四季发财 May you prosper in all the four seasons

五福临门 May five blessings abound in your family

六六大顺 May things go smoothly in six (many) ways

七星高照 May seven stars shine upon you

八面临风 May you have *guanxi* (social relationships) from eight (all) directions

九九归真 May you remember your pure origin nine times out of ten

十全十美 May you have a perfect life ten out of ten

万事如意 May all your wishes come true (May everything come your way)

Shèngdàn Jié: Dāng Shèngdàn Jié zhōngshēng xiǎngqǐ de nà yí kè,　qīn'ài de,　wǒ xiǎng
圣诞　节：当　圣诞　节　钟声　响起 的那一刻，亲爱的，我 想

duì nǐ shuō sān ge zì　(jīntiān bú shì Qíngrén Jié,　bié wùhuì),　wǒ yào gàosu nǐ de sān ge zì
对你 说 三个字（今天不是 情人 节，别误会），我 要 告诉你的三个字

shì —— lǐwù ne?
是——礼物呢？

Christmas: The moment the bell rings on Christmas, my dear, I would like to tell you three words (Don't be mistaken. Today is not Valentine's Day). The three words that I want to tell you are: "Where's my gift?"

学唱中文歌
Sing a song

康定 情歌
Kāngdìng Qínggē
A Love Song of Kangding

 2-10-09

四川民歌

稍慢　饱满地

1=F

3 5 6 65　6. 3 2　　3 5 6 65　6　3.

跑 马 溜 溜 的　　山　上，　　一 朵 溜 溜 的　　云　哟，
Pǎo mǎ liū liū de　shān shang,　yì duǒ liū liū de　yún yo,

李 家 溜 溜 的　　大　姐，　　人 才 溜 溜 的　　好　哟，
Lǐ jiā liū liū de　dàjiě,　　réncái liū liū de　hǎo yo,

一 来 溜 溜 的　　看　上，　　人 才 溜 溜 的　　好　哟，
Yī lái liū liū de　kànshang,　réncái liū liū de　hǎo yo,

世 间 溜 溜 的　　女　子，　　任 我 溜 溜 的　　爱　哟，
Shìjiān liū liū de　nǚzǐ,　　rèn wǒ liū liū de　ài yo,

3 5 6 65　6. 3 2　　5 3 23 21　2　6.

端 端 溜 溜 的　　照　在，　　康 定 溜 溜 的　　城　哟！
duān duān liū liū de　zhào zài,　Kāngdìng liū liū de　chéng yo!

张 家 溜 溜 的　　大　哥，　　看 上 溜 溜 的　　她　哟！
Zhāng jiā liū liū de　dàgē,　　kànshang liū liū de　tā yo!

二 来 溜 溜 的　　看　上，　　会 当 溜 溜 的　　家　哟！
Èr lái liū liū de　kànshang,　huì dāng liū liū de　jiā yo!

世 间 溜 溜 的　　男　子，　　任 你 溜 溜 的　　求　哟！
shìjiān liū liū de　nánzǐ,　　rèn nǐ liū liū de　qiú yo!

6 2.　5 3.　2 1 6.　　5 3 23 21　2　6.

月 亮　弯　　弯，　　康 定 溜 溜 的 城 哟！
Yuèliang　wān　　wān,　　Kāngdìng liū liū de chéng yo!

月 亮　弯　　弯，　　看 上 溜 溜 的 她 哟！
Yuèliang　wān　　wān,　　kànshang liū liū de tā yo!

月 亮　弯　　弯，　　会 当 溜 溜 的 家 哟！
Yuèliang　wān　　wān,　　huì dāng liū liū de jiā yo!

月 亮　弯　　弯，　　任 你 溜 溜 的 求 哟！
Yuèliang　wān　　wān,　　rèn nǐ liū liū de qiú yo!

附录 1 | 语法术语缩略形式一览表
Appendix 1 | Abbreviations for Grammar Terms

缩略形式 *Abbreviations*	英文翻译 *Grammar Terms in English*	中文名称 *Grammar Terms in Chinese*	拼音 *Grammar Terms in Pīnyīn*
A	Adjective	形容词	xíngróngcí
Adv	Adverb	副词	fùcí
AsPt	Aspect Particle	动态助词	dòngtài zhùcí
Conj	Conjunction	连词	liáncí
IE	Idiomatic Expression	习惯用语	xíguàn yòngyǔ
Int	Interjection	叹词	tàncí
M	Measure Word	量词	liàngcí
MdPt	Modal Particle	语气助词	yǔqì zhùcí
N	Noun	名词	míngcí
NP	Noun Phrase	名词词组	míngcí cízǔ
Nu	Numeral	数词	shùcí
O	Object	宾语	bīnyǔ
Ono	Onomatopoeia	象声词	xiàngshēngcí
OpV	Optative Verb	能愿动词	néngyuàn dòngcí
P	Predicate	谓语	wèiyǔ
PN	Proper Noun	专有名词	zhuānyǒu míngcí
Pr	Pronoun	代词	dàicí
Pref	Prefix	词头	cítóu
Prep	Preposition	介词	jiècí
Pt	Particle	助词	zhùcí
PW	Place Word	地点词	dìdiǎncí
QPr	Question Pronoun	疑问代词	yíwèn dàicí
QPt	Question Particle	疑问助词	yíwèn zhùcí
S	Subject	主语	zhǔyǔ
StPt	Structural Particle	结构助词	jiégòu zhùcí
Suf	Suffix	词尾	cíwěi
TW	Time Word	时间词	shíjiāncí
V	Verb	动词	dòngcí
VC	Verb plus Complement	动词与补语	dòngcí yǔ bǔyǔ
VO	Verb plus Object	动宾式动词	dòngbīnshì dòngcí
VP	Verb Phrase	动词词组	dòngcí cízǔ

A

啊	啊	a	MdPt	*attached to a verb, adjective, or the end of a sentence as a sign of confirmation*	3
爱	愛	ài	V	to love	10
爱人	愛人	àiren	N	husband or wife	10

B

爸爸	爸爸	bàba	N	dad; father	2
吧	吧	ba	MdPt	*a modal particle used at the end of a sentence to indicate consultation, suggestion, request, etc.*	4
百	百	bǎi	Nu	hundred	7
班	班	bān	N	class	4
办公	辦公	bàngōng	VO	to handle official business; to work (usu. in an office)	6
办公楼	辦公樓	bàngōnglóu	N	office building; administration building	6
半	半	bàn	Nu	half	4
帮	幫	bāng	V	to help	10
包子	包子	bāozi	N	*baozi*; steamed stuffed bun	2
报告	報告	bàogào	N	speech; lecture; report	10
北	北	běi	N	north	6
北边	北邊	běibian	N	north (side)	6
北京	北京	Běijīng	PN	Beijing	2
贝贝	貝貝	Bèibei	PN	Beibei, a name	3
别	別	bié	Adv	don't	6
病	病	bìng	N/V	illness / to be sick	8
博物馆	博物館	bówùguǎn	N	museum	9
不错	不錯	búcuò	A	pretty good	7
不客气	不客氣	bú kèqi	IE	you are welcome	5
不用	不用	búyòng	Adv	no need	8
不	不	bù	Adv	not; no	1
不好意思	不好意思	bù hǎoyìsi	IE	(to be) sorry; to feel embarrassed	5

C

参加	參加	cānjiā	V	to participate; to attend	5
草莓	草莓	cǎoméi	N	strawberry	7
层	層	céng	M	floor	8
茶	茶	chá	N	tea	3
差	差	chà	V	to be short of; to lack	4
尝	嘗	cháng	V	to taste	7
常	常	cháng	Adv	often	5
常常	常常	chángcháng	Adv	often	5
唱	唱	chàng	V	to sing	5
唱歌	唱歌	chàng gē	V O	to sing (a song)	5
超市	超市	chāoshì	N	supermarket	6
车	車	chē	N	vehicle	9
陈	陳	Chén	PN	Chen, a surname	2
衬衫	襯衫	chènshān	N	shirt; blouse	7
吃	吃	chī	V	to eat	2
出生	出生	chūshēng	V	to be born	5
穿	穿	chuān	V	to wear (clothing); to put on	8
床	床	chuáng	N	bed	8
春节	春節	Chūnjié	PN	Spring Festival; Chinese New Year	10
春天	春天	chūntiān	N	spring	9
词典	詞典	cídiǎn	N	dictionary	10
错	錯	cuò	A	wrong	7

D

打车	打車	dǎchē	VO	to take a taxi; (to go somewhere) by taxi	9
打电话	打電話	dǎ diànhuà	V O	to call someone	10
打折	打折	dǎzhé	VO	to offer a discount	7
打针	打針	dǎzhēn	VO	to give an injection; to get a shot	8
大	大	dà	A	big	2
大家	大家	dàjiā	Pr	everyone	5
大夫	大夫	dàifu	N	doctor	8
蛋糕	蛋糕	dàngāo	N	cake	5
当然	當然	dāngrán	Adv	of course	7
到	到	dào	V	to reach; to arrive	2
的	的	de	StPt	*a possessive or modifying particle*	3
等	等	děng	V	to wait	6
地方	地方	dìfang	N	place; region	6

地铁	地鐵	dìtiě	N	subway	9
地图	地圖	dìtú	N	map	6
弟弟	弟弟	dìdi	N	younger brother	3
点心	點心	diǎnxin	N	snacks; dim sum	2
点（钟）	點（鐘）	diǎn (zhōng)	M	o'clock	4
电话	電話	diànhuà	N	telephone	10
电影	電影	diànyǐng	N	movie	4
店	店	diàn	N	shop; store	10
丁力波	丁力波	Dīng Lìbō	PN	Ding Libo, name of a Canadian student	1
丁云	丁雲	Dīng Yún	PN	Ding Yun, Chinese name of Ding Libo's mother	10
东	東	dōng	N	east	6
东边	東邊	dōngbian	N	east (side)	6
冬天	冬天	dōngtiān	N	winter	9
都	都	dōu	Adv	all; both	2
堵	堵	dǔ	V	to block	9
堵车	堵車	dǔchē	VO	to be congested with traffic; to be in a traffic jam	9
度	度	dù	M	degree	8
短	短	duǎn	A	short	10
短信	短信	duǎnxìn	N	text message	10
对	對	duì	A	right; correct	4
对不起	對不起	duìbuqǐ	V	(to be) sorry	8
对了	對了	duìle	V	(*an expression to change the subject of a conversation or to remind the listener of a new subject*) by the way; well, yes	4
对面	對面	duìmiàn	N	opposite; across (from)	6
多	多	duō	A/Adv	many; much; more	4
多大	多大	duō dà	IE	how old	5
多少	多少	duōshao	QPr	how many; how much	4

E

饿	餓	è	A	hungry	9
儿子	兒子	érzi	N	son	10

F

发炎	發炎	fāyán	VO	to be inflamed	8
饭	飯	fàn	N	(cooked) rice; meal	2
饭馆	飯館	fànguǎn	N	restaurant	6
飞机	飛機	fēijī	N	airplane	9

（飞）机票	（飛）機票	(fēi) jīpiào	N	airplane ticket	9
分	分	fēn	M	minute	4
风	風	fēng	N	wind	9
复习	複習	fùxí	V	to review	10

G

该	該	gāi	OpV	should	8
干杯	乾杯	gānbēi	VO	to drink a toast; cheers; bottoms up	5
刚	剛	gāng	Adv	just	2
刚才	剛才	gāngcái	N	just now	10
钢琴	鋼琴	gāngqín	N	piano	3
高兴	高興	gāoxìng	A	happy	1
哥哥	哥哥	gēge	N	elder brother	3
歌	歌	gē	N	song	5
个	個	gè	M	*a measure word for general use*	3
给	給	gěi	Prep	to; for	6
给	給	gěi	V	to give	7
跟	跟	gēn	Prep	with	6
工作	工作	gōngzuò	V/N	to work / work; job	3
公共	公共	gōnggòng	A	public	9
公共汽车	公共汽車	gōnggòng qìchē	N	bus	9
狗	狗	gǒu	N	dog	3
古波	古波	Gǔ Bō	PN	Gu Bo, Chinese name of Ding Libo's father	10
刮风	颳風	guā fēng	VO	to be windy	9
挂	掛	guà	V	to register (in a hospital)	8
挂号	掛號	guàhào	VO	to register (in a hospital)	8
贵	貴	guì	A	expensive	7
贵姓	貴姓	guìxìng	N	one's (honorable) surname	2
国	國	guó	N	country	2
过	過	guò	V	to cross; to pass	6
过	過	guò	V	to spend (time)	10
过节	過節	guòjié	OV	to spend a holiday; to celebrate a festival	10

H

还	還	hái	Adv	in addition	3
还是	還是	háishi	Conj	*(used in a choice-type question)* or	8
孩子	孩子	háizi	N	child	3
汉语	漢語	Hànyǔ	N	Chinese (usually referring to Mandarin)	2
汉字	漢字	Hànzì	N	Chinese character	4

好	好	hǎo	A	good; well; fine; OK	1
好吃	好吃	hǎochī	A	delicious; tasty	2
好久	好久	hǎojiǔ	A	very long; for a long time	10
好久不见	好久不見	hǎojiǔ bú jiàn	IE	long time no see	10
号	號	hào	N	day of the month; date; size	5
喝	喝	hē	V	to drink	3
合适	合適	héshì	A	suitable; fitting	7
和	和	hé	Conj	and	2
盒	盒	hé	N	box	5
黑	黑	hēi	A	black	7
黑色	黑色	hēisè	N	black	7
很	很	hěn	Adv	very	1
后	後	hòu	N	back	6
后边	後邊	hòubian	N	back; behind; rear	6
胡同	胡同	hútòng	N	hutong; alley	6
滑雪	滑雪	huáxuě	VO	to ski	9
欢迎	歡迎	huānyíng	V	to welcome	5
换	換	huàn	V	to transfer; to change	9
回	回	huí	V	to return	4
会	會	huì	OpV/V	can; to be able to / to have knowledge of	9
活动	活動	huódòng	N	activity; event	4

J

几	幾	jǐ	QPr	how many	3
季节	季節	jìjié	N	season	9
寄	寄	jì	V	to post; to mail	10
加拿大	加拿大	Jiānádà	PN	Canada	10
家	家	jiā	N	family; home	3
家乡	家鄉	jiāxiāng	N	hometown	9
驾照	駕照	jiàzhào	N	license	9
件	件	jiàn	M	item/article (of clothing)	7
教	教	jiāo	V	to teach	5
饺子	餃子	jiǎozi	N	jiaozi; dumpling	2
叫	叫	jiào	V	to be called; to call	1
教授	教授	jiàoshòu	N	professor	10
教学	教學	jiàoxué	N	teaching and learning	6
街	街	jiē	N	street	6
街道	街道	jiēdào	N	street	6

节	節	jié	N	holiday; festival	10
节日	節日	jiérì	N	festival; holiday	10
姐姐	姐姐	jiějie	N	elder sister	3
介绍	介紹	jièshào	V	to introduce	5
斤	斤	jīn	M	*jin* (500g)	7
今年	今年	jīnnián	N	this year	3
今天	今天	jīntiān	N	today	3
进	進	jìn	V	to enter	1
就	就	jiù	Adv	exactly	5
聚会	聚會	jùhuì	N	get-together; party	5
决定	決定	juédìng	V	to decide	10

K

咖啡	咖啡	kāfēi	N	coffee	3
卡	卡	kǎ	N	card	7
开	開	kāi	V	to drive	9
开车	開車	kāichē	VO	to drive a car (or any type of vehicle)	9
看	看	kàn	V	to look at; to see	2
看	看	kàn	V	to see; to visit (someone)	10
看病	看病	kànbìng	VO	to see a doctor	8
科	科	kē	N	department	8
可能	可能	kěnéng	OpV	may; maybe; (to be) possible	9
可是	可是	kěshì	Conj	but	8
可惜	可惜	kěxī	A	it's a pity	5
可以	可以	kěyǐ	OpV	may; can	7
刻	刻	kè	M	quarter (of an hour)	4
客气	客氣	kèqi	A	polite	5
课	課	kè	N	class; lesson; course	3
课文	課文	kèwén	N	text	10
空气	空氣	kōngqì	N	air	9
恐怕	恐怕	kǒngpà	Adv	(*indicating an estimation*) I'm afraid that…	4
口	口	kǒu	M	*a measure word mainly for the number of people in a family*	3
口语	口語	kǒuyǔ	N	spoken language	4
块（钱）	塊（錢）	kuài (qián)	M	*kuai (a colloquial measure word for dollar)*	7
快	快	kuài	Adv/A	quickly / quick	8
快乐	快樂	kuàilè	A	happy	5

L

| 来 | 來 | lái | V | to come | 4 |

老	老	lǎo	A	old	6
老板	老闆	lǎobǎn	N	shopkeeper; proprietor; boss	7
老师	老師	lǎoshī	N	teacher	2
了	了	le	Pt	*an aspect particle indicating something that has happened or a change*	9
累	累	lèi	A	tired; exhausted	4
冷	冷	lěng	A	cold	8
礼物	禮物	lǐwù	N	gift; present	5
里	裏 / 裡	lǐ	N	in; inside	6
里边	裏邊 / 裡邊	lǐbian	N	in; inside	6
练习	練習	liànxí	V/N	to practice / exercise	4
凉快	凉快	liángkuai	A	cool	9
量	量	liáng	V	to measure	8
两	兩	liǎng	Nu	two	3
林娜	林娜	Lín Nà	PN	Lin Na, name of a British student	1
林强	林强	Lín Qiáng	PN	Lin Qiang, name of a British student, Lin Na's elder brother	5
零	零	líng	Nu	zero	7
龙	龍	lóng	N	dragon	5
楼	樓	lóu	N	building	6
陆雨平	陸雨平	Lù Yǔpíng	PN	Lu Yuping, name of a Chinese reporter	3
路	路	lù	N	road; way; path	6
路	路	lù	N	route; road	9
路上	路上	lùshang	N	on the way	9
旅行	旅行	lǚxíng	V	to travel	10
绿	綠	lǜ	A	green	7
绿色	綠色	lǜsè	N	green	7

M

妈妈	媽媽	māma	N	mom; mother	2
马大为	馬大為	Mǎ Dàwéi	PN	Ma Dawei, name of an American student	1
马路	馬路	mǎlù	N	road; street	6
吗	嗎	ma	QPt	*a modal particle used for a question expecting a yes-no answer*	1
买	買	mǎi	V	to buy	7
卖	賣	mài	V	to sell	7
慢	慢	màn	A	slow	9
忙	忙	máng	A	busy	1

没	没	méi	Adv	not	3
没关系	没關係	méi guānxi	IE	it doesn't matter; never mind	8
没问题	没問題	méi wèntí	IE	no problem	7
每	每	měi	Pr	each; every	8
美国	美國	Měiguó	PN	the United States	2
妹妹	妹妹	mèimei	N	younger sister	3
门	門	mén	N	door; gate; entrance	6
们	們	men	Suf	*plural suffix*	2
米饭	米飯	mǐfàn	N	(cooked) rice	2
面条	麵條	miàntiáo	N	noodles	2
名字	名字	míngzi	N	name	1
明天	明天	míngtiān	N	tomorrow	4

N

哪	哪	nǎ	QPr	which	2
哪儿	哪兒	nǎr	QPr	where	6
哪里	哪裏 / 哪裡	nǎli	IE	(*an expression of modesty*) not at all	7
那	那	nà	Pr	that	2
男	男	nán	A	male	4
男生	男生	nánshēng	N	male student	4
呢	呢	ne	QPt	*a modal particle used for an elliptical question*	1
内	内	nèi	N	internal; inside	8
内科	内科	nèikē	N	department of internal medicine	8
能	能	néng	OpV	can; to be able to	8
你	你	nǐ	Pr	you (*singular*)	1
你们	你們	nǐmen	Pr	you (*plural*)	2
年	年	nián	N	year	3
年轻	年輕	niánqīng	A	young	10
您	您	nín	Pr	you (*singular, polite form*)	2
牛仔裤	牛仔褲	niúzǎikù	N	jeans	7
女	女	nǚ	A	female	3
女儿	女兒	nǚ'ér	N	daughter	3
女生	女生	nǚshēng	N	female student	4
暖和	暖和	nuǎnhuo	A	warm	9

P

旁边	旁邊	pángbiān	N	side; beside	6
朋友	朋友	péngyou	N	friend	2
便宜	便宜	piányi	A	inexpensive; cheap	7

票	票	piào	N	ticket	9
漂亮	漂亮	piàoliang	A	beautiful; pretty	3
苹果	蘋果	píngguǒ	N	apple	7
苹果园	蘋果園	Píngguǒyuán	PN	Pingguoyuan (Apple Orchard, name of a subway station in Beijing)	9

Q

起床	起床	qǐchuáng	VO	to get up	8
汽车	汽車	qìchē	N	vehicle; car	9
千	千	qiān	Nu	thousand	7
前	前	qián	N	front	6
前边	前邊	qiánbian	N	front; in front of	6
钱	錢	qián	N	money	7
巧克力	巧克力	qiǎokèlì	N	chocolate	5
请	請	qǐng	V	please; to request; to invite	1
请问	請問	qǐngwèn	V	may I ask; excuse me	1
秋天	秋天	qiūtiān	N	autumn; fall	9
去	去	qù	V	to go	4
全	全	quán	A	whole; complete; total	8
全身	全身	quánshēn	N	the whole body; all over	8

R

让	讓	ràng	V	to let; to allow	10
热	熱	rè	A	hot	9
人	人	rén	N	person	2
认识	認識	rènshi	V	to know	1
日	日	rì	N	day	5

S

嗓子	嗓子	sǎngzi	N	throat	8
商店	商店	shāngdiàn	N	shop; store	10
上	上	shàng	N	above; preceding; previous	4
上海	上海	Shànghǎi	PN	Shanghai	2
上课	上課	shàngkè	VO	to go to class	8
上网	上網	shàngwǎng	VO	to go online; to go on the Internet	10
上午	上午	shàngwǔ	N	morning; before noon	4
少	少	shǎo	A	few; little	4
谁	誰	shéi	QPr	who; whom	3
身体	身體	shēntǐ	N	body; health	8
什么	什麼／甚麼	shénme	QPr	what	1
生日	生日	shēngrì	N	birthday	5

圣诞节	聖誕節	Shèngdàn Jié	PN	Christmas; Christmas Day	10
时候	時候	shíhou	N	time; moment	9
时间	時間	shíjiān	N	time	4
食堂	食堂	shítáng	N	cafeteria; dining hall	6
事儿	事兒	shìr	N	matter; thing	5
试	試	shì	V	to try; to try on	7
是	是	shì	V	to be; is/am/are...	2
手	手	shǒu	N	hand	10
手机	手機	shǒujī	N	cell phone	10
寿面	壽麵	shòumiàn	N	(birthday) longevity noodles	5
售货员	售貨員	shòuhuòyuán	N	salesperson	7
书	書	shū	N	book	6
舒服	舒服	shūfu	A	comfortable	8
属	屬	shǔ	V	to be born in the year of (one of the 12 animals in the Chinese zodiac)	5
树	樹	shù	N	tree	9
刷卡	刷卡	shuākǎ	VO	to pay with a credit/debit card	7
水	水	shuǐ	N	water	8
睡	睡	shuì	V	to sleep	8
睡觉	睡覺	shuìjiào	VO	to sleep; to go to bed	8
说	説	shuō	V	to say; to speak	4
宋华	宋華	Sòng Huá	PN	Song Hua, name of a Chinese student	1
送	送	sòng	V	to give (as a gift); to deliver	5
宿舍	宿舍	sùshè	N	dormitory	6
岁	歲	suì	M	year (of age)	3

T

他	他	tā	Pr	he; him	1
她	她	tā	Pr	she; her	2
太	太	tài	Adv	too; extremely	1
特别	特別	tèbié	Adv	especially	4
疼	疼	téng	A	painful	8
体温	體溫	tǐwēn	N	body temperature	8
体育	體育	tǐyù	N	physical education; physical training	6
体育馆	體育館	tǐyùguǎn	N	gym; stadium	6
天	天	tiān	N	day	3
天安门	天安門	Tiān'ān Mén	PN	Tian'anmen	9
天气	天氣	tiānqì	N	weather	8
条	條	tiáo	M	(a measure word for something long, narrow or thin, like rivers, dragons, trousers, etc.) strip; long narrow piece	6

跳	跳	tiào	V	to jump	5
跳舞	跳舞	tiàowǔ	VO	to dance	5
听	聽	tīng	V	to listen	4
听说	聽説	tīngshuō	V	to be told; to hear of	4
同学	同學	tóngxué	N	classmate; schoolmate	6
头	頭	tóu	N	head	8
图书馆	圖書館	túshūguǎn	N	library	6

W

外婆	外婆	wàipó	N	(maternal) grandmother	10
晚	晚	wǎn	A	late	3
晚上	晚上	wǎnshang	N	evening	3
王府井	王府井	Wángfǔjǐng	PN	Wangfujing, a famous shopping area in Beijing	10
王小云	王小雲	Wáng Xiǎoyún	PN	Wang Xiaoyun, name of a Chinese student	2
网	網	wǎng	N	net; Internet	10
为什么	為什麼 / 為甚麼	wèi shénme	QPr	why	8
喂	喂	wèi	Int	(usually on the phone) hello	10
文学	文學	wénxué	N	literature	10
问	問	wèn	V	to ask	1
问好	問好	wènhǎo	VO	to send one's regards (to someone); to say hello (to someone)	10
问题	問題	wèntí	N	question; problem; issue	7
我	我	wǒ	Pr	I; me	1
舞	舞	wǔ	N	dance	5

X

西	西	xī	N	west	6
西边	西邊	xībian	N	west (side)	6
西方	西方	Xīfāng	N	the West	10
喜欢	喜歡	xǐhuan	V	to like	2
下	下	xià	N	below; next; latter	4
下午	下午	xiàwǔ	N	afternoon	4
下雪	下雪	xià xuě	V O	to snow	9
下雨	下雨	xià yǔ	V O	to rain	9
夏天	夏天	xiàtiān	N	summer	9
先	先	xiān	Adv	first; before	6
先生	先生	xiānsheng	N	sir; Mr.	7
现在	現在	xiànzài	N	now	4

线	綫	xiàn	N	line; route	9
响	響	xiǎng	V	to ring	10
想	想	xiǎng	V/OpV	to think; to think about / to want; would like	7
想	想	xiǎng	V	to miss	10
小	小	xiǎo	A	small	2
小姐	小姐	xiǎojiě	N	Miss; young lady	6
校门	校門	xiàomén	N	school gate; campus entrance	6
些	些	xiē	M	some; a few	7
写	寫	xiě	V	to write	5
血	血	xiě	N	blood	8
谢谢	謝謝	xièxie	V	to thank	1
新	新	xīn	A	new	6
星期	星期	xīngqī	N	week	5
星期日	星期日	Xīngqīrì	N	Sunday	5
行	行	xíng	V	to be OK	4
姓	姓	xìng	V/N	one's surname is / surname	1
休息	休息	xiūxi	V	to rest; to take a break	8
学	學	xué	V	to study (usually with an object)	2
学生	學生	xuésheng	N	student	4
学习	學習	xuéxí	V	to study; to learn	2
学校	學校	xuéxiào	N	school	4
学院	學院	xuéyuàn	N	institute; college	10
雪	雪	xuě	N	snow	9

Y

验血	驗血	yànxiě	VO	to have a blood test	8
药	藥	yào	N	medicine	8
要	要	yào	V	to want; would like	2
也	也	yě	Adv	also; too	1
衣服	衣服	yīfu	N	clothing	7
医生	醫生	yīshēng	N	doctor	3
医院	醫院	yīyuàn	N	hospital	8
一共	一共	yígòng	Adv	altogether	3
一会儿	一會兒	yíhuìr	Nu-M	in a little while	5
一下	一下	yíxià	Nu-M	*used after a verb to indicate a short or informal action*	5
以前	以前	yǐqián	N	before; previously	9
（一）点儿	（一）點兒	(yì) diǎnr	Nu-M	a little; some	7

一起	一起	yìqǐ	Adv	together	4
意思	意思	yìsi	N	meaning	4
银行	銀行	yínháng	N	bank	6
应该	應該	yīnggāi	OpV	should; ought to	8
英国	英國	Yīngguó	PN	United Kingdom; England	5
英语	英語	Yīngyǔ	N	English (language)	3
用	用	yòng	V	to use	10
游泳	游泳	yóuyǒng	VO	to swim	9
有	有	yǒu	V	to have; there is/are	3
有（一）点儿	有（一）點兒	yǒu (yì) diǎnr	Adv	somewhat; a little	8
有意思	有意思	yǒu yìsi		interesting	4
右	右	yòu	N	right	6
右边	右邊	yòubian	N	right (side)	6
羽绒服	羽絨服	yǔróngfú	N	down coat; down jacket	7
雨	雨	yǔ	N	rain	9
语法	語法	yǔfǎ	N	grammar	4
语言	語言	yǔyán	N	language	10
员	員	yuán	Suf	(*a suffix attached to persons in certain fields*) person	7
月	月	yuè	N	month	5
运动	運動	yùndòng	V	to do sports; to take exercise	8

Z

再	再	zài	Adv	again	7
再见	再見	zàijiàn	V	goodbye	2
在	在	zài	V	to be (here, there); to be (in, on, at)	1
在	在	zài	Prep	at, in, on	8
咱们	咱們	zánmen	Pr	we; us	5
早	早	zǎo	A	early	2
早上	早上	zǎoshang	N	morning	2
怎么	怎麼	zěnme	QPr	how	7
怎么样	怎麼樣	zěnmeyàng	QPr	how (is, are); how about	1
展览	展覽	zhǎnlǎn	V	to exhibit	9
张	張	zhāng	M	*a measure word for flat objects*	3
着急	着急	zháojí	A	worried; anxious	6
找	找	zhǎo	V	to give change	7
照片	照片	zhàopiàn	N	picture; photo	3
这	這	zhè	Pr	this	2
这儿	這兒	zhèr	Pr	here	6

针	針	zhēn	N	injection	8
真	真	zhēn	Adv/A	really / real	3
知道	知道	zhīdào	V	to know	6
只	祇	zhǐ	Adv	only	4
中国	中國	Zhōngguó	PN	China	3
中文	中文	Zhōngwén	N	Chinese (language)	5
中药	中藥	zhōngyào	N	traditional Chinese medicine	8
重要	重要	zhòngyào	A	important	10
主意	主意	zhǔyi	N	idea	4
住	住	zhù	V	to live	10
祝	祝	zhù	V	to wish	5
专业	專業	zhuānyè	N	major (subject)	4
最	最	zuì	Adv	most; to the highest degree	9
最近	最近	zuìjìn	Adv	lately; recently	1
昨天	昨天	zuótiān	N	yesterday	5
左	左	zuǒ	N	left	7
左边	左邊	zuǒbian	N	left (side)	7
坐	坐	zuò	V	to sit	1
坐	坐	zuò	V	to sit; to go/travel somewhere by means of	9
做	做	zuò	V	to do; to make	3

补充生词 / 補充生詞
Supplementary Words

A

埃及	埃及	Āijí	PN	Egypt	2
澳大利亚	澳大利亞	Àodàlìyà	PN	Australia	2

B

白色	白色	báisè	N	white	7
杯	杯	bēi	N	cup; glass; mug	3
比萨饼	比薩餅	bǐsàbǐng	N	pizza	2
脖子	脖子	bózi	N	neck	8

C

参观	參觀	cānguān	V	to visit (a place)	9
操场	操場	cāochǎng	N	sports field	6
称呼	稱呼	chēnghu	V	to call; to address	7
城里	城裏 / 城裡	chéngli	N	city; town	9
橙汁	橙汁	chéngzhī	N	orange juice	3
橙子	橙子	chéngzi	N	orange	7
厨房	廚房	chúfáng	N	kitchen	6
穿	穿	chuān	V	to wear; to put on	7
船	船	chuán	N	ship; boat	9

D

打球	打球	dǎ qiú	V O	to play ball	4
大便	大便	dàbiàn	N	feces, stool	8
德国	德國	Déguó	PN	Germany	2
第一次	第一次	dì-yī cì		the first time	10
电脑	電腦	diànnǎo	N	computer	10
电视	電視	diànshì	N	television; TV	4
电子邮件	電子郵件	diànzǐ yóujiàn		e-mail	10
豆浆	豆漿	dòujiāng	N	soyabean milk	3
端午节	端午節	Duānwǔ Jié	PN	Dragon Boat Festival	10

E

俄罗斯	俄羅斯	Éluósī	PN	Russia	2
饿	餓	è	A	hungry	1
儿童节	兒童節	Értóng Jié	PN	Children's Day	10

F

发	發	fā	V	to send	10
发烧	發燒	fāshāo	VO	to have a fever	8
法国	法國	Fǎguó	PN	France	2
分	分	fēn	M	*fen (a measure word for one cent)*	7
服务员	服務員	fúwùyuán	N	waiter; waitress; server	3
复活节	復活節	Fùhuó Jié	PN	Easter	10

G

感冒	感冒	gǎnmào	V	to have a cold	8
胳膊	胳膊	gēbo	N	arm	8
工程师	工程師	gōngchéngshī	N	engineer	3
公园	公園	gōngyuán	N	park	9
国庆节	國慶節	Guóqìng Jié	PN	National Day	10

H

还行	還行	hái xíng		not bad	1
韩国	韓國	Hánguó	PN	South Korea	2
汉堡包	漢堡包	hànbǎobāo	N	hamburger	2
红色	紅色	hóngsè	N	red	7
猴	猴	hóu	N	monkey	5
后天	後天	hòutiān	N	the day after tomorrow	5
滑冰	滑冰	huábīng	VO	to go ice-skating; to skate	9
火车	火車	huǒchē	N	train	9
火车站	火車站	huǒchēzhàn	N	railway station	9
火锅	火鍋	huǒguō	N	hot pot	10

J

机场	機場	jīchǎng	N	airport	9
鸡	鷄	jī	N	chicken; rooster	5
急诊	急診	jízhěn	N	emergency	8
记者	記者	jìzhě	N	reporter	3
加拿大	加拿大	Jiānádà	PN	Canada	2
角	角	jiǎo	M	*jiao (the official measure word for 10 cents)*	7
京剧	京劇	jīngjù	N	Peking opera	10
经济	經濟	jīngjì	N	economics; economy	4
经理	經理	jīnglǐ	N	manager	3
惊喜	驚喜	jīngxǐ	N	surprise	10
酒吧	酒吧	jiǔbā	N	bar	6

K

咖啡厅	咖啡廳	kāfēitīng	N	coffee shop; café	6
可乐	可樂	kělè	N	Coke; cola	3
渴	渴	kě	A	thirsty	1
客厅	客廳	kètīng	N	living room	6
困	睏	kùn	A	sleepy	1

L

拉肚子	拉肚子	lā dùzi	V O	to have loose bowels; to have diarrhea	8
篮球	籃球	lánqiú	N	basketball	9
劳动节	勞動節	Láodòng Jié	PN	Labor Day	10
老虎	老虎	lǎohǔ	N	tiger	5
老鼠	老鼠	lǎoshǔ	N	rat; mouse	5
累	纍	lèi	A	tired	1
历史	歷史	lìshǐ	N	history	4
录音	錄音	lùyīn	N	recording	10
律师	律師	lǜshī	N	lawyer	3

M

马	馬	mǎ	N	horse	5
马马虎虎	馬馬虎虎	mǎmǎhūhū	A	so-so	1
毛	毛	máo	M	*mao (a colloquial measure word for 10 cents)*	7
美术馆	美術館	měishùguǎn	N	art gallery	9
面包	麵包	miànbāo	N	bread	2

N

那儿	那兒	nàr	Pr	there	6
男朋友	男朋友	nánpéngyou	N	boyfriend	3
难	難	nán	A	difficult	4
牛	牛	niú	N	cow; ox	5
牛奶	牛奶	niúnǎi	N	milk	3
女朋友	女朋友	nǚpéngyou	N	girlfriend	3

P

拍照	拍照	pāizhào	VO	to take a picture	7
排球	排球	páiqiú	N	volleyball	9
跑步	跑步	pǎobù	VO	to run; to jog	4
葡萄	葡萄	pútao	N	grape	7

Q

| 骑 | 騎 | qí | V | to ride (a bicycle or horse) | 9 |
| 起床 | 起床 | qǐchuáng | VO | to get up | 4 |

前天	前天	qiántiān	N	the day before yesterday	5
轻松	輕鬆	qīngsōng	A	relaxed	10
清明节	清明節	Qīngmíng Jié	PN	Qingming Festival; Tomb Sweeping Day	10
清真餐厅	清真餐廳	qīngzhēn cāntīng		Muslim restaurant; halal restaurant	6
情人节	情人節	Qíngrén Jié	PN	Valentine's Day	10
晴	晴	qíng	A	sunny	10
裙子	裙子	qúnzi	N	skirt	7

R

日本	日本	Rìběn	PN	Japan	2
日记	日記	rìjì	N	diary	10
容易	容易	róngyì	A	easy	4

S

商人	商人	shāngrén	N	business person	3
上边	上邊	shàngbian	N	above; over; on top of	6
上个月	上個月	shàng ge yuè		last month	5
上星期一	上星期一	shàng Xīngqīyī		last Monday; Monday last week	5
蛇	蛇	shé	N	snake	5
师傅	師傅	shīfu	N	(a respectful form of address for workers, e.g., drivers, etc.) master	9
售票员	售票員	shòupiàoyuán	N	ticket seller; (of a bus) conductor; box-office clerk	9
书房	書房	shūfáng	N	study	6
帅	帥	shuài	A	handsome	3
水	水	shuǐ	N	water	3
水果	水果	shuǐguǒ	N	fruit	7
睡觉	睡覺	shuìjiào	VO	to sleep; to go to bed	4

T

T恤	T恤	T xù	N	T-shirt	7
她	她	tā	Pr	she; her	1
太太	太太	tàitai	N	Mrs.; madam; wife	3
泰国	泰國	Tàiguó	PN	Thailand	2
踢	踢	tī	V	to kick; to play (soccer, etc.)	9
听力	聽力	tīnglì	N	listening	4
通	通	tōng	V	to connect	10
同学	同學	tóngxué	N	classmate; schoolmate; fellow student	2
透视	透視	tòushì	V	to have an X-ray exam	8
腿	腿	tuǐ	N	leg	8

W

外边	外邊	wàibian	N	outside	6
外科	外科	wàikē	N	surgical department	8
晚饭	晚飯	wǎnfàn	N	supper; dinner	4
卫生间	衛生間	wèishēngjiān	N	washroom; bathroom	6
胃	胃	wèi	N	stomach	8
文化	文化	wénhuà	N	culture	4
文学	文學	wénxué	N	literature	4
卧室	臥室	wòshì	N	bedroom	6
午饭	午飯	wǔfàn	N	lunch	4

X

西班牙	西班牙	Xībānyá	PN	Spain	2
西药	西藥	xīyào	N	Western medicine	8
吸烟	吸煙	xī yān	V O	to smoke	7
下边	下邊	xiàbian	N	below; under; underneath	6
下个月	下個月	xià ge yuè		next month	5
下星期一	下星期一	xià Xīngqīyī		next Monday; Monday next week	5
先生	先生	xiānsheng	N	Mr.; sir; gentleman; husband	3
香蕉	香蕉	xiāngjiāo	N	banana	7
小便	小便	xiǎobiàn	N	urine	8
新年	新年	xīnnián	N	New Year	10
学生	學生	xuésheng	N	student	3

Y

牙	牙	yá	N	tooth	8
眼睛	眼睛	yǎnjing	N	eye	8
羊	羊	yáng	N	sheep; goat	5
阳台	陽臺	yángtái	N	balcony	6
腰	腰	yāo	N	lower back; waist	8
音乐会	音樂會	yīnyuèhuì	N	concert	5
印度	印度	Yìndù	PN	India	2
英国	英國	Yīngguó	PN	United Kingdom; England	2
樱桃	櫻桃	yīngtao	N	cherry	7
语言	語言	yǔyán	N	language	4
元	元	yuán	M	*yuan (the official measure word for dollar)*	7
运动	運動	yùndòng	N/V	sports; exercise / to do physical exercise	4

Z

早饭	早飯	zǎofàn	N	breakfast	4
针灸	針灸	zhēnjiǔ	N	acupuncture and moxibustion	8
中国	中國	Zhōngguó	PN	China	2
中秋节	中秋節	Zhōngqiū Jié	PN	Mid-Autumn Festival; Moon Festival	10
祝贺	祝賀	zhùhè	V	to congratulate	10
自行车	自行車	zìxíngchē	N	bicycle	9
走路	走路	zǒulù	VO	to walk	9
足球	足球	zúqiú	N	soccer	9
左边	左邊	zuǒbian	N	left (side)	6
作业	作業	zuòyè	N	homework	10

B

半	bàn	4
帮	bāng	10
贝	bèi	2
匕	bǐ	2
别	bié	4
病	bìng	8

C

草	cǎo	7
茶	chá	3
超	chāo	6
车	chē	9
衬	chèn	7
虫	chóng	5
出	chū	5
穿	chuān	8
床	chuáng	8
寸	cùn	4

D

打	dǎ	7
蛋	dàn	5
刀	dāo	4
等	děng	6
电	diàn	4
东	dōng	6
冬	dōng	9
肚	dù	8
度	dù	8

E

| 儿 | ér | 3 |
| 耳 | ěr | 5 |

F

饭	fàn	2
方	fāng	6
分	fēn	4
夫	fū	8
复	fù	10

G

戈	gē	10
跟	gēn	6
工	gōng	3
弓	gōng	3
狗	gǒu	3
古	gǔ	10
贵	guì	2
国	guó	2
果	guǒ	7

H

禾	hé	9
盒	hé	5
滑	huá	9
火	huǒ	8

J

寄	jì	10
家	jiā	3
见	jiàn	2

叫	jiào	1		凉	liáng	9		秋	qiū	9

叫	jiào	1	凉	liáng	9	秋	qiū	9
教	jiào	10	林	lín	1	**R**		
街	jiē	6	路	lù	6	热	rè	9
巾	jīn	10	**M**			人	rén	1
进	jìn	1	么	me	1	认	rèn	1
近	jìn	1	米	mǐ	2	日	rì	4
井	jǐng	1	皿	mǐn	5	**S**		
聚	jù	5	名	míng	1	山	shān	3
K			明	míng	4	衫	shān	7
开	kāi	9	木	mù	1	上	shàng	2
看	kàn	2	目	mù	2	舌	shé	6
可	kě	10	**N**			舍	shě	6
刻	kè	4	男	nán	4	身	shēn	8
空	kōng	9	牛	niú	4	生	shēng	1
裤	kù	7	**Q**			尸	shī	5
快	kuài	5	期	qī	5	时	shí	4
L			其	qí	5	识	shí	1
老	lǎo	2	气	qì	5	矢	shǐ	6
礼	lǐ	5	汽	qì	9	事	shì	10
力	lì	1	钱	qián	7	手	shǒu	7
立	lì	4	且	qiě	7	书	shū	6

属	shǔ	5		心	xīn	2		又	yòu	2

属	shǔ	5
水	shuǐ	9
睡	shuì	8
岁	suì	3

T

特	tè	4
疼	téng	8
天	tiān	3
田	tián	4
头	tóu	8
土	tǔ	1

W

王	wáng	2
文	wén	5

X

西	xī	6
惜	xī	5
下	xià	4
夏	xià	10
线	xiàn	9

心	xīn	2
行	xíng	6
姓	xìng	1
穴	xué	9
雪	xuě	9

Y

牙	yá	8
言	yán	1
炎	yán	8
羊	yáng	1
样	yàng	1
衣	yī	7
宜	yí	7
意	yì	4
应	yīng	8
英	yīng	3
泳	yǒng	9
游	yóu	9
友	yǒu	2
有	yǒu	3

又	yòu	2
雨	yǔ	9
语	yǔ	3
玉	yù	2
月	yuè	4
云	yún	2

Z

张	zhāng	3
找	zhǎo	10
折	zhé	7
知	zhī	6
中	zhōng	3
竹	zhú	6
祝	zhù	5
走	zǒu	6
足	zú	6
最	zuì	1
坐	zuò	1

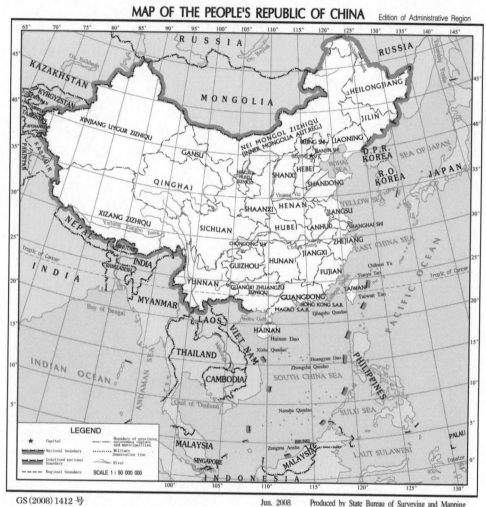

GS (2008) 1412 号

Jun. 2008   Produced by State Bureau of Surveying and Mapping